Landscape Construction and Detailing

Landscape Construction and Detailing

Alan Blanc

B. T. Batsford Ltd · London

First published 1996

© Alan Blanc 1996

Typeset through World Print, Hong Kong

and printed in Hong Kong

Published by
B. T. Batsford Ltd
4 Fitzhardinge Street
London W1H 0AH

A CIP catalogue record for this book is available
from the British Library

ISBN 0 7134 6922 6

Publisher's note
Alan Blanc had supervised the early stages of the
production of *Landscape Construction and Detailing* before
his sudden death in May 1995. In preparing the final
proofs for press, the publishers gratefully acknowledge
the assistance of his wife Sylvia Blanc.

CONTENTS

ACKNOWLEDGEMENTS

We have tried as far as possible to trace the holders of copyright material and sources of previously published material.
The illustrations would never have seen the light of day without the generous help given by Leo Pemberton at the Royal Botanic Gardens, Kew, who assisted with funds for the original sketch material. Thanks are also due to countless suppliers who over the years have furnished catalogues that were the inspiration for technical content. Former students will now be able to read the drawing notes due to the valiant efforts of Batsford to convert my unreadable scrawl into perfect lettering. Photographs are by the author unless otherwise credited.

There is finally the generous help from other sources where illustrations have been used:

2.05a   Aitken Spence Printing (PVT) Ltd, Sri Lanka.

2.05b−c *Treppen*, Franz Schuster, published by Julius Hoffman, Stuttgart (1949).

2.06f   *Italian Gardens of the Renaissance*, JC Shepherd and GA Jellicoe, Princeton Architectural Press, Princeton, US.

2.10i   Tim Blanc.

2.11a−c *The Building Regulations Explained and Illustrated*, Vincent Powell−Smith and MJ Billington, Blackwell Scientific Publications, Oxford, 1992.

5.05g   *The Concise Townscape* by Gordon Cullen Publisher Architectural Press, London, 1971.

6.01g   *Town Planning in Practice* by
10.04a   Raymond Unwin, 2nd edition, 1911, concerning Hampstead Garden Suburb, London.

8.02e−g Orsogril Sarl (UK Department, c/o McArthur Group Ltd, Geddings Road, Hoddesdon, Herts, EN11 0NZ).

10.03d   Sir Norman Foster Associates.

14.10a   *An Illustrated History of Gardening* by Anthony Huxley, Paddington Press, 1978.

15.1   Abacus Municipal Ltd, Sutton−
15.2   in-Ashfield, Notts, NG17 3FT.

FOREWORD

This book is in the tradition of Elizabeth Beazley's early standard reference work for landscape designers, *The Design and Detail of the Space between Buildings*, published in 1960 by the Architectural Press. It was one of the most useful and readable books on landscape construction of the period, not least because it combined landscape context with a wealth of in depth knowledge of landscape detailing. The author of *Landscape Construction and Detailing* adopts a similar approach. The wide range of illustrations also follows the Beazley formula of both freehand and ruled drawings and a selection of photographs, thus avoiding a stereotyped format.

Alan Blanc shows the need for a thorough understanding of the implications and interaction of construction details and their relevance to design. Throughout the text the connection is made between design considerations and construction techniques. Like Beazley, he sees each detail in an appropriate setting and serving a particular purpose. The book aims to provide the reader with an understanding of construction principles, but it still addresses the minutiae of construction. The author has travelled widely and with discretion recorded what he has seen. The material presented is based on his serial lectures to students at the School of Horticulture, Royal Botanic Gardens, Kew, from 1964 to 1990. The School in those days had the inspired leadership of Leo Pemberton who permitted 'Construction' to occupy a lecture block of forty-four hours which could embrace design history and context as part of the syllabus spread over two years. Those days are sadly past, with hard landscape detailing now reduced to a few hours per annum. The text is enriched by contextual and historical references accompanied by a generous number of illustrations allowing the reader to appreciate the construction described. Nevertheless, the emphasis is on the practitioner to produce appropriate details rather than copy slavishly. The readers are clearly expected to think for themselves. Former students who have already seen the redrawn material say it is a valuable refresher and a delight at last to read the captions instead of the dreadful handwriting from times past.

The contents cover the range of 'hard' construction techniques available to the designer. There is clearly more written about paving and walls than other building forms due to the wide choice available. Material selection is disposed of largely in the chapter devoted to surfaces, so that Chapter One becomes the primer when considering masonry elements or mass materials like concrete. Continuity is ensured by grouping ramps, steps and edging in the ensuing pages. Cross references are given to assist those looking for comprehensive solutions. The index has also been prepared with this in mind. The surfaces considered range from reinforced grass, sand and gravel and unit paviours to in-situ concrete paving, macadam and terrazzo tiling and many others. Many of the finer points of paving details are discussed in relation to such matters as tree preservation, safety, the need for maintenance and other factors. The difficult subject of bedding and jointing to paved surfaces is dealt with in depth. Chapter Two deals with ramps and steps where there is a useful introduction dealing with current UK legislation in relation to safety and step access to buildings. In addition to discussing the technical aspects of construction, there is a resume of the importance of monumental stair construction throughout history, particularly its association with formal settings and religious symbolism.

Water in the Landscape is a subject which has received much attention in professional publications, with technical information available from specialist firms. The author describes a wide range of water retention techniques but concentrates particularly on the finer points of construction and their aesthetic effects. Since water in the landscape is often intended to be a solely visual and stimulating experience a thorough understanding of the aesthetics of water in the landscape is essential.

Barriers and fencing are dealt with extensively in five chapters – Markers, Rail Fencing, Agricultural, Security and Palisade. A considerable variety of fencing types are illustrated and their appropriate uses considered in both the domestic and public domains. There is a great deal of useful information on the advantages and disadvantages of the various kinds. The fencing chapters also serve as primers in the selection of timbers and metals in external details as well as gates and fastenings. Examples referred to include the Royal Parks, Garden Cities and examples from France, Germany, Holland, Scandinavia and the USA.

Another far ranging chapter is dedicated to walling and shows the author's familiarity with the qualities of the basic materials of an architect's profession. Categories of brick are concisely described and the complexity of mortar jointing explained. The potential problems of building freestanding external walls are highlighted and an unusually wide range of wall types are described. Undoubtedly, this is one of the most valuable sections in the book for those responsible for external works involving masonry and retaining structures. Preceding the chapter on walls there is a short section dealing with the use of the ha-ha, this most self-effacing element in landscape construction. Modern designs are illustrated as well as the familiar historic examples.

Trellises and pergolas are dealt with in two highly detailed chapters. The former emphasises the range of imaginative uses for trelliswork ranging from architectural treatments at Chatsworth, Potsdam and Otterloo to their use as plant supports at Hever Castle and Milton Keynes. The descriptions of pergola designs are supported by a wealth of constructional details. Fixings and joint construction between different materials are explained at length with the emphasis on durability. Standard pergola kits are also described.

The specialised technical requirements for garden lighting will be available from manufacturers. Thus the main qualities of different types of lighting are described. This section also concentrates on the characteristics and detailed application of a wide range of luminaires. The requirements of licensing authorities are also considered.

The final chapter deals with surface water and field drainage. Flow characteristics are explained and aspects of channels, drainage, grids, access chambers and types of pipes are considered at length.

The writing is supported by references to the relevant sources and British Standards are identified as appropriate. The implications of maintenance in respect of particular types of construction are recognised and discussed. There is a generous quantity of drawn and photographic material and many of the detail drawings are three dimensional. This makes them particularly helpful for students and self-builders who may find the ubiquitous section and elevation drawing more difficult to grasp.

Writing from the viewpoint of a practising landscape architect, I believe this book will be of interest both to students and practitioners not only for its comprehensive coverage, but also because a potentially 'dry' subject is made interesting. It captures the flavour of an impressive lecture series given at Kew Gardens.

Michael Branch
August 1994

INTRODUCTION

Why another book on landscape construction? Firstly, a number of existing guides simply relate to the minimum standard required by governmental/federal or public authority/state regulations. Secondly, the European publications leading the field have little regard for economy. German work of the recent past, for example, relied on cheap labour from 'guest-workers' to provide the handwork forms familiar in publications like *Garten und Landschaft*. The designer in the 1990s may assume that some handwork will be available from job creation schemes and the like, but it will be largely unskilled — a far cry from the masonry traditions of the guest-workers from Greece, Spain and Portugal who have served in Germany. Thirdly, there is a potential for bias from sources like the cement and brick industries. Their publicity efforts tend to be self-cancelling, for neither will admit that a co-ordinated use of concrete and brick with other materials is desirable. In the same way, semi-soft materials like gravel or shingle are not going to be promoted by trade associations representing macadam/tar surfacing or block paving. A similar complaint can be made about the propaganda for forest products in landscape construction, which shows little regard for 'green' policies.

There is, finally, the writer's vanity in wishing to see the sum of 26 years' lecturing at the Royal Botanic Gardens at Kew, London, appearing between two covers! The material presented stems from a lecture series given at Kew Gardens for the School of Horticulture, and also successful trials with the lecture material in the USA. The technical handouts have been redrawn and the 5000 slides weeded down to acceptable limits for publication. The core of the Kew course was landscape design and management, and initially the construction element ran parallel with the Institute of Landscape Architects course at Hammersmith College of Art and Building, London. That is no longer the case, but it is hoped that the data given will nevertheless be useful to all designers, whether they be architects, landscape architects or horticulturalists involved with the external environment. Furthermore, to help the do-it-yourself enthusiast, some of the complicated details presented here are broken down as a building process in sketch form. There are gaps in the contents: one omission is the skill

formalists inspired by Ricardo Bofill or Albert Speer.

The author's approach is to counter the notion that this or that construction must be worthy of 'quality assurance' or else be totally banned. Landscape construction can leak and settle, and more relaxed standards apply to its design. The design process is certainly more easygoing, allowing the use of a rectangle or circle, without recourse to T-squares or compasses. The edge or trim can be sketched in notebook form for a particular location and then applied on site with the minimum of drawing board effort.

A significant aspect of post-war work in the former West Germany is the high standard of woodworking skills still employed, which extends to custom-made designs for items like park benches, bins or simply wooden railings. Blacksmith's work is also preferred for gates and guardrails, instead of catalogue items. Recent pricing on private work shows that custom-made triprails cost no more than proprietary patterns, the reason being the effect of inflation on manufacturers, who prefer to fabricate to order rather than to maintain stock. Under these circumstances landscape components in metal or timber do not have to be catalogue items, but simply assemblies of standard profiles and sections.

The selling off of public housing in the UK, and greater leisure time, have led to a boom in garden construction, as indicated by the growth of garden centres/nurseries offering design packages as well as pallets of pavers and bundles of garden trellises. The BBC TV programme *Gardener's World* enjoys the highest rating of all BBC TV evening programmes in the UK. Similar trends are likely to develop in Eastern Europe as the spaces around public housing become private spaces, even though 'digging for food' is currently more of a priority than patio paving, judging by housing estates outside Moscow.

involved in levelling and grading, or in laying out sports grounds. These were taught by a surveyor at Kew Gardens, and the author recommends the excellent texts that already exist on those topics.[1]

The choice offered is wide but not exclusive, the intent being that the reader will learn to look and look again, and to consider the advice offered as a primer and not a foregone conclusion. The other hope in putting together a book of details is that readers will formulate their own ideas and never forget a sense of fun in the process of creativity. Crazy/random paving or tile creasings are not covered, on the grounds that nothing need be that ugly!

The pious hopes that created the cultural centre on London's South Bank finally expired in acres of concrete-covered ground, either precast or poured on site. Portmeirion in Wales and the ideas of Gordon Cullen are much more beguiling, and (thank heaven) have been more influential in landscape design than the

Any landscape, whether hard or soft, needs love, care and maintenance, and the visitor to many showpieces of municipal design (Figures 1.1–1.2) comes away with the impression of private splendour contrasted with public squalor, the ill-kempt local government elements suffering as much from the disease of official neglect as from vandalism. The Dutch manage these things better by operating a graduated scale of taxes and/or rents according to the standard of upkeep desired by the residents. This is a policy that London boroughs might like to copy instead of adopting the lowest common denominator of slum-style management (Figure 1.3). The nineteenth-century Peabody estates in London are an extreme example of parsimony, the space between buildings being reduced to macadam/tar surfacing, grass and perhaps trees. The City of Birmingham, England, has taken this theme even further by proposing the use of plastic trees.

This book describes another world, but it illustrates examples from places barely 200 miles apart, whether in Byker in Newcastle, England or Zutphen, the Netherlands, where the community and their servants in the environment game have created architecture at street level (Figure 1.4). If English or Dutch communities can achieve such qualities in the matrix imposed by their townscape, then so can others.

This book has been great fun to put together, and it is hoped that its use as a textbook will make lecturing more enjoyable, and sharpen the eyes of the environmental designer.

1.04 Raked shingle patterns symbolizing water movement around rocks. Japanese Garden,
University of British Columbia, Vancouver

1   SURFACES

1.1 Soft Surfaces

Reinforced grass

The most popular 'soft' surface for landscape is probably a green sward. The failure of turf under heavy pedestrian or wheeled traffic is no doubt the reason why designers seek to reinforce the sub-base of lawns or rough grassland to maintain a surface that will green itself — road verges/shoulders are a typical example. Traditional solutions have included shingle or gravel rolled into the top surface before seeding. Compacted gravel driveways and paths will grass over unless the surface is kept raked, and the lack of kerbs in a lawn setting will mean that root spread will quickly develop from the surrounding turf. Gravel has the advantage that a surface coating of 75 mm over consolidated hardcore of 100 to 150 mm can cope with a wide range of vehicle loads even though grassed over, but it is wise to employ seed rather than turf to prevent scuffing. This solution works well with garden paths and accessways for tractors, or for feeder routes in grassed car parks.

The public parking problem in garden or rural situations is often a seasonal event, with winter and spring being the period when 'green' surfaces can recover. This concept has been applied by the National Trust to some of their key locations in the UK. The seasonal flux of visitors is parked largely on grassland where the whole area has been reinforced by galvanized chain link or plastic mesh laid over raked ground. There is a topping of 75 mm compacted sand/gravel and soil mix, which is subsequently seeded. Wear and tear takes place at feeder routes, but it is a simple matter to refurbish in the winter cycle of maintenance. Figure 1.01, shows a summer view with erosion exposing the mesh underlay, which in turn prevents wheelslip. The layout should be so arranged that exits from the parking spaces and egress routes are downhill to minimize problems of moving traffic in wet weather. The general effect is far superior to 'crib paving' (described later in Figure 1.16a) and much easier to walk over.

It is worth emphasizing that the strengthening of grass surfacing may need drastic management measures to be successful. Limitations on wheel loads will be needed, and alternative routes designed for grassed footpaths so that green areas have a better chance to recover. Demarking of strengthened grass may need signing for vehicles, but with pedestrians it should be sufficient to define areas by close mowing. At Kew Gardens metal hoops are employed to discourage access to lawn walks that are out of bounds (see Section 6.1).

A final word of warning is required concerning soft surfaces in car parks. Neither gravel nor mesh-reinforced sub-bases will prevent soil compaction, which can be very injurious to existing trees. At Beaulieu National Motor Museum, Hampshire, a car park made of gravel surfacing below the canopy of mature chestnuts eventually killed all the trees. Much-maligned macadam/tar coated stone in these circumstances would have saved the trees due to the load-spreading qualities of a bonded surface coating, provided that wheel loads had been kept 2.5 m clear of the trunks.

Sand

Sand forms the ideal material for play areas, though care is needed in the specification and in providing effective drainage. 'Play pit' sand is a

1.01 Use of mesh reinforcement below grassed car park surface

specific product and should be a naturally-occurring 'soft' sand that has been washed to remove loam or other staining agents. Sharp or crushed sands should be avoided to prevent injury (Figure 1.02). The example illustrates a play equipment area where the sand thickness was 450 mm over a soft sub-base.

The underlay can be plastic mesh or stout perforated sheeting laid over sand blinding and loose gravel to 150 mm thickness. The subsoil should be compacted and graded to fall away from the play area to French drains – pebble-filled drains instead of conventional land drains

that will become blocked (refer to Section 16.6 for full details).

'Play pit' sand is far too expensive to use over a whole playground and is usually contained within kerbs for specific activities with sand and water. A typical installation resembles the concrete work employed for a formal pool (see Figure 4.02c) except that the base slab will have perforations made by embedding vertical land drains that allow generous drainage to a loose gravel underlay falling away to French drains as already described. 'Play pit' sand will need replacement from time to time, and the exclusion of cats and dogs from the play area will alleviate the hygiene problem.

Adventure playgrounds also need a soft stone-free surface. The usual specification is garden soil that has been sieved through a 10 mm mesh. An alternative material is shredded timber bark for ground cover below playground constructions. Sawmill waste should be avoided due to problems with splintered wood and nails. Proprietary play equipment is commonly installed over shock-absorbent carpets.

Shingle

Shingle is one of the cheapest materials to lay, and provides the easiest solution to the instant tidying of a building site. There are two forms of shingle: naturally-occurring rounded pebbles, and fine crushed aggregate known as pea shingle. The rounded form is to be preferred where child safety is important. Crushed aggregate is cheaper and has the advantage that it can be reused for making concrete if the ground works are of a temporary nature.

There are many applications where shingle provides a perfectly adequate long-term surfacing around buildings, and particularly for anti-splash margins against façades and walls. Figures 3.08–3.10 reveal the way self-draining shingle beds can be arranged at such critical locations, where vegetation might fail or where solid paving would look inappropriate. Figure 1.03 features the shingle margins of St Catherine's College, Oxford, which have been in place for 30 years. Shingle is often provided as solar insulation above flat roofs. A light-weight form with vermiculite beds of 75 mm thickness should be considered where super-loading is a problem.

1.02 Soft washed sand used in play park, with a depth of 300 mm

1.03 Shingle margins installed at St Catherine's College, Oxford, in the early 1960s. Architect: Arne Jacobsen

'Instant' gardeners are probably the keenest users of shingle beds, since they can be used to mask the unsightly scars contractors leave when they quit building sites. A 100 mm depth of pea shingle is usually adequate for camouflage and can be combined with planters and paving stones to give the impression of a terrace. Consolidation is difficult on shingle areas, and overlaid paving slabs are features to be seen rather than used. The ultimate visual designs are the raked pebble surfaces that originate in the temple gardens of Japan, where the pattern often forms symbolic waves and water reflections (Figure 1.04).

Gravel

Gravel is favoured by gardeners due to the ease of laying and adapting to the site, the soft nature of the finish also complementing plant material better than hard surfaces like concrete or stone slabs. Gravel suitable for this purpose is naturally-occurring and is found in the upper layers of gravel workings, the supply situation changing with the opening of new pits. It is important to find current sources within reasonable distance from the site rather than specifying an ideal surfacing that is unavailable. The colour range varies from cream and silver through sandy colours to dark ochres and sienna browns. The quality should permit compaction into a firm matrix of pebble, sand and loam binders. A visit to the supplier's pit is essential to check that the qualities of the dug gravel are appropriate to the surfacing required.

Success with gravelled drives and paths depends upon constructional detail as well as careful specification. Drainage and falls are just as important as for other trafficways. Ponding has to be avoided as otherwise the surface disintegrates and forms craters, while run-off will seriously erode the wearing coat down to the hardcore bed. A common mistake is to lay gravel level or near-level without adequate falls; the other error is to construct kerbs in such a way that storm water is trapped. Figure 1.05 portrays a typical failure with gravel laid level and without proper drainage. An ideal solution is to allow the gravelled work to follow natural inclines. It also helps if paths wider than 1 m have a cross-fall and those wider than 3 m have two-way falls. The falls should be 1:30 or 1:40 to be effective. Containment at the edges is important, since

1.05 Failed gravel surfaces without falls or adequate drainage

gravel is rolled into place and will be dressed and rerolled from time to time to repair the finish. Timber edges, granite setts or pavers are used for this purpose, and have the added virtue of isolating vegetation roots to prevent them from colonizing gravel beds.

Preparation should be as follows — excavation, compaction of the sub-base and laying of hardcore, then provision of kerbs, consolidation of hardcore to 150 mm thickness and overlaying with 75 to 100 mm of gravel to the gradients required. The kerbs could be a stout batten of 100 × 38 mm treated softwood nailed to stakes at 1.2 m centres. This detail should last ten years or so, to be replaced by setts or brick margins. More permanent kerbs are best laid on a bed of 100 mm lean-mix concrete and haunched to provide a firm edging. Figures 1.06a–d give four solutions, which range from garden paths to drives and roadways. Wide expanses of gravel will need draining to central points or to a series of gullies arranged on a grid giving a 'quilted' pattern to the surface. Technically these are termed 'reverse pyramid falls' and are shown in Figure 1.13f and 16.01. FIGURE 1.25g also portrays a gully surround and the way a stone slab can be used instead of iron gratings.

The maintenance of gravel and the problems arising with the 'walking in' of loose stone to lawns or to interiors of buildings are common complaints. Nothing is maintenance-free, and gravelled surfaces need treatment with weed killers and a twice-yearly dressing

a Wood battens

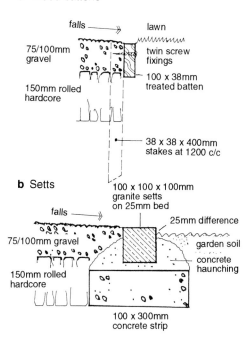

falls →
lawn
75/100mm gravel
twin screw fixings
100 x 38mm treated batten
150mm rolled hardcore
38 x 38 x 400mm stakes at 1200 c/c

b Setts

100 x 100 x 100mm granite setts on 25mm bed
falls →
25mm difference
75/100mm gravel
garden soil
concrete haunching
150mm rolled hardcore
100 x 300mm concrete strip

c Channel for wide path or drive

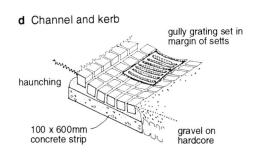

100 x 100 x 100mm granite setts as channel with falls in length to gullies
falls →
75/100mm gravel
haunching
150mm rolled hardcore
100 x 600mm concrete strip

d Channel and kerb

gully grating set in margin of setts
haunching
100 x 600mm concrete strip
gravel on hardcore

1.06 Kerbs for gravel paths and drives

1.07 The gravel paradise which surrounds the Palace of Versailles
a Tracing of paths and routes in wide terraces. Note stone slab covers to gulleys
b Raking patterns to Orangery terrace
c Parterre with gravel surfaces

of grit rolled in wet into the wearing coat. Wide kerbs or margins of alternative paving will serve as grit barriers for lawns or building entrances, as will grids at entry doors (see Chapter 2).

The low initial cost and minimal maintenance involved with gravel work explains its continuous employment in château gardens in France. It is also commonly used in urban spaces such as the gardens of the Louvre, Paris. Stone paving the vast areas of avenues and terraces of Versailles was beyond the budget of Louis XIV, and thankfully they have been left as a raked and rolled gravelly paradise ever since. Figures 1.07a−c give some idea of the scale and detail and the way stone dressing and raking is used for the Orangery terrace. Another visual advantage is the way graduations in texture develop with traffic so that bland expanses are delineated by traces of footsteps or vehicle tracks. All these signs help to indicate the varying importance of routes within the landscape. Similar qualities in walkways can be perceived in the gravel work beyond the garden front at Hampton Court Palace, London, which contrasts sadly with the characterless and dingy macadam/tar coated stone that was substituted for the main west entry. One final advantage of gravel in relation to domestic driveways needs to be emphasized. My house drive, constructed in 1957, has only had two resurfacings, granite sett kerbs being added in 1972, and a new dressing of Breden gravel in 1991. The neighbours' drives laid in macadam have to be extensively patched or resurfaced after every severe winter. Macadam is probably three times more expensive than gravel over 35 years.

1.2 Flexible Surfaces

The flexibility depends upon the sub-base. Sand and hardcore beds will improve this, but concrete bedding gives the same firmness as a concrete road deck.

Pebble

Pebble is probably one of the earliest methods devised for ground surfacing. There is certainly evidence on the sites of Mycenaean towns, for example, the alleyways of Gournia (see Figure 2.05d). The historic settings of Chinese houses and temples have patterned pebble designs which are reinforced by artists' paintings from the distant past. The Mediterranean tradition continues today with pebble pavements restored at the gardens of the Alhambra, Grenada, and in the old Jewish quarters of Cordoba and Seville. The related Portuguese tradition has been transferred to Brazil and is the inspiration for the work by Burle Marx in the remade promenade of Copacabana, Rio de Janeiro. A selection of these design sources is given in Figures 1.08a–c.

Pebbles are usually found in gravel pits, and represent the larger stones that are often marketed as 'rejects', namely flint nodules that are too expensive to crush into regular-sized aggregate. Chalk beds are another source. The use of beach pebble is not usually permitted due to risks of coastal erosion. The nodules can be screened to provide pebble diameters between 25 and 75 mm, often egg-shaped. The material stems from silica nodules found in chalk or deposited in shingle beds, which are extremely durable. The method of laying consists of hammering the stones with a wooden mallet into a matrix of gravel or a mixture of dry sand and cement. This needs to be laid over a hardcore sub-base, the total thickness of pebbles, matrix and hardcore being 200–250 mm. Watering by spray will assist the consolidation and will set cement-based beds into a solid mass. In garden work, natural gravel and pebble will provide a semi-permeable paving and one that will respond to settlement and frost heave without breaking up. Cement bonding implies a hard surface that will need efficient drainage (see Section 16.1). Cracking will occur, but it will be

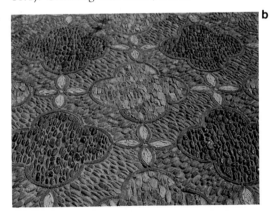

1.08 Historic references to pebble paving
a Gardens of Souchow, China (historic replica)
b Generalife, Grenada (circa 1400)
c Jewish Quarter, Cordoba (circa 1400)

1.09 Present-day applications of pebble paving
a Hostile paving at Kimbolton village, Huntingdon, Cambridgeshire
b Moulded surfaces, St John's College, Cambridge
c Poorly-laid pebbles, spaced too far apart in bed of concrete
d Contrasting scale and texture. Court of suburban house in Zurich

masked by the pebble texture. Jointing should be provided by a dry mixture of sand brushed between the stones, pointing or grouting being totally avoided.

Pebble surfaces are often regarded as a hazard area – a hostile paving to discourage pedestrians or vehicles. They are certainly employed in that capacity at Oxford and Cambridge colleges, where swathes of pebbles are laid next to windows at street level to direct traffic to the smooth stone slabs 2 m or more away. It is a ground treatment that is often used in main roads running through small village to 'distance' pavement users from the properties adjacent (Figure 1.09a). Pebble is much easier to maintain than loose gravel, and has the advantage that ground modelling can adopt sophisticated forms that emulate drainage channels, multiple falls in pyramid or reverse pyramid forms. Figure 1.09b demonstrates the way pebble textures can surmount banks and modify the ugly instrusion of inspection covers.

One disadvantage is slipperiness in places that become heavily used, in which case granite

setts need to be considered as infilling. The other problems include vandalism, as gravel-bedded areas can readily be lifted by budding 'Davids' seeking stones for their slings. Cement-bound pebble can also be dislodged by determined vandals, and this paving finish is discouraged by many police forces in the UK and elsewhere.

In the private domain, pebble does seem to be a perfect finish for many difficult areas in the individual garden where excessive dryness, shade or wet conditions prevent use of vegetation. One needs to appreciate the way varied pebble textures can blend with other paving, nearby vegetation or water. Pebble margins also make an attractive device below the shaded areas caused by roof overhangs, and make an excellent tree guard to discourage people and vehicles that will otherwise cause root damage. The hazard element is valuable at path junctions to prevent corner-cutting. The contrast in garden scale is another feature, the rounded forms looking more sympathetic than so-called 'rock gardens' which too often resemble builders' rubbish left over on site.

1.10 Granite setts, sizes and laying patterns
a Circular paving in three shades (white, grey and lavender) at Vallingby, Stockholm (circa 1953–5)

b Common shapes and sizes
(note: 100 x 100 x 100 and larger sizes replicated in precast concrete)

large setts

usual size

often curved top

size 200/250 x 150

150 x 150 cubes

100 x 100 cubes

50 x 50 cubes

c Laying process and patterns

The sett laying process

phase 5: watering

phase 4: dry sand & mortar mix brushed into joints

phase 3: working forward in metre bays

gullies completed later

phase 2: bedding laid to falls and setts laid

phase 1: sub-base and kerbs

kerb blocks

50mm step

simple sett kerb

25mm step

haunching

macadam

splayed setts

100mm concrete bed

25mm step

setts for parking bays

stretcher bond

direction of road

broken bond

square bond to margins

fall in length

dividers for parking bays

margins to gullies

fantail form

armlength radius

d Sett-laying by hand
e Setts laid in grass to form a terrace by Olympic Stadium, Munich (1972)
f Setts laid in graduated spacing to mask a wide path in a memorial garden. War memorial, Aarhus, Denmark (1950s)

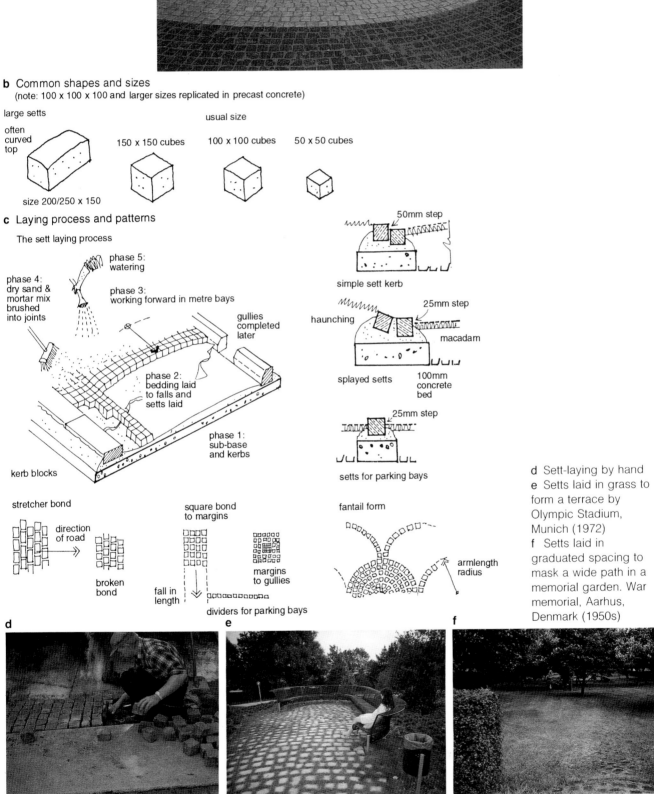

d

e

f

Figures 1.09a–d show advantages and disadvantages of pebble paving. Retaining features can be made from pebbles bound together in wire cages, called 'gambions' (see Section 11.18 for details).

Granite setts

Setts and pebbles share many similar qualities in paving techniques, and they can both be arranged in complex shapes. The laying process follows that already described, with a dry matrix of gravel or sand and cement that is watered in. The finishing work is undertaken with the same materials, moistened with a hose fitted with a sprinkler attachment. Once again, pointing or grouting with a ribbon of cement and sand has to be avoided to preserve the colour and texture of the setts.

Stone paving should be selected for hard-wearing and frostproof qualities. An igneous stone like granite is the most appropriate, and of these basalt is most difficult to cut. Sedimentary stones such as limestone or sandstone are often trimmed down to paving blocks, but they do not have the durability of setts under hard traffic. An outline comparison of building stones is presented in Section 1.4. Granite blocks are split into slabs (50, 75,

100, 125 or 150 mm thickness) and sawn into strips and then into small cubes or blocks. The split face guarantees a non-slip surface. Related stones like basalt are more suitable for tooling to produce slightly rounded forms or else to be cut into small slabs that can be grooved or textured for the traffic face. There is a wide colour range, and attractive designs can be made which depend upon contrasting shades, such as the white, grey or lavender featured at the shopping centre at Vallingby, Stockholm (Figure 1.10a). The common sizes and laying patterns are shown in Figures 1.10b–c. Tapered cubes were devised by Roman road builders to ensure a better fit under loading.

Fan-shaped layouts are arranged to combat the stresses caused by turning-wheel traffic – the interaction between the angled blocks prevents rucking of the surface. The radius of fanwork is dictated by arm length, as the paviour works back from the laying edge. Typical handwork is shown in Figure 1.10d. Granite setts laid with wide joints using earth infilling and grass seed will produce a reinforced lawn with subtle qualities. There are many locations, such as firefighter's paving or where crowds need to be accommodated occasionally, when grass-surrounded setts provide the right balance between firmness and softness in paving. Figures 1.10e–f provide two examples. The former is the pedestrian area close by the main stadium at the Munich Olympic site. Here, informal seating has reinforced grass for terracing. The other design demonstrates the full potential in graduated effects where a serpentine path runs through a war memorial garden, with the setts placed close together to trace the primary route, while the margins have wider and wider spacings to lose the total area of paving within the lawn. The route is in a significant position, the paving serving to accommodate crowds at ceremonies or just a few that pass through this corner of the public park. The bronze sculptures are placed within the grass and would have been totally overscaled by 4 m widths of unbroken hard surfacing in their proximity.

Granite setts are associated with the cobbled streets of inner cities. In such places the variety of paving pattern and texture can define differing uses, for example, crossovers (at entries to side streets or driveways), margins, gutters and kerbs, pathways and

1.11 Definition of uses

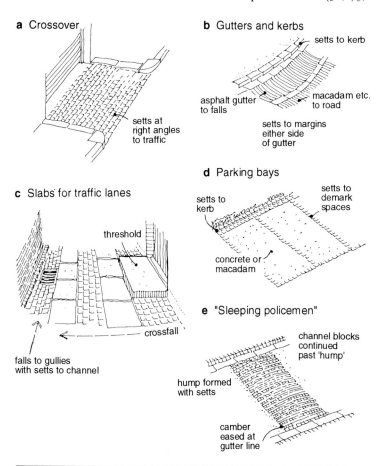

a Crossover

setts at right angles to traffic

b Gutters and kerbs

setts to kerb

asphalt gutter to falls

macadam etc. to road

setts to margins either side of gutter

c Slabs for traffic lanes

threshold

crossfall

falls to gullies with setts to channel

d Parking bays

setts to kerb

setts to demark spaces

concrete or macadam

e "Sleeping policemen"

channel blocks continued past 'hump'

hump formed with setts

camber eased at gutter line

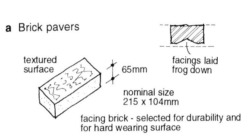

1.12 Cobbles and setts in historic context
a Paving in the domain of Edinburgh Castle: living rock, paving and cobbles burnished by time
b Gutters and kerbs in New Town, Edinburgh (Note scale of detail and neat combination of gutter and kerb)
c Enhancement by resurfacing the space between buildings, with textures to define uses, Thorn, Limburg, Holland (1975)

ramps, parking bays, roads and sleeping policemen speed bumps (Figures 1.11a−e). The dense, compact surface of setts means a complete system of surface drainage has to be designed, similar to that for impermeable concrete or macadam/tar coated stone given in Section 1.5. Figures 1.12a−c take these themes from a number of historic settings associated with granite sett paving. The Edinburgh New Town setts are distinguished by a bold scale and by a functional line to the combined gutters and kerbs. The old town of Thorn, in Limburg, Holland, was totally repaved for Architectural Heritage Year in 1975. Each part of the hard landscape is articulated, both in terms of the purpose and use of components. The threshold marker, the vehicleway, the footpath and subdivisions demark the architectural cadences in the space between buildings.

Setts have a high second-hand value and should be saved for reuse instead of thrown away or broken up for hardcoring, and the Dutch scheme already described used quantities of salvaged material.

The slipperiness which develops under heavy vehicle traffic can be countered by cutting grooves at 50 mm centres using rollers mounted with abrasive diamond cutters.

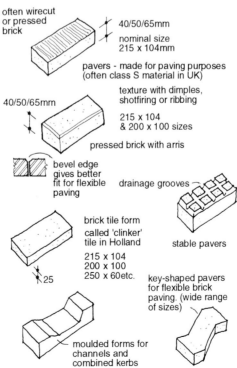

a Brick pavers

textured surface
65mm
facings laid frog down
nominal size 215 x 104mm
facing brick - selected for durability and for hard wearing surface

often wirecut or pressed brick
40/50/65mm
nominal size 215 x 104mm
pavers - made for paving purposes (often class S material in UK)

40/50/65mm
texture with dimples, shotfiring or ribbing
215 x 104 & 200 x 100 sizes
pressed brick with arris

bevel edge gives better fit for flexible paving

drainage grooves

brick tile form called 'clinker' tile in Holland
215 x 104
200 x 100
250 x 60etc.
25

stable pavers

key-shaped pavers for flexible brick paving. (wide range of sizes)

moulded forms for channels and combined kerbs

1.13 Brick and block flexible paving

1.13b Typical concrete block units

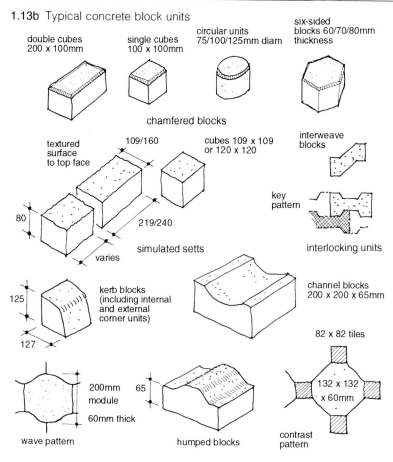

double cubes
200 x 100mm

single cubes
100 x 100mm

circular units
75/100/125mm diam

six-sided
blocks 60/70/80mm
thickness

chamfered blocks

textured
surface
to top face

109/160

80

219/240

varies

cubes 109 x 109
or 120 x 120

simulated setts

interweave
blocks

key
pattern

interlocking units

125

127

kerb blocks
(including internal
and external
corner units)

channel blocks
200 x 200 x 65mm

200mm
module

60mm thick

wave pattern

65

humped blocks

82 x 82 tiles

132 x 132
x 60mm

contrast
pattern

c Pedestrian & lightly loaded areas

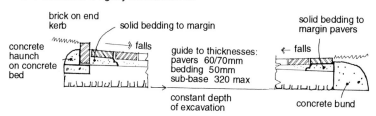

brick on end
kerb

solid bedding to margin

falls

concrete
haunch
on concrete
bed

guide to thicknesses:
pavers 60/70mm
bedding 50mm
sub-base 320 max

constant depth
of excavation

solid bedding to
margin pavers

falls

concrete bund

d Commercial traffic areas

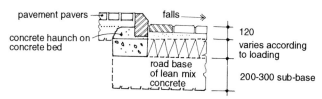

pavement pavers

falls

concrete haunch on
concrete bed

road base
of lean mix
concrete

120

varies according
to loading

200-300 sub-base

e Paving patterns

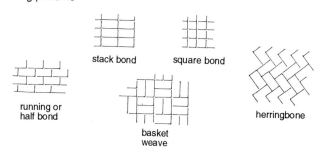

stack bond

square bond

running or
half bond

basket
weave

herringbone

1.13f Arranging falls : see also illustration 1601
Note: brick or block paving units require 1:40 falls

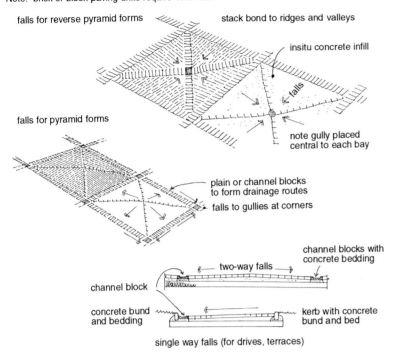

falls for reverse pyramid forms

stack bond to ridges and valleys

insitu concrete infill

falls

falls for pyramid forms

note gully placed
central to each bay

plain or channel blocks
to form drainage routes

falls to gullies at corners

channel blocks with
concrete bedding

two-way falls

channel block

concrete bund
and bedding

kerb with concrete
bund and bed

single way falls (for drives, terraces)

This is to be preferred to the coating of grit-finished asphalt favoured by traffic engineers.

Block and brick paving

Brick-paved paths and roads are associated with Flanders and the Netherlands, where this old method of paving is used to overcome the softness of silt or loam-based soils. The continuous settlement problems with reclaimed polderland in the Netherlands oblige road builders to re-lay paved surfaces every few years, using sand bedding to facilitate lifting and relaying. Flexible paving with clay or concrete pavers is today an accepted method regardless of site conditions, and unit costs are no more that 10% over macadam. To make the comparison one is looking at macadam with a consolidated sub-base of hardcore and lean-mix concrete. The loading capacity can be broadly defined as PA (pedestrians, cars and light vans) or PB (including public transport and commercial road vehicles)[1]. Bricks or blocks need to be specified to PA or PB standards, and the sub-base prepared to specific load-bearing capacities. Other factors are frost- and skid-resistance, and, of course dimensions. [2 and 3] Figures 1.13a–f highlight the key details of flexible paving in clay brick or concrete block and the typical units available. The broad classification for clay or silicate pavers or concrete blocks would be 'engineering class',

that category covering strength and frost-resistance for use in pavements.[3] Many clay facing bricks can fulfil this role if laid frog downwards and may be cheaper to obtain if facing quantities are simply over-ordered. However, brick makers make pavers specifically for that use, and it will be easier to obtain guarantees for these. Belgian and Dutch producers offer a wide range of small-scale clay units (50 × 200 mm on face) that form such an attractive feature in the Dutch townscape.

The reduced scale of such pavers enhances the appearance of small spaces or narrow paths (see Figure 1.14e), and they also permit three-dimensional modelling, as with pebbles and setts.

Compaction and consolidation is an important element in the laying process, the finishing operation being carried out with a plate vibrator which ensures that the pavers are compacted into their sand bedding, forcing the bed material into all unit joints (Figure 1.14a).

Chamfered edges to pavers improve the surface drainage and allow for individual units to settle against one another, with less risk of spalling at extreme corners. The rough texture and unevenness of flexible paving implies steeper falls than for asphalt or concrete – 1:40 is the recommended minimum fall. It is difficult to lay standard-size units (225 × 112 mm on face) to three-dimensional falls or to pyramid forms unless the ridges or valleys

1.14 Flexible paving
in use
a Plate vibrator with
concrete pavers laid by
hand over compressed
sand topping and
hardcore
b Inspection cover
raised above settled
pavers
c Cement-pointed
London stocks in a
Cambridge garden
d The same path with
sand joints and
extensive moss growth
e Typical Dutch pavers
in characteristic small
scale
f Failed facings used
as pavers at Jyvaskyla,
Finland

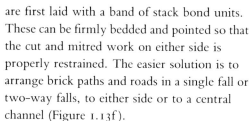

are first laid with a band of stack bond units.
These can be firmly bedded and pointed so that
the cut and mitred work on either side is
properly restrained. The easier solution is to
arrange brick paths and roads in a single fall or
two-way falls, to either side or to a central
channel (Figure 1.13f).

Sand-bedded pavers settle slightly under
traffic, which means that gully tops or
inspection covers need to be placed 10 mm or
so below the laid work, otherwise gratings no
longer work or covers become a hazard, as
shown in Figure 1.14b. The spreading of
pavers into the surrounding ground due to
laying or traffic loads is prevented by laying
solid kerbs to all outside edges (see Figures
1.13c−d for light and heavy applications).
The spread of lichen and moss depends upon
the exposure and type of vegetation − mortar
pointing certainly discourages moss growth,
Figure 1.14c shows yellow stock bricks
pointed in cement and Figure 1.14d shows the
same path left sand-jointed. Stock bricks are

very absorbent, hence problems with moss,
but the same difficulties can be experienced
with some silicate bricks due to the lime sand
content, which encourages lichen. Designers
should check that the specified brick has
previously performed well as pavers at similar
locations. Frost-resistance in protected walling
is not a reliable indicator, as shown by the
pressed clay facings at Jyvaskyla, Finland,
chosen by Aalto for the college buildings,
where the same bricks fail miserably as terrace
paving (Figure 1.14f).

It is a simple matter to re-lay totally flexible
paving, but difficult to persuade utility
undertakings to neatly patch and stitch
together pavers other than with the iniquitous
smudge of black macadam/tar surfacing
wherever electricity, gas, telephone or water
pipes are installed. The interlocking of setts to
resist turning-wheel loads has been mentioned,
and concrete block products achieve similar
ends, either with a key or wave pattern (see
Figure 1.13b). Concrete blocks depend upon

pattern and texture for their visual effect; the colour range is, however, drab compared with brick, and tends to darken with ageing. The aggregate selection is crucial – crushed granite wears well and provides a finish which improves with wearing despite fading of the cement mix, usually white, grey, buff or black upon manufacture. For further details on concrete finishes refer to Section 1.3.

Blocks are usually of a stouter profile than brick, 100 × 100 mm being a popular cross-section. The formats include cube and cylindrical blocks which simulate cobbles and pebble paving, and also tapered components, which enable radius work to be laid without having to cut the paving blocks. Figures 1.15a–d demonstrate the decorative possibilities. The juxtaposition of differing-sized blocks enables the designer to achieve complex modelling in imitation of setts.

The other advantage of concrete products is the standardization in thickness, which enables layouts to be made in differing patterns but to a constant depth. This speeds laying since the compacted sand bed can be laid and then overlaid in one continuous operation. The use of block paving in 300 mm squares is fast replacing the 600 × 750 × 50 mm slabs that were popular in the UK, due to its superior performance under wheel loads. It is true that the slab form was designated only for footpaths, but urban paving is increasingly in mixed traffic use, where load capacities of 7.6 tonnes gross load should be allowed for unless bollards/posts restrict vehicle use (see Section 5.2).

1.3 Cellular or Crib Paving

These forms resemble concrete block but have been modified to provide a cellular surface that will encourage grass or other plant life. The purpose is to strengthen lawn areas for emergency traffic like fire tenders or fire escape paths, and another use is to reinforce soft areas for occasional traffic and car parking. A further possibility is to use honeycomb blocks as tree guards or as reinforcement for river banks to prevent erosion.

Figures 1.16a–f depict differing forms. The cellular unit which carried the original patent of 'Bg Slab' has an interesting history. The designer had decided to improve a shady courtyard at his studio and make lawns with a bay of granite setts for car parking. He noted that the grass died off except between the setts. Compaction and dryness killed the unprotected lawn while the setts protected roots and allowed whatever rain fell to be distributed without caking or ponding. The 'Bg unit' simulates this effect by giving a robust grid to support pedestrians and vehicles, while the filling of loam, peat and sand supports vegetation. The car park at the Southwark sports centre shown is a fine example of greening a service route with cellular pavings (see Figure 1.16b); the river-bank reinforcement as at the tide mill at Woodbridge, Suffolk, is another application (Figure 1.16c). Other applications include highway work where soft verges/shoulders need to be strengthened or where underground services need to be demarked and protected by

1.15 Decorative block paving
a Round units
b Tapered units
c Mixture of differing patterns
d One of the earliest applications, at the Swiss National Exhibition at Lausanne (1964)

1.16 Cellular and crib paving

a Cellular units ('Monoslabs' reproduced by permission of Marshall Mono Ltd)

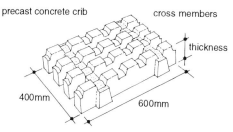

precast concrete crib   cross members

thickness

400mm   600mm

typical crib unit for fire brigade paving (type F) or for hardstanding in car parks or service roads

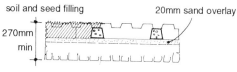

soil and seed filling   20mm sand overlay

270mm min

125mm consolidated sub-base. (for type F)   increase sub-base according to traffic loading

pattern	thickness mm	size mm
F	125	400x600
G	125	400x600
E	110	400x600
G90	95	300x500
F90	110	300x500

c

d

e

b Service route. Architect: Sir Peter Shepheard
c Riverbank reinforcement with units
d Thin PVC mould for in-situ concrete cellular paving
e Eventual effect when the PVC is cut away and the concrete work is soiled and seeded (In-situ bays on the left, crib paving on the right)

b

f 'Geoblock' reinforced polyethylene grid units (reproduced by kind permission of Cooper Clark PLC)

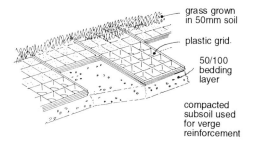

grass grown in 50mm soil

plastic grid.

50/100 bedding layer

compacted subsoil used for verge reinforcement

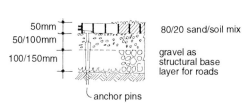

50mm
50/100mm
100/150mm

80/20 sand/soil mix

gravel as structural base layer for roads

anchor pins

non-grid paving. Some local/municipal regulations require greater definition for a fire path, and here poured concrete with temporary plastic moulds provides the answer (Figures 1.16d—e). Note that the thin PVC mould is used as shuttering for concrete. The hollow plastic portion is cutaway for soil filling. A sub-base of consolidated hardcore is needed for drainage and support. The containing margin of plain concrete is laid as a mowing edge for adjacent lawns and to act as a visual reminder to the fire brigade. Poured concrete with plant pockets has the advantage that it is vandalproof.

A 'green' solution which avoids the use of precast or poured in-situ concrete is provided by a plastic grid which presents an open area of 81% for plant material (Figure 1.16f). The grids measure 925 × 310 × 50 mm and interlock on all edges to give a reinforced polyethylene mattress. The specification for the sub-base will provide traffic loading of 1.5 tonnes axle load 'parking' to 7.6 tonnes (service roads) and 30 tonnes (fire access).

Cellular paving is not a comfortable surface to walk over, even when the grass is fully established. Heavy wear, for example on public footpaths, entails gravel reinforcement, which recovers faster than soil contained within concrete or plastic grids that tend to stand proud of the eroded ground.

1.4 Firm Surfaces

These are wearing surfaces consisting of slabs or solid-bedded bricks and blocks, and where the sub-base is concrete or heavily-compacted material.

In-situ concrete paving

Cast in place or 'in-situ' concrete paving is the cheapest form of permanent surfacing. Cheapness is no excuse for such a utilitarian material to be poorly detailed or finished roughly in unattractive textures. The cementacious quality of concrete mixtures and their limitations have to be understood. The structural mixes used for paving work have a proportion of cement, sand and ballast of 1:2:4, the cement colour imparting greyness to the resultant concrete unless white or coloured cement is substituted. The aggregate tones are far more important since wearing will expose these to view. It is worth casting trial panels if extensive work is to be undertaken. Crushed granite has more interesting textures than gravel-based aggregates, and a greater colour range (silver, lavender, reddish brown and blue grey).

Cast concrete suffers from irreversible drying shrinkage over a considerable period, which has to be allowed for in the process of forming bays. The bay joints should occur at 3–4.4 m intervals in either direction and can be

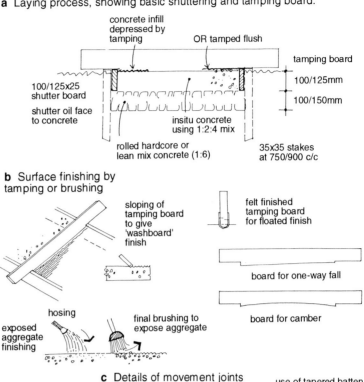

a Laying process, showing basic shuttering and tamping board.

b Surface finishing by tamping or brushing

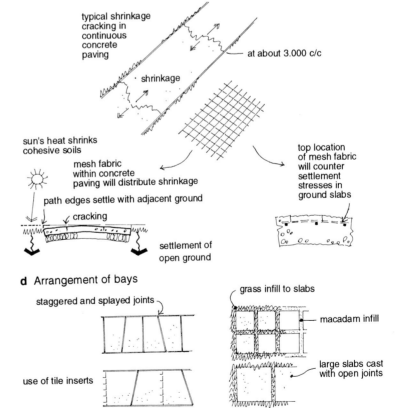

c Details of movement joints

e Role of mesh reinforcement

d Arrangement of bays

1.17 Details of in-situ concrete paving

arranged by placing concrete in alternate areas and then filling in later. Continuous pouring can be achieved, but the upper half of the slab thickness needs to be divided by wood rules which can later be withdrawn to give effective break joints. The various methods are shown in Figures 1.17a–e.

Cast concrete can be made crack-free by embedding steel mesh reinforcement to distribute loading and shrinkage stresses. Ground slabs tend to settle at their edges due to drying adjacent subsoil, and reinforcement can be incorporated in the upper portion of the slab to counter bending stresses and to limit shrinkage cracking. Such considerations need to be addressed in the construction of road surfaces or wide expanses of concrete paving laid over made-up ground, where engineering advice should be sought.

The texture of the wearing surface can be enhanced by tamping to produce a 'washboard' surface, rolling to give an indented pattern, or by scouring with a brush using a circular movement. Exposing the aggregate will provide the best finish, the process relying on carefully-timed light hosing (using a sprinkler attachment) and then brushing to clear off the surface latence of cement paste. It is also possible to use a mechanical hammer to break away the surface to expose the aggregate core. This technique may also help remedy poorly-executed work. Other textures include decorative roller treatment with imprinted textures which simulate brick pavers, setts and wood planks. Patented finishes from the USA include colour injection to reproduce tints and tones of brick and stone. The final touch is to cement point the joints to complete the deceit. Such paving concepts are featured in Disneyland, and they are chosen for the ease of cleaning and repair and with the fact that waxed polishing makes cement paving suitable for covered areas. Scoured or tooled work and 'Disneyland' finishes are shown in Figures 1.18a–c. Figures 1.18d–e reveal the results of long-term exposure of well-laid concrete paving. The technique involved casting slabs of concrete on site, with the wearing face

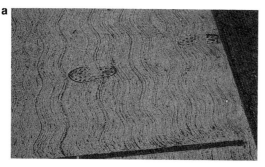

1.18 Textured finishes **a** Scoured finish (including footprints) **b** Use of electrical bush hammer to expose aggregate **c** Textured concrete using patent rollers with coloured dye keep (as used at Disneyland) **d** In-situ slabs by Aarhus Town Hall, Denmark (photographed after 25 years' exposure). Architect: Arne Jacobsen **e** Cast slabs with textured infill units, in the quads of St Catherine's College, Oxford (photographed after 30 years' exposure)

textured by brushing. The indented blocks used as 3 m spacers at St Catherine's College were cast against ribbed rubber moulds and turned over for laying as infilling elements. The Aarhus paving was in excellent order after 25 years' exposure. The St Catherine's paving has also worn well, apart from settlement caused by nearby planting or by botched repairs.

Garden paths employing cast in-situ concrete can use locally-dug material where gravel pockets exist. Sir Frederick Gibberd's garden at Harlow, Essex, relied on local material, with the wheelbarrow and other access routes formed with concrete having an exposed aggregate finish, the shrinkage joints hidden by brick or quarry tile inserts. The simplicity of this idea allows the brick or tile to interplay with the concrete and to take a dominant role for important areas such as steps or terracing (Figures 1.19a—b).

The movement joints discussed will handle shrinkage, but larger soft-filled joints will be required to counter thermally-induced movement. The spacing depends upon solar exposure, but large areas of concrete will need thermal expansion joints at 20–30 m intervals. The detail involves a 20 mm gap which can be filled with a soft gasket and mastic.

Paving over concrete sub-bases

This procedure is adopted where the finished surface needs continuous support and is subject to stresses caused by settlement or wheel loads causing breakdown (as with asphalt) or fractures (as occur with thin slabs of precast

a Asphalt

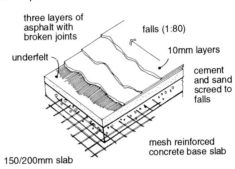

three layers of asphalt with broken joints
falls (1:80)
underfelt
10mm layers
cement and sand screed to falls
mesh reinforced concrete base slab
150/200mm slab

1.20 Slab, tile and other paving finishes for solid bedding

concrete, natural stone or tile). Many of the paving materials already discussed (pebble, setts and brick pavers) can be laid solid-bedded over concrete. The key difference between flexible bedding and solid work is the need for thermal movement joints, say 25 mm per 20–30 m.

An outline of other finishes for laying in solid beds of mortar is given in Figures 1.20a–e, with a summary below.

a Joint handling

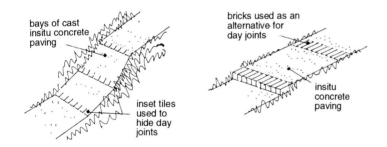

bays of cast insitu concrete paving
inset tiles used to hide day joints
bricks used as an alternative for day joints
insitu concrete paving

b Interplay of materials

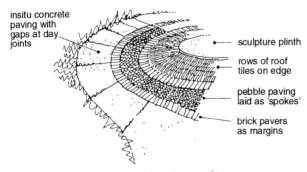

insitu concrete paving with gaps at day joints
sculpture plinth
rows of roof tiles on edge
pebble paving laid as 'spokes'
brick pavers as margins

1.19 Details of Sir Frederick Gibberd's garden

1.20b Ceramic tile and brick pavers

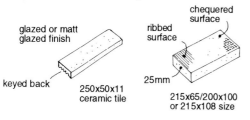

glazed or matt
glazed finish

keyed back

250x50x11
ceramic tile

ribbed
surface

chequered
surface

25mm

215x65/200x100
or 215x108 size

c Insitu and precast Terrazzo

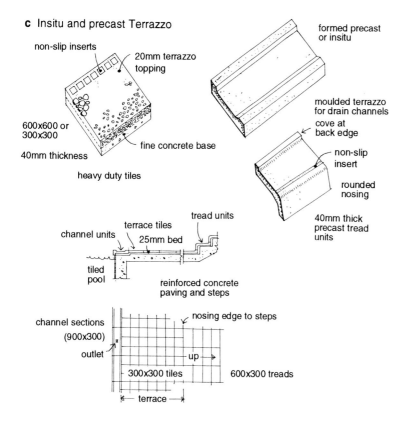

non-slip inserts

20mm terrazzo
topping

600x600 or
300x300

40mm thickness

fine concrete base

heavy duty tiles

formed precast
or insitu

moulded terrazzo
for drain channels

cove at
back edge

non-slip
insert

rounded
nosing

40mm thick
precast tread
units

channel units

terrace tiles

25mm bed

tread units

tiled
pool

reinforced concrete
paving and steps

channel sections
(900x300)

outlet

nosing edge to steps

up

300x300 tiles

600x300 treads

terrace

d Marble and slate

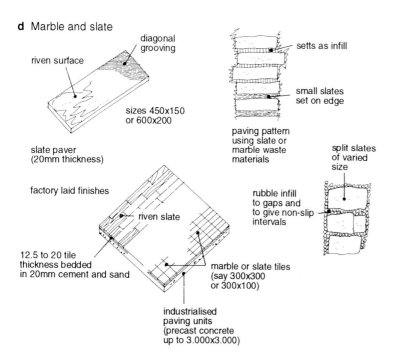

riven surface

diagonal
grooving

sizes 450x150
or 600x200

slate paver
(20mm thickness)

factory laid finishes

riven slate

12.5 to 20 tile
thickness bedded
in 20mm cement and sand

industrialised
paving units
(precast concrete
up to 3.000x3.000)

marble or slate tiles
(say 300x300
or 300x100)

setts as infill

small slates
set on edge

paving pattern
using slate or
marble waste
materials

split slates
of varied
size

rubble infill
to gaps and
to give non-slip
intervals

a Asphalt and asphaltic coatings

Asphalt paving is reserved for watertight surfaces and where a totally inert finish is needed. It is used for tanking below water features, the usual thicknesses are three 10 mm coats laid with lapping joints. Asphaltic mixes can contain crushed granite to provide a richer colour and texture to roads or driveways. The total thickness over concrete bedding is 60 mm, allowing for two-coat work. The immediate underlay has to be well-laid concrete screeding run to accurate falls, since it is not possible to taper asphaltic coatings. The smooth quality of finish means that slopes as shallow as 1:80 are feasible; it is wise, however, to add a further 25 mm to falls to allow for tolerances in the sub-base.

b Ceramic tiles

Paving tiles need to be guaranteed frostproof. Laying depends upon rich cement mortar beds and pointing with 1:1 to 1:3 mixes of cement and sand, plus additives for colouring and water proofing. Precise specifications are needed for work on paving, steps and pool surrounds, and advice should be obtained in writing from tile suppliers, with names of approved fixers.

The sub-base has to be fine concrete screeding in 1:1:3 mixes, laid to accurate falls and shapes. Chicken wire or thin mesh reinforcement is essential to distribute shrinkage stresses in screeds, while thermal expansion joints have to be designed to occur immediately adjacent in decking/vertical surfaces and the finished tile work. Advice on these technical measures can be sought from the leading manufacturers or their trade council.[4] The problem is complicated by the long-term expansion of ceramic products in contact with cement mortar, which entails laying external tiled paving in broken bays of 10–12 m squares with soft mastic joints at those extremities which extend through the screed layer.

Tiled work in swimming pools is a specialist problem outside the scope of this book.[5]

Selecting external tile pavers is not an easy task, the points to look for are:

- Guarantees; ● Non-slip surfaces;
- Robustness to withstand foot traffic and impact from garden furniture.

1.20e stone slabs

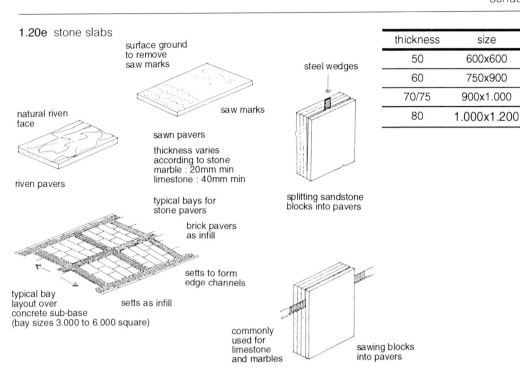

thickness	size
50	600x600
60	750x900
70/75	900x1.000
80	1.000x1.200

surface ground
to remove
saw marks

saw marks

natural riven
face

riven pavers

sawn pavers

thickness varies
according to stone
marble : 20mm min
limestone : 40mm min

typical bays for
stone pavers

brick pavers
as infill

setts to form
edge channels

typical bay
layout over
concrete sub-base
(bay sizes 3.000 to 6.000 square)

setts as infill

steel wedges

splitting sandstone
blocks into pavers

commonly
used for
limestone
and marbles

sawing blocks
into pavers

It is useful to look at installations completed a decade ago. The liability laws vary, but in the UK one needs to consider a 16-year period of liability. The types of tile fall into three basic forms. First and foremost, fully-vitrified ceramic tiles, which resemble engineering-quality brick and are termed 'quarry tiles' or 'klinker tiles'. In broad terms, the hardest-wearing have the darkest colours, so that black, blue black and brown are superior to red and buff-bodied components. Secondly, there are glazed versions of dark-bodied tiles which have frostproof qualities. Finally, there are tiles fired from mud-clays which produce a softer and light-coloured body, such as traditional Mediterranean or Mexican pavers, available in natural colours or glazed. They have more attractive proportions and textures than quarry tiles, but guarantees may not be forthcoming. Refer to Figures 1.21a–c for sizes, and Figure 1.21d for an example of a tiled fountain. In this location Italian terracotta units were made in special sizes to form the fountain surrounds. Terracotta or faience tile is a form of fired ceramic which can be made in large units. The body of the tile blocks is usually hollow or perforated, so firing is effective throughout the profile, and the finishes are natural colour or glazed. A final word of warning: most glazed tiles eventually craze when used externally. Defenders of the faience industry will say this is part of the natural charm of porcelain, and refer to antique Chinese vases, but your clients may have other expectations.

Brick pavers have already been discussed in terms of flexible surfaces. The difference between solid-bedding and pointing derives from the long-term expansion of ceramic products embedded in mortar, subdivided areas being needed as for external tilework. Thinner units can be used due to the continuous support of a concrete sub-base, the industry having responded by making 25 mm thick brick pavers, known as brick tiles. Non-slip versions exist with dimpled or ribbed textures, or with chequered grooves to improve drainage. Kerb and channel units are also manufactured for road verges or for draining terraces, as shown in Figure 1.22. Falls for smooth tiles and bricks can be 1:80 or 1:60 for textured faces.

c Terrazzo: tile and cast in-situ work

This application resembles the examples given for ceramic tile paving, namely steps and pool surrounds. It is best undertaken by specialist sub-contractors, and the firms engaged should be made responsible for the screed sub-base and for the finished terrazzo work, since bonding between the two elements is crucial. The basis for terrazzo, whether precast tile or cast in-situ, is a fine concrete mixture comprising cement (often coloured), marble/ stone dust and broken marble. The surface colour and finish is derived by grinding and polishing the surface. Tiles can be made up to 900 mm square, though smaller units, such as

1.21 Details of ceramic tiles

a Quarry tile components

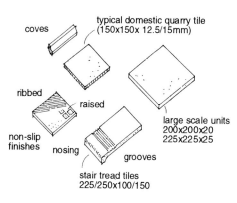

coves

typical domestic quarry tile (150x150x 12.5/15mm)

ribbed

raised

non-slip finishes

nosing

grooves

stair tread tiles 225/250x100/150

large scale units 200x200x20 225x225x25

b Glazed tiles

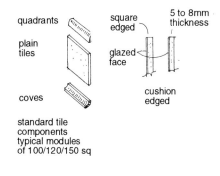

quadrants

plain tiles

square edged

5 to 8mm thickness

glazed face

coves

cushion edged

standard tile components typical modules of 100/120/150 sq

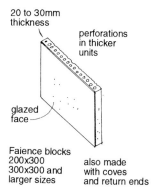

20 to 30mm thickness

perforations in thicker units

glazed face

Faience blocks 200x300 300x300 and larger sizes

also made with coves and return ends

c Traditional mediterranean pavers

25mm thick

colour through cut tile

typical uneven hand-made form 225/300 square

25/40 mm thick

10mm thick for coloured material

glazed cement tile (wide range of sizes)

interlocking forms

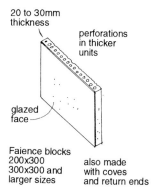

d Glazed tile using terracotta units for the fountain surrounds at Sutton Place, Surrey (1981). Architect: Sir Geoffrey Jellicoe

300 and 450 mm square, are standard. The advantage of terrazzo units over ceramic tiles rests in the complex shaping that can be arranged, which makes it ideal for pool surrounds. Cast in-situ terrazzo can match precast work, which means that a continuous surface can be provided for wet areas. Guarantees are available for frost-resistance and durability. It is easy to maintain and can be reground and repolished to restore to its original condition. Falls can be 1:80.

The technique dates back to Roman times when flooring surfaces were formed as conglomerates of concrete and marble fragments, often in the form of mosaic pavements. Figures 1.23a−c show three present-day examples.

d Marble and slate paving

These expensive stones are cut into thin slabs and used as a paving veneer, or as a facing to steps and garden plinths − 20 or 25 mm thicknesses should be regarded as the minimum externally, though thin tile versions exist which rely on 10 or 12 mm of stone bonded to a cement base. Such tiles relate only to interior work. Marbles must be carefully selected where frost-resistance is required, and have additional protection with winter covering or by waxing to aid their preservation in severe winters. It is true that Roman examples in travertine marble date back 2000 years, but these are solid paving blocks, often 450 mm thick, not just the 20 mm veneer common today.

Brick gutters and kerbs
alternative forms

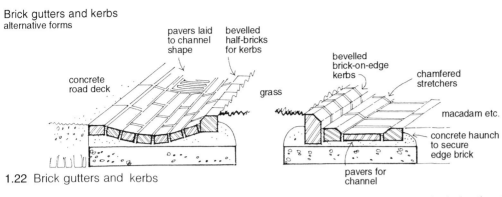

1.22 Brick gutters and kerbs

Split slate slabs have been utilized for paving wherever slate is quarried.
A characteristic in the Lake District and other parts of north-west England is the use of Westmoreland slate for general building (roofing and walling) as well as for garden construction. A great deal of waste material is generated by quarrying, and attempts have been made to promote pavers which comprise cast concrete slabs faced with a random mix of broken slate. Figure 1.20d shows this

experiment at Liverpool Cathedral. The riven finish has been selected to provide a non-slip surface. Polished marble and slate both become slippery when wet, and such finishes might be considered for decorative surfaces rather than regular pavements. The geological factors affecting the selection of marble and slate are as follows:

Marbles and Slates Both are metamorphic rocks formed by transformation of sedementary rocks within the earth's crust by the processes of heat, pressure and chemical changes. Slate is evolved from mudstones and shales. The original mineral matter is partly transferred into planes at angles to the pressure bed, and the presence of mica means that the rock can be easily split. British sources are the Lake District (blue greys, greens and silver grey), North Wales (blues, blue blacks) and Cornwall (multi-coloured). Marble is limestone that has wholly recrystallized, and no true marble will contain fossils. The principal sources are France, Italy, Portugal and Spain. Thin slabs of marble can distort under freezing/thawing conditions. Hollow bedding with mortar dots to carry the corners of slabs will quickly fail under pedestrian traffic.

To avoid slipperiness, both materials need textured finishes — say riven for slate, grit-blasted for marble, or grooved to provide additional drainage. Close bands of smooth and textured strips is another possibility. A dry, warm setting is ideal, and Figures 1.23b—c highlight the decorative quality of well-chosen marble paving. The historic context should be emphasized, as should the way contrasting colours of travertine marble and granite have been used by Palladio in the piazza in front of St Giorgio Maggiore, Venice (Figure 1.24a). Another example is Michelangelo's design in similar contrasts for the Capitol, Rome, which was not constructed until 1936 (Figure 1.24b).

1.23 Terrazzo paving mixed with marble or granite
a Precast terrazzo units as a pool surround at the Christian Science Center, Boston (1970). Architect: Pei Associates
b Terrazzo and marble mosaic as a pool surround at San Simeon, California (1919—39). Architect: Julia Morgan
c Terrazzo and marble slabs at Getty Museum, California (1972—3). Consultant architect: Stephen Garrett

1.24 Marble in historical context
a Travertine and granite paving piazza in front of St Giorgio's, Venice (1560–75). Architect: Palladio
b Similar contrasts in pattern and material, the Capitol, Rome

a

b

e   Other stone paving

The choice of other building stones for paving is as follows, and is based upon sedimentary stones.

Sandstone An arenaceous rock formed by the compaction and natural bonding of grains of quartz and other minerals. The varieties are classified according to the cementing material and presence of other materials. For example, when the bonding agent is quartz the rock is known as a quartzite. Durable sandstones are composed of silica material bound together with a siliceous cement. The silica element is indestructible, failure of sandstones resulting from the de-bonding of the layers, and impurities such as clay or mica which weather badly. These durable stones are ideally suited for paving since they can be split in large-dimension units from 1.2–2.4 m square. The colour range is silver grey or buff to shades of pink and red brown.

Limestone A calcareous rock, composed mainly of the mineral calcite and usually containing fossil. The principal sources in the UK are the South-West, the Cotswolds and the limestone ridge which runs through Oxfordshire, Northamptonshire and Lincolnshire. The stone is generally less durable than sandstone, and care should be taken with selection for frost-resistance when used in paving or steps. The colour range is near-white to cream and honey-coloured tones. Grey and blue grey limestone is also available from Derbyshire and Yorkshire quarries.

Natural bed in sedimentary stones The natural bed is that plane in which the original sedimentation occurred – this need not be horizontal since strata are often inclined or upright due to bed disturbance during their geological formation. In paving work the bed is often parallel to the wearing face due to the ease of splitting sandstones along the natural bedding plane. Frost action and wear will gradually crater or flake the wearing face, which means reversing slabs to extend their life span. Severe wear in ramps or steps means placing stone with the natural bed in a vertical plane to increase the wearing resistance. Sawn blocks of this pattern are used like granite setts for roads and crossovers.

The primary working of stone occurs near the quarry, as splitting and cutting is easier while quarry sap is still present in the freshly-quarried material. Sandstone blocks are split and trimmed, the riven face providing a non-slip surface. Production is batched so that thicknesses and girths can be matched. See Figure 1.25a for typical batches of sandstone pavers (commonly called Yorkstone paving in the UK). A smooth finish is obtained by grinding or sawing, and the sawn texture can be left or alternatively ground smooth. Thicknesses vary with unit sizes, and obviously affect cost per slab, apart from the labour charges inherent in laying heavy slabs on site. For example, two masons will be needed to shift one slab measuring $750 \times 75-80\,mm$ thick, while a single worker can handle slabs $750 \times 600 \times 45-50\,mm$ thick; the larger sizes of stone slabs need mechanical handling. A recent example is the repaving of Trafalgar Square, London, with blocks which replicated the original nineteenth-century work using 2.4 m squares of Yorkstone (Figures 1.25b–c). The source was the Scoutmoor quarry near Halifax, Yorkshire, and the blocks were of the same quality as the original Silex stone used. The present contract involves a concrete sub-base to cope with pedestrian and service traffic.

Suction pads were used for lifting and placing slabs onto location blocks, thus enabling the pressure cement grouting to be completed without the risk of hollow beds occurring. The edges of slabs need to be spaced to prevent spalling under impact, and to be neatly pointed with cement and stone dust, moistened and brushed into the joint.

The erosion pattern of flaking has already been mentioned, and the visual effect can be seen in Figures 1.25d–e.

Sandstone paving can be severely eroded by the run-off from adjacent limestone surfaces, particularly building façades. The layout should allow for this defect by using an isolating surface of setts or pebbles to absorb the run-off, complete with gullies if needed. Limestone and sandstone slabs laid next to one another can cause localized decay – for example, Portland stone steps discharging on to a 'Yorkstone' terrace.

Limestone paving is usually selected where a light-reflective stone is needed, or where, as in the Cotswolds, a local material is used to guarantee a homogeneous and natural character in paving and walling. Algae and lichen flourish on limestone surfaces, so slipperiness can be a serious problem. Cement grouting, as with brick pavers, can counter moss growth, but regular dressing with moss killers may be necessary.

Limestones such as Shelley Portland resemble the marble travertine, where the honeycomb nature of the stone produces a natural non-slip surface. Large blocks up to 2.4 m long can be obtained, which makes it a popular material for steps and kerbs. Weathering increases the textural quality and enhances the surface with white highlights. An elegant example is shown in Figure 1.25f.

Owing to their dimensions, paving slabs have to be laid in simple and regular falls of approximately 1:40, either one- or two-way, with channels formed in granite setts. A more expensive solution is to shape thicker blocks of stone to form integral channels with longitudinal falls to gullies (see Figure 1.25g–h which detail drainage channels and a carved gully cover).

f   Precast paving

The casting and making of concrete paving has already been explained. Precast manufacture uses similar materials, but involves factory

1.25 Other stone paving
a Typical batches of sandstone pavers
b Laying procedure for large slabs. Repaving of Trafalgar Square, London (1989). Architect: Donald Insall and Partners

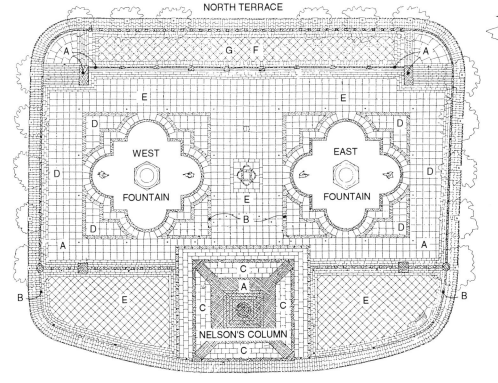

c Typical paving bay layout at Trafalgar Square
d Renewed Yorkstone at the Temple, City of London (1964). Architect: Hubert Worthington
e The same paving today with flaking of surface due to erosion
f Shelley Portand stone as long blocks of paving in the forecourt of the Economist Building, London (1964). Architects: Alison and Peter Smithson in association with Maurice Bebb

A existing Granite
B new Granite border
C Cromwell Buff York stone
D re-used York stone
E new Scout Moor Blue York stone
F Portland stone
G Mansfield stone

d

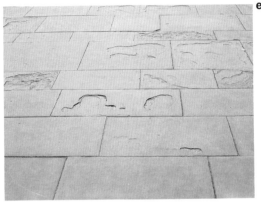

e

f

g

h

Figure 1.26a for typical patterns and sizes. Typical finishes are:

- Smooth (normally bearing the imprint of steel plate texture);
- Simulated (depends upon the mould plates, which give a riven or weathered effect);
- Textured (ribbed or rough-textured due to grit-blasting or acid etching);
- Chequered (regular patterns from metal rollers to imitate setts or brick pavers);
- Non-slip (with inclusions of carborandum dust, or non-slip inserts, or grooved).

The colour and natural texture depends, as with in-situ work, upon cement colour, the aggregates used and the degree of aggregate exposure.

The bedding and laying process is similar to stone paving but is speedier due to the regular sizes and thicknesses. The simulated slabs made with buff-coloured cement and stone aggregate are very close in appearance to natural stone pavers and can be installed at one-third the cost.

g Portland stone drainage channel and gulley cover. King George VI Memorial steps. Carlton Gardens, London (late 1950s). Architect: Louis de Soissons

h Stone gully cover in gravel paving, Versailles

production in steel moulds. Compaction is achieved by mechanical pressure, and the curing improved by autoclaves. The resultant product complies with given compressive strengths and wearing resistance.[6] Domestic paving is thinner (about 38 mm) and made with concrete cast in vibrated moulds. These have limited resistance to cracking.

The slab modules relate to batch sizes of 600 mm girth and 50 mm thickness. Refer to

1.26 Precast paving compared with natural stone

a Precast paving : typical patterns & sizes

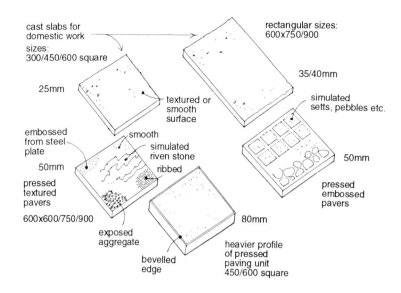

cast slabs for domestic work
sizes:
300/450/600 square

25mm

textured or smooth surface

rectangular sizes:
600x750/900

35/40mm

simulated setts, pebbles etc.

embossed from steel plate

smooth

simulated riven stone

ribbed

50mm

50mm

pressed textured pavers

600x600/750/900

exposed aggregate

bevelled edge

80mm

heavier profile of pressed paving unit 450/600 square

pressed embossed pavers

b Regular grid layouts with precast paving of differing textures
c Interweaving slabs of differing sizes

b

c

d Typical standard channel blocks and kerbs

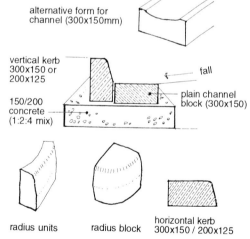

alternative form for channel (300x150mm)

vertical kerb 300x150 or 200x125

fall

150/200 concrete (1:2:4 mix)

plain channel block (300x150)

radius units

radius block

horizontal kerb 300x150 / 200x125

The repetitive aspect of the product can be used to advantage by devising patterns based upon regular geometry, as shown in Figures 1.26b–c. The bland appearance can be alleviated by interspersing with clay or smaller concrete block pavers to give a contrast in colour, scale and texture. Precast components have also supplanted granite or natural stone kerbs and channels, and once again the standardized product is covered by British Standards specifications or their equivalents.[7] Figure 1.26d shows typical details, and Figure 1.26e shows an example of an application.

Solid-bedding of slabs over a lean-mix concrete sub-base without hardcore is current practice for roadside pavements/sidewalks. The solidity improves the bearing capacity for vehicles which may park on the kerb or drive across footways for deliveries. Heavy road traffic produces a sideways vibration that is readily transferred to the continuous concrete bedding, hence soft-packed material is used between the pavement and building frontage. Kerbing by service vehicles can convey a direct thrust upon building walls, which has to be countered by non-rigid fillings, such as butyl mastics.

Public footways have pavers laid at right-angles to improve non-slip qualities and to ease the difficulty of cutting curved layouts at kerbs and frontages. The slabs are laid broken-joint to facilitate lifting with a crowbar forced against a solid portion when lifting, which overcomes fragility at points where four slabs meet in square bond patterns (Figure 1.26f). Square bond patterns look better, but should ideally be reserved for rectangular paving areas that are free from wheel loads. Hexagonal pavers are available, but also need care in laying out, since curved or splayed cuts prove to be very wasteful.

Increasingly, traffic engineers are looking towards smaller and shorter precast blocks for solid-bedded pavements to avoid the fracturing problems that beset thin slabs of 45–50 mm thickness laid in batches of 600 mm girth. The standard of pavement/sidewalk maintenance in the UK has fallen sharply, assisted by the lowering of legal requirements governing differing levels between adjoining pavers. These are now permitted to be 15 mm steps as compared with plus or minus 2 mm in the 1970s. This is markedly different to procedures in Germany.[8]

The relative ease in laying and patching macadam/tar surfacing as a replacement for slab pavers is one of the main reasons for its continued use even though the cost is within 10% of concrete paving. Ponding is one of the main criticisms where falls are shallower than 1:30, and substitution for slabs laid at 1:40 to 1:50 falls often leads to a disappointing surface unless regrading can take place. Fuller consideration of macadam is given in Section 1.7.

1.5 Garden Paving

Sections 1.1 and 1.2 discuss at length the soft and flexible surfaces that are associated with garden works. Many forms of slab and precast paving are equally suitable and will provide adequate service on flexible beds if vehicle traffic is excluded from the pathways or terraces. The usual preparation is to excavate to a 250–300 mm depth, to compact the subsoil

e Public pavement using natural stone pavers

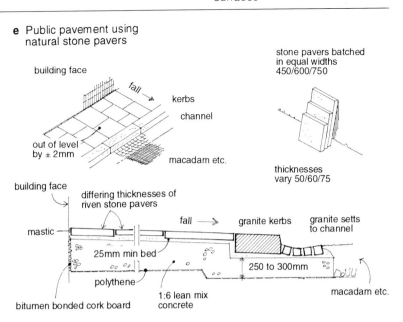

Pavements between buildings

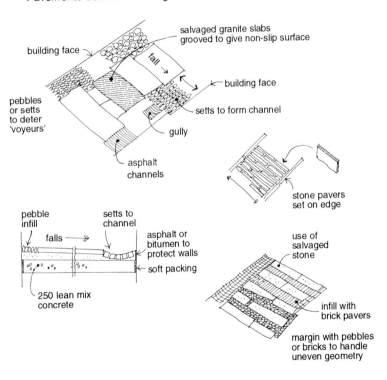

f Broken joint versus square bonding pattern

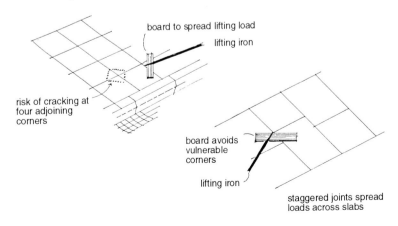

and to overlay with consolidated hardcore, blinded with crushed stone or fine gravel. The slabs are laid in a dry sand/lime mix and pointed or left with wide margins to allow for soiling and seeding. Large paving slabs are cut or riven thicker than small units, and a layout with both patterns will need extra bedding to make up the difference.

The patterns of material and configuration of units are as described for stone and precast slabs in Sections 1.4e & f. The concept of a more relaxed layout with winding paths or irregular margins to accommodate planting material may lead the designer to seek a more natural line than the geometric or grid paving associated with public spaces. Natural materials with riven or sawn faces look better in a landscape setting than smooth-faced or polished slabs and will not be so troublesome in terms of attack from lichen or moss. Figures 1.27a–g show examples of garden paths displaying features designed to fit a natural setting.

Quarried stone can be sawn into batches, but assorted sizes are easier to handle in a free layout. The designs by Sir Geoffrey Jellicoe at Sutton Place, Surrey, use larger and smaller units, with the large slabs turned at an angle to crenellate the path edge at borders. Some stones are difficult to trim in a regular fashion, or are available as quarry waste, which is the origin of crazy paving. The natural form can be seen at Hidcote, Gloucestershire, where small pieces of Cotswold limestone have been used

to good effect. Materials, like quartz or slate have a fine appearance in random sizes, and suit infilling with pebble or granite setts to emphasize the contrasting shapes. The Nut Walk at Sissinghurst, East Sussex, is another example, where the interface between the stones is gradually filled with plants as paving and borders merge. Paving for private gardens like Sissinghurst, which are later opened to the public, may have to withstand the onslaught of 120,000 visitors per year in contrast to family and friends of yesteryear. At Sissinghurst the Nicholsons laid out grass paths, but designed brick and stone paving as replacements in anticipation of future crowds. The National Trust have adopted these designs, which successfully manage the transformation from private to public paths without losing a garden scale. Old stone flags laid on lime/sand beds disintegrate under heavy traffic and have to be relaid on newly-consolidated hardcore. Figures 1.27a–g reveal the damage that can be caused to old paving laid on soft bedding.

1.6 Timber Paving

Timber use and the woodworking skills involved in paving are an extension of the construction methods employed for fences and retaining features. The materials are often recycled railway sleepers or woodland trimmings. The choice of timber species

1.27 Garden paving
a Irregular layout as laid at Sutton Place, Surrey (1982). Architect: Sir Geoffrey Jellicoe
b Same layout after naturalization by planting

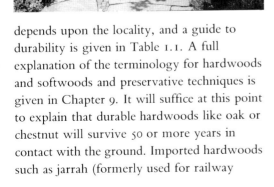

c Random arrangement in new paving laid at the Royal Horticultural Society Gardens, Wisley, Surrey
d Paving made from quarry waste, Hidcote, Gloucestershire
e Quartz slabs infilled with granite setts. Public park in Alstatten, Switzerland
f Limestone slabs laid to cross-falls, Haddon Hall, Derbyshire. Note how the path is deforming under heavy use, and the unsightly eroded edge to the lawn
g Nicholson's design scheme for brick and stone paths to replace grass paths at Sissinghurst, East Sussex

depends upon the locality, and a guide to durability is given in Table 1.1. A full explanation of the terminology for hardwoods and softwoods and preservative techniques is given in Chapter 9. It will suffice at this point to explain that durable hardwoods like oak or chestnut will survive 50 or more years in contact with the ground. Imported hardwoods such as jarrah (formerly used for railway sleepers) are also highly durable. Softwoods are far less durable unless one can afford Californian redwood, Russian larch or Western red cedar. All other softwoods used for paving work depend upon full preservative treatment to give resistance to wet rot beyond five to ten years. Sleepers have also been made from Douglas fir or larch, and were usually preserved in tar-based solutions.

Table 1.1 Durability and permeability ratings for some structural hardwoods

Timber species	Country of origin	Durability	Permeability
Afrormosia *Pericopsis elata*	W Africa	Durable	Extremely resistant
Afzelia *Afzelia* spp	W Africa	Very durable	Extremely resistant
Ash − European *Fraxinus excelsior*	Europe	Perishable	Moderately resistant
Balau *Shorea* spp	S E Asia	Durable	Extremely resistant
Balau red *Shorea* spp	S E Asia	Moderately durable	Extremely resistant
Basralocus *Dicorynia guianensis*	Surinam & F Guyana	Durable	Extremely resistant
Beech − European *Fagus sylvatica*	Europe	Perishable	Permeable
Belian *Eusideroxylon zwageri*	S E Asia	Very durable	Resistant
Bintangor *Calophyllum curtisii* *C. inophyllum, C. retusum*	S E Asia	Moderately durable	Moderately resistant
Bitis *Madhuca utilis,* *Palaquium ridleyi*	S E Asia	Very durable	Moderately resistant
Dahoma *Piptadeniastrum* *afrcanum*	W, C & E Africa	Durable	Very resistant
Danta *Nesogordonia* *papaverifera*	W Africa	Moderately durable	Resistant
Ekki *Lophira alata*	W Africa	Very durable	Extremely resistant
Elm *Ulmus procera,* *Ulmus hollandica*	Europe	Non-durable	Resistant
Greenheart *Ocotea rodiaei*	Guyana	Very durable	Extremely resistant
Idigbo *Terminalia ivorensis*	W Africa	Durable/Moderately durable	Extremely resistant
Iroko *Milicia excelsa* *(Chlorophora excelsa)*	W Africa	Very durable/Durable	Extremely resistant
Jarrah *Eucalyptus marginata*	Australia	Very durable	Extremely resistant

Kapur *Dryobalanops* spp	S E Asia	Very durable/Durable	Extremely resistant
Karri *Eucalyptus diversicolor*	Australia	Durable	Extremely resistant
Kempas *Koompassia malaccensis*	S E Asia	Durable	Resistant
Keruing *Dipterocarpus* spp	S E Asia	Moderately durable	Resistant
Makoré *Tieghemella heckelii*	W Africa	Very durable	Extremely resistant
Mengkulang *Heritiera* spp	S E Asia	Non-durable	Resistant
Meranti-dark red (also includes dark red seraya & dark red lauan) *Shorea* spp	S E Asia	Variable-generally Non-durable/Durable	Resistant/Extremely resistant
Merbau *Intsia* spp	S E Asia	Durable	Extremely resistant
Missanda *Erythrophleum* spp	W Africa	Very durable	Very/Extremely resistant
Mora *Mora excelsa*	C America	Very durable	Very/Extremely resistant
Nargusta *Terminalia amazonia*	C America	Very durable	Very resistant
Niangon *Heritiera utilis*	W Africa	Moderately durable	Extremely resistant
Oak – European *Quercus petraea,* *Q robur*	Europe	Durable	Extremely resistant
Okan *Cylicodiscus gabunensis*	W Africa	Very durable	Extremely resistant
Opepe *Nauclea diderrichii*	W Africa	Very durable	Moderately resistant
Padauk, African *Pterocarpus soyauxii*	W Africa	Very durable	Moderately resistant/Resistant
Purpleheart *Peltogyne* spp	S America	Durable/Moderately durable	Extremely resistant
Sepetir *Sindora* spp	S E Asia	Durable	Extremely resistant
Teak *Tectona grandis*	S E Asia	Very durable	Extremely resistant

Note Many of the above mentioned tropical hardwoods are from endangered species.
Specifiers should check that their selection comes from plantation sources where authentic forest
conservation exists.

1.28 Sleeper and log paving

a Sleeper and log steps

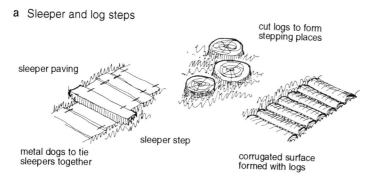

sleeper paving

cut logs to form
stepping places

metal dogs to tie
sleepers together

sleeper step

corrugated surface
formed with logs

b Simple steps using sleepers

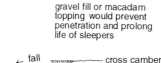

gravel fill or macadam
topping would prevent
penetration and prolong
life of sleepers

gravel over broken
brick hardcore
as infill to path

cross
camber

← fall

← fall

cross camber

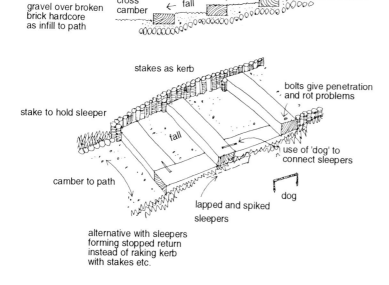

stakes as kerb

bolts give penetration
and rot problems

stake to hold sleeper

fall

use of 'dog' to
connect sleepers

camber to path

dog

lapped and spiked
sleepers

alternative with sleepers
forming stopped return
instead of raking kerb
with stakes etc.

c Simple steps or ramped
steps using Larch stakes

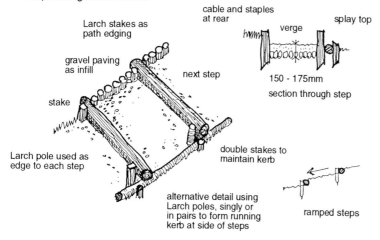

cable and staples
at rear

splay top

Larch stakes as
path edging

verge

gravel paving
as infill

next step

150 - 175mm

section through step

stake

Larch pole used as
edge to each step

double stakes to
maintain kerb

alternative detail using
Larch poles, singly or
in pairs to form running
kerb at side of steps

ramped steps

d Cut log paving in sand.
Oriental landscaped area at Swiss National
Exhibition, Laussane (1964)

e Demonstration Japanese house and
duckboard terrace. (Portland, Oregon USA)

Sleeper paths

Recycled sleepers are generally available as
balks measuring 300 × 150 × 2400 mm. The
original impregnation can still be injurious to
planting, and plastic lining will have to be used
at vertical edges. The bedding should be self-
draining with gravel and/or hardcore, and the
levels so arranged that 1:40 cross or
longitudinal falls exist to prevent ponding. The
sleepers are laid at right-angles to the track to
spread wheel loads. 'Iron dogs' (double-spiked
staples) can be hammered home to improve
stability. Log paths are laid in a similar
manner. The key advantage is minimal cost in
comparison with firm materials, and this is
often the best solution where a short to
medium-term result is required, which is to be
replaced in due course by more permanent
materials. Sleepers are ideal for forming
stepped features in gravel paths, and can be
combined to make abutments and short
retaining features. Figures 1.28a−c show key
details.

Cut log paving is usually associated with
gardeners, footholds in borders, but can form
an interesting texture to ground modelling

inspired by Oriental gardens, as shown in Figure 1.28c. Cut logs of this pattern are driven into 300–450 mm of silver sand and are more usual as a visual surface than practical paving.

Timber decking

Decking or duckboard terracing also has its origins in Chinese and Japanese landscape design, and is the corollary to timber-framed architecture where floors and terraces are placed above the ground and supported on intermediate framing. A typical Japanese terrace is featured in Figure 1.28e, the constructional sketches which follow explaining the supporting framework of joints and posts. The exposed deck is made self-draining to save the cost of waterproof decking, with plywood, felt roofing and gutters, etc. Slatted battens are fixed by non-ferrous screws or screw nails to the joists, and the slats have to be durable and splinter-free. Hardwoods such as oak, keruing, iroko, or teak have been the traditional choice. Conservation policies will probably mean using oak or iroko in future.

The joist framework can be constructed from a mixture of timber species: oak or iroko for posts, with impregnated Douglas fir or larch for framing. Ideally, the posts should be tar-painted where buried in the ground, or else placed on concrete pads with a separating layer of bituthene or lead (code 4 in UK). The ground left below the decking should be blinded with shingle to facilitate weed clearance.

A housing project in Lewisham, London, is constructed on this principle of raised floors and decks, and some residents have enclosed the space below their houses with mesh to form a spacious home for rabbits!

The popularity of decks owes a great deal to the persuasive writing of Thomas Church, the ideas also embracing duckboard trellises that could be laid in sand or placed over unsightly paving.[9] Such components are now widely marketed on both sides of the Atlantic.

Wood block paving dates back to the days of horse-drawn traffic, to deaden the noise of hooves and iron-shod wheels. The blocks were oak, chestnut or jarrah, and tar-impregnated, with a tar and sand coating. They are sometimes used to recreate historic settings for *porte-cochère* or stable entries.

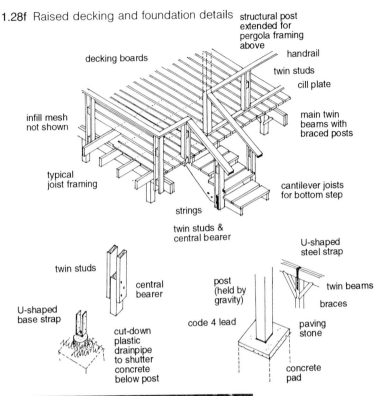

1.28f Raised decking and foundation details

g Duckboard trellises used over concrete paving. Demonstration garden at Bonn International Garden Show (1979)

Timber species and their durability externally

Grade of durability	Approximate life in contact with ground (years)
Very durable	more than 25
Durable	15–25
Moderately durable	10–15
Non-durable	5–10
Perishable	Less than 5

1.7 Other Surfaces

The host of specialist techniques in athletics and sports ground construction is beyond the scope of this book. There are many valuable references to be obtained from Sports Councils and similar organizations and from contractors specializing in this work.[10]

- General points – *Specification for outdoor sports and recreational facilities*, National Playing Fields Association, 1980.
  A. E. Weddle (ed.), *Landscape Techniques*, Heinemann, 1979.
- Specialist firms – *Landscape Specification*, 3rd edn, Landscape Promotions, 1991.
- Advice – Sports Council Technical Unit for Sport, 16 Upper Woburn Place, London WC1H 0QP.

Consideration of highway construction is also beyond the scope of this book, which may help explain the scant regard given to 'black top' or tar surfacing. The unpopularity of this surface results from the way the coating replaces gravel, granite setts or other natural materials with a non-reflective and characterless mess. Coating over gravel is a short-term remedy since frosts will rapidly lift the coating. Dressing with rolled stone will improve the colouring but reduce stormwater flow, Chemical bonding with stone granules provides a fine-grained surface, but at a cost that equals brick or block pavers.

The utilitarian quality of basic macadam/tar surfacing dictates its choice for service areas and parking bays, and especially where River or Water regulations forbid the laying of porous paving which will leach oil or pollutants to the subsoil.

Figures 1.29a–d are devoted to the design and construction problems of laying out car parks to soften their impact upon the environment. Layouts should be planted to form a surrounding framework and as subdivisions to give definition to the parking bays. Drainage channels should be located away from planting strips to prevent pollution, perhaps ideally at the centre of trafficways to

1.29 Car park construction

a Trees and bollards in parking areas

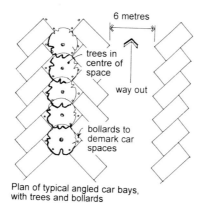

6 metres

trees in centre of space

way out

bollards to demark car spaces

Plan of typical angled car bays, with trees and bollards

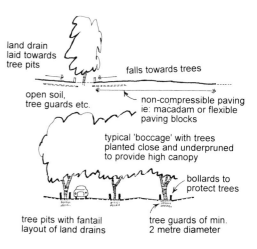

land drain laid towards tree pits

falls towards trees

open soil, tree guards etc.

non-compressible paving ie: macadam or flexible paving blocks

typical 'boccage' with trees planted close and underpruned to provide high canopy

bollards to protect trees

tree pits with fantail layout of land drains

tree guards of min. 2 metre diameter

b Kerbs and bollards for parking areas

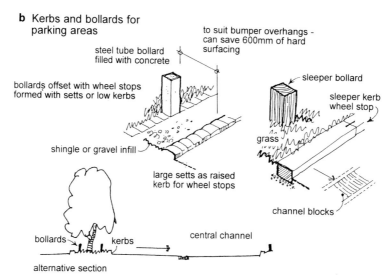

to suit bumper overhangs - can save 600mm of hard surfacing

steel tube bollard filled with concrete

bollards offset with wheel stops formed with setts or low kerbs

sleeper bollard

sleeper kerb wheel stop

grass

shingle or gravel infill

large setts as raised kerb for wheel stops

channel blocks

bollards   kerbs   central channel

alternative section

keep parking areas as dry as possible. Different colouring for the wearing coat of macadam can distinguish parking areas from roads, grey or black being more suitable for the former since it masks oil slick. Slightly lowering the car park level and using the surplus soil to mound the surroundings will also assist.

Plantings and tree pits must have protection from vehicles and people, and here raised planters, bollards or robust triprails can be used. Tree guards, which assist with watering and provide a surface hostile to pedestrians, are another solution.

Tree guards protect newly-planted material and existing trees in various ways. Firstly, they prevent soil compaction around the main roots and provide a protective zone that is clearly demarked. Secondly, the surface treatment can serve as a water catchment area and be reinforced by irrigation pipes built into the planting pit. Thirdly, the infill paving can be loose shingle, perforated blocks or loose setts, all of which permit growth and allow for relaying or adjustment for root spread. Details are provided in Figures 1.30a–d for tree pits in relation to new planting, as well as typical grids or loose paving which can be employed as surface finishes near trees. The following notes summarize the key design points.

Tree pits for new planting

The pits (Figure 1.30a) need to be dug at least 225 mm deeper than the root ball, and prepared after breaking the ground for a further 225 mm depth. Site drainage is improved by shaping the pit floor with falls to the edges, with, say, a 150 mm depth of gravel. Land drains can be laid running away from this zone in heavy soils. More commonly, irrigation pipes are needed to facilitate watering in dry spells, usually of perforated plastic, rising to the surface on either side of the planting area.

Tree pits in artificial conditions

This example (Figures 1.30b–c) shows a precast concrete tree pit used for a rooftop car park. The construction involves an extensive area of rubble infill covering an underground

1.30 Tree pits and tree guards

a Tree pit variations

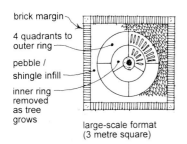

detail of land
drains and
water point

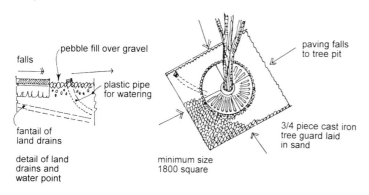

falls

pebble fill over gravel

plastic pipe
for watering

fantail of
land drains

paving falls
to tree pit

3/4 piece cast iron
tree guard laid
in sand

minimum size
1800 square

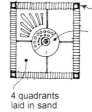

brick margin

4 quadrants to
outer ring

pebble /
shingle infill

inner ring
removed
as tree
grows

large-scale format
(3 metre square)

bollards at corners
in traffic areas

2-ring
centre
piece

sizes
2.100 to
2.400 square

4 quadrants
laid in sand

b Tree guard materials

	type	appraisal	problems
a	shingle	good short term material	easily vandalised
b	pebble over shingle	more stable	ditto
c	gravel	ideal, vis a vis drainage	ditto: and can be compacted for heavy traffic
d	brick or setts over gravel	gives reasonable surface but needs periodic relaying	sub-base needs to be designed for traffic loads
e	hollow brick or block	ditto: has advantage of being difficult to "lift" in vandal-prone areas	ditto
f	cast iron tree guards	excellent traditional method: anchored by driving home bent steel bars	nil
g	precast version	excellent - but difficult to adjust as trees grow	nil
h	grid units	"BG"slabs or similar are excellent	expensive to relay

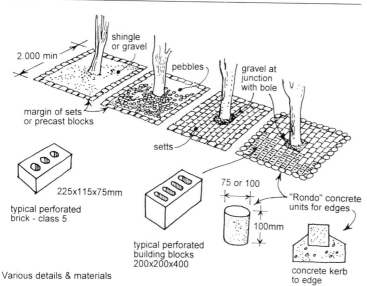

2.000 min

shingle
or gravel

pebbles

gravel at
junction
with bole

margin of sets
or precast blocks

setts

225x115x75mm

typical perforated
brick - class 5

typical perforated
building blocks
200x200x400

75 or 100

100mm

"Rondo" concrete
units for edges

concrete kerb
to edge

Various details & materials

c

d

e

Tree guard materials

The sketches (Figure 1.30d) show some of the proprietary forms of cast iron and precast concrete tree guards available. The cast iron frets provide greater drainage areas and are available as double rings so that the inner sections can be removed as the tree's bole increases in girth. Precast units have the advantage that they can be laid integral with paving units, though they need to be relaid as settlement or root heave recurs. Alternative treatments with pebbles or loose-laid granite setts perform just as well but are more readily vandalized.

Sectional cast iron tree guards

Two traditional examples are shown (Figures 1.30e−f) which reveal the range of attractive castings available. It is helpful from the point of view of maintenance to contain the grids within a margin of cemented paving. Security can be enhanced by holding down the grids using high-tensile steel 'dogs' hammered into the ground.

Precast hollow blocks for tree surrounds

This simple example (Figure 1.30g) shows an economic solution employing standard building blocks, with the perforations acting as irrigation holes for the planting pits.

railway station. The tree pits are planters, and serve as divisions to the surface car park, which relates to street level. Tree grids are provided as a galvanized steel frame infilled with perforated blocks. The ultimate surfacing is formed with granite setts, the drainage measures comprising gullies feeding irrigation pipes to the planted areas.

2.01 The grand stairs, Versailles (1661–87). Architect: André Lenôtre
a The grand stairs close by the main terrace
b Reconstruction of steps

Legislation on disabled access calls for ramped access. In general terms, this relates to entry points for public buildings and the provision of alternative routes to steps in public spaces. Ramps are also used to form emergency escape paths.

Space is not usually at a premium in garden or landscape design, and it is relatively easy to extend a ramped path to negotiate changes of level. Safety requirements in the UK call for 1:12 slopes with continuous lengths limited to 5 m between changes of direction; the length can be 10 m for 1:15 ramps. Guardrails are needed if the ramp has vertical edges, with heights standardized at 900 mm for slopes and 1.1 m at level landings. The strength of guardrails has to be agreed with local regulations.

Typical figures for Uniformly Distributed Loads at the top of guardrails (applied horizontally) are:

- Residential (private houses) 0.36 kN/m (stairs and ramps);
- Residential (institutional) 0.74 kN/m;
- Places of public assembly 3.0 kN/m.

Guardrails for the disabled should extend 300 mm beyond the length of the ramp to give extra safety. This is a wise precaution in any case, and one neglected elsewhere in the standard UK Building Regulations, which permit podiums or ramps to be unguarded for vertical edges up to 380 mm in public areas — high enough to break a leg amongst the able-bodied! Surfaces for ramps should be non-slip, and this can be achieved using the paving materials reviewed in Chapter 1, polished marble or glazed tiles being the obvious exceptions.

Steps in landscape can be divided into three categories: firstly, garden steps to negotiate minor changes within a garden setting; secondly, steps related to building entrances, which are bound by UK building regulations and codes of practice;[1] thirdly, monumental steps in landscape, such as those in the grounds of Versailles (Figures 2.01a−b). There are also the commonplace derivatives of the formal tradition where flights of external steps are needed in public spaces.

2.1   Simple Garden Steps

The sleeper steps shown in Figures 1.29 could be remade in permanent materials, such as second-hand granite or sandstone kerbs. The self-weight and stability of such blocks of stone ensures that these elements can be ground-bedded on compacted soil with a layer of sand or fine gravel to assist levelling. Single blocks can be butted together for longer runs beyond 900 or 1200 mm, pointing or cement mortar beds being totally avoided. The ends of the individual steps can be expressed in various ways, either projecting from the ground slope or else recessed between sloping kerbs. Comparisons are shown in Figures 2.02a−b.

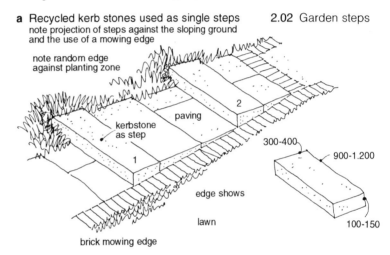

a Recycled kerb stones used as single steps   2.02 Garden steps
note projection of steps against the sloping ground and the use of a mowing edge

note random edge against planting zone

paving

kerbstone as step

brick mowing edge

edge shows

lawn

300-400

900-1.200

100-150

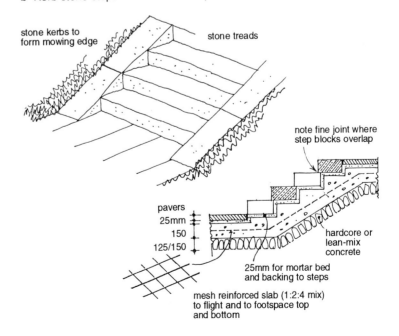

b Kerb stone steps recessed into slope

stone kerbs to form mowing edge

stone treads

note fine joint where step blocks overlap

pavers 25mm

150

125/150

hardcore or lean-mix concrete

25mm for mortar bed and backing to steps

mesh reinforced slab (1:2:4 mix) to flight and to footspace top and bottom

2.02c Layouts for ramped paths related to contours

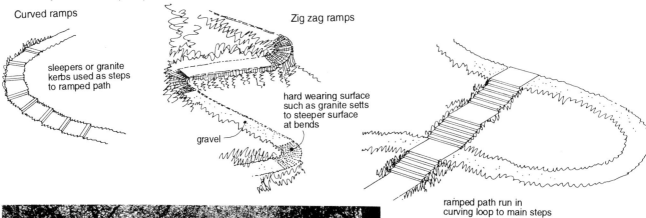

Curved ramps

sleepers or granite kerbs used as steps to ramped path

Zig zag ramps

hard wearing surface such as granite setts to steeper surface at bends

gravel

ramped path run in curving loop to main steps

d Granite setts for ramped steps. Woodland path to Kennedy Memorial, Runnymede (1965). Architect: Sir Geoffrey Jellicoe
e Same location but showing Shelley Portland stone step slabs by memorial stone. Note the delicate treatment of setts used as step ends
f Use of large sandstone paving stones to provide simple steps. Rhine Park' Cologne International Gardenshow (mid-1950s)

Stepped ramps can be blended with sloping ground by varying the frequency of steps or by winding the path to suit the contours. Small ramped pieces of stone could be placed at each step to assist wheelchair users, and gardeners with wheelbarrows. Figures 2.02c−f show such details, and Figures 2.02d−e feature the ramps and steps at the Kennedy Memorial, Runnymede, near the Thames; where considerable care has been taken to model the ascending steps into the landscape. The outdoor scale is well-captured in Sir Geoffrey Jellicoe's design, with a generous proportion to the tread−riser relationship. It should be remembered that internal stairs, at their most generous, are often 300×150 mm (tread to riser) while externally the ideal proportions should be shallower to reflect the horizontal character or spreading lines of landscape. The Spanish Steps in Rome have a proportion of 400×100 mm (see Figure 2.06e). The 100 mm riser should be treated as a minimum from the safety point of view. Step ratios are not arbitrary but are controlled by proportion rules which date back to antiquity. Such rules are today mandatory under building codes, and the UK regulations lay down the following rules for flights of steps:

- Minimum of two risers (except for building entries where one riser is permitted);
- Maximum of 16 risers for public stairs between landings;
- The ratios of maximum rise to minimum pitch (namely angle of nosing line to horizontal plane) are laid down according to building use.[2] In essence, all ratios have to fall within the range of twice the riser plus the tread dimensions to equal 550−700 mm. The maximum pitch for private residential

stairs is 42°, while all other stairs (means of escape, places of public assembly, etc.) may not be steeper than 35°.

Clearly, ramped steps fall outside these rules, but common sense should prevail to ensure that the 'footspace' between risers accommodates one or two paces or more. The average pace is 600 mm, and riser spacing should relate to that dimension. Vitruvius writes of Roman temples having three, five or seven steps in order that a symmetry in footsteps could be maintained – right foot forward at the entry and departure to each flight. By the same argument, ramped steps should have two paces between each riser, with treads of 1.2 m girth and arranged in uneven numbers.

Granite setts or brick pavers form excellent non-slip surfaces for ramped steps, but the leading edge will need stabilizing with mortar bedding and setting. The detailing at Runnymede (see Figure 2.02d) depends upon two rows of long setts at the risers, say 300 × 100 × 100 mm buried end-on and solidly bedded in cement mortar (1:3). A dry mix of cement and sand can be also be used for general work in laying granite sett ramps, the moistening being carried out with a sprinkler as the laying proceeds, with the dry mix brushed between the joints. Brick paving could be treated similarly with two courses of brick-on-end pavers used at risers. Pointing the riser bricks will prevent the moss growth encouraged by the calcium and sodium sulphate in rich mortars.

Gardens often need occasional steps, and a large slab of stone with the full thickness exposed at the riser face can be effective. Figure 2.02f shows sandstone paving stones of substantial size used for this purpose. Laying such slabs to a slight fall towards the front edge will prevent ponding and slipperiness. Chemical washing of sandstones will normally cure mould problems. Limestone slabs look more attractive as they encourage lichens, but can prove very treacherous in use due to moss growth.

Brick steps should be laid on end or on edge and will only be effective in the long term if laid over concrete bedding to cope with settlement. Curved plan forms are easy to make, and a double or treble line of bricks will give a more comfortable foothold of 450 or 675 mm than the minimal brick size of 225 mm (see Figure 2.03c). Pointed brickwork at such

2.03 Building entries

a Steps and ramps to public buildings

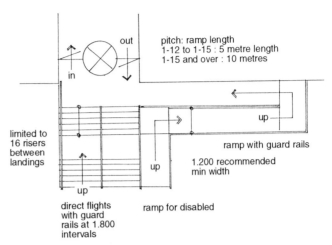

b Ramp at flush building entry

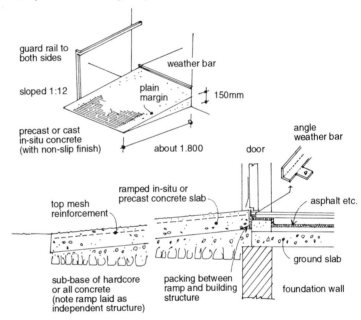

c Concrete or brick thresholds at flush building entry

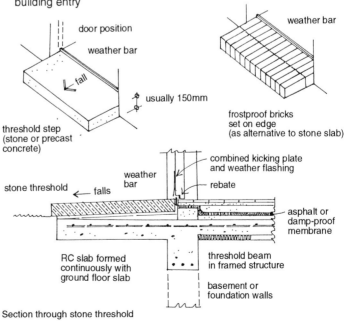

locations, will improve stability under hard wearing conditions and, as already explained, will inhibit mould growing over the steps.

2.03d Temporary steps using chequer plate

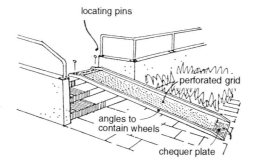

e Step and porch in village housing at London, Norfolk (1950s). Architects: Taylor and Green

f Public building entrances, with handrail lighting

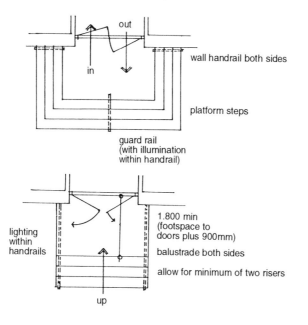

2.2 Building Entries

A primary design factor is the requirement for building floors to be constructed at a higher plane than the external ground. The minimum difference in the UK is 150 mm, and this can be solved with a ramped path at 1:12 slope which absorbs 1.8 m run of paving. The surface needs to be textured so that it can be identified by the sightless and partially sighted. Such a feature will solve disabled access for public buildings and could be applied to all categories of building use. Typical details and layouts are given in Figures 2.03a–d which elaborate on the present requirements under the national regulations in the UK. Similar rules apply in the USA.

The construction can be achieved with a slab of precast or in-situ concrete. (The term 'in-situ' means concrete cast within temporary shuttering on site, and the general construction method follows that described for concrete paving in Section 1.4.) In either case, the concrete work should be considered as a ground-based slab which is made separate to the building structure. The majority of building entries for private use will be made with a single step. Such steps can always be adapted with a temporary steel chequer-plate ramp if required. In domestic work it is worth studying in detail the house and garden relationship at doorways, and more generally to look at building entries and their setting.

Step slabs should be in scale with the door, the depth providing a comfortable footspace of 450 mm, as shown in Figure 2.03c. It should be noted that a 125 to 150 mm high step will combat driving rain, further protection can be given by a 'weather bar' inserted within the door sill. Engineering-class bricks make an excellent step, but a block of granite, sandstone or well-made precast concrete would also serve. Ideally entrances should have two-person girth – say 900 mm of paving projecting beyond the face of the wall. Post-war prefabricated buildings in the UK were well thought out for courting couples, Gibberd's steel houses having a 900 mm height railing to lean against, and Figure 2.03e shows a development of this idea. Public entrances may have outward-opening doors, which implies allowing space for door swings and a space before the first riser, say a distance of 1.8 m. Flights of steps should have balustrade protection to both sides of guardrails where

a Standard grit box and grid

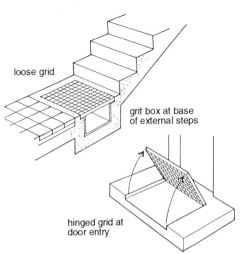

loose grid

grit box at base
of external steps

hinged grid at
door entry

2.04 Self-draining
details for building
entrances

b Duckboard terrace
against sliding doors

c Typical channel and grid
covers at flush building entries

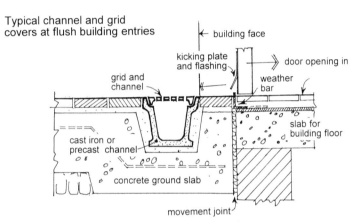

building face

kicking plate
and flashing

door opening in

grid and
channel

weather
bar

cast iron or
precast channel

slab for
building floor

concrete ground slab

movement joint

d Terrace slabs with gap at patio doors

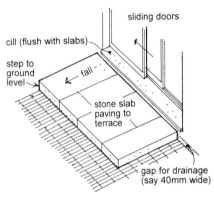

sliding doors

cill (flush with slabs)

step to
ground
level

fall

stone slab
paving to
terrace

gap for drainage
(say 40mm wide)

platform stairs are employed, as in Figure 2.03f. An external step which combines a foot scraper and drainage sump has a number of advantages, particularly where heavy snowfall occurs. The detail featured in Figure 2.04a is a standard product in Scandinavia and would be worthwhile marketing further afield, with perhaps a ramped grid to provide a universal threshold for building entries. Timber-framed thresholds are associated with Oriental and Japanese architecture, the construction reflecting the free-standing wooden building frames utilized in traditional houses and temples. It is cheaper to construct extensive raised terraces as timber decking, and this overcomes the problems of forming extensive ground slabs and surface drainage in proximity to doorways (see Section 1.6b and Figures 1.28e–g for examples of timber decking). The difference between the ground floor (US first floor) level of buildings and the surroundings can easily overcome by decking, and this permits floor levels to be taken through from inside to outside due to the slatted surface,

which is self-draining. A typical duckboard terrace with sliding doors is shown in Figure 2.04b.

There are clearly circumstances where more permanent materials are needed, such as terrace paving related to restaurant doors or foyer space. In these circumstances an adequate drainage channel will be needed to separate the terrace from the building interior to prevent flooding during rainstorms. The same precautions have to be taken with ramped entries for disabled access, since areas of paving will be laid flush with interior levels at such thresholds. The details are shown in Figure 2.04c. The considerable variety of channel drains used in paved areas is dealt with in Section 16.2. It is a wise precaution against flooding and rain splash to use such devices wherever extensive paving or wide steps adjoin doors or extensive fenestration. In domestic construction, it is usually sufficient to 'gap' the terrace slabs from the base patio doors (Figure 2.04d) provided a full drainage zone is left adjacent.

2.05 Monumental steps in landscape

2.3 Formal and Monumental Steps in Landscape

There are symbolic undertones to monumental steps in landscape architecture. Many Buddhist temples are constructed in the form of 'steps to heaven'. A key example is Adam's Peak, Sri Lanka, where a mountain rising to a height of 2240 m is seen in symbolic terms as the ascent of life itself. There are lesser shrines and pauses in the long ascent, the conical summit having an oblong platform, within which there is a hollow resembling the imprint of a human foot, though of substantial dimensions (1500 × 750 mm). The footprint is ascribed to Adam, to Gautama and to Siva, and held in veneration by Muslims, Buddhists and Hindus alike. The heavy chains on the south-west face, which are said to have been left there by Alexander the Great, are mentioned by Marco Polo as indicating the original ascent. Figures 2.05a−c show details of Adam's Peak and the use of mountain steps leading to a Buddhist shrine of Tai Shan in Shantung, China.

The reverence inspired by a temple mount can also pertain to more modest themes, as witnessed by the Kennedy Memorial, Runnymede (Figure 2.02d−e). The stepped ramps that occur in landscape have also existed in townscape from the beginning of time. The Minoan city of Gournia in Crete has a stepped alleyway design for the cross-streets that is characteristic of Mediterranean hill towns built over the past three millenia. Yemen Moshe outside the walls of Jerusalem has been rebuilt on the original pattern using stepped limestone blocks. Comparisons between these various traditions can be seen in Figures 2.05d−h.

Figures 2.05f−g showing the Acropolis, exemplify the constructional problems to be overcome when reconstructing steps and ramps for tourism today. The old rock paths and steps which climbed up the slopes of the Acropolis had either been worn dangerously smooth and slippery or were entirely broken by the volume of traffic. Archaeological references do not exist, though historical records refer to ramps and steps made in the Roman period. The landscape architect maintained the traditional route and utilized silver grey dolomite limestone paving associated with the site. The laying technique involved edge-laid units for ramps, with block paving for steps and terraces. The rock

substrata were not disturbed, the rebuilt work being constructed as an overlying surface with substantial kerbs to demark the reconstruction from the antiquities and the 'living' rock of the site. The blocks were solid-bedded due to the heavy traffic anticipated, but care was taken to recess the mortar joints to emphasize texture. In a dry situation like Athens, durable, hard dolomite limestones perform well in external steps. In the UK the natural texture of 'oolitic' stones such as Shelley Portland would have to be used to give inherent non-slip qualities, and it is a popular material for formal work, such as the plinths at the Kennedy Memorial, Runnymede. Another example, this time from the 1960s, is the steps and surroundings to the Economist Tower off St James's Street, London, shown in Figure 2.05h.

Mention must be made of the Italianate tradition which dominates the Renaissance and Baroque handling of steps in landscape. Complexity of layout and immense scale of design are the overriding factors. In essence, the outdoor space of an Italian garden is compartmented into 'rooms and passages' laid out across sloping land, with stairs and ramped paths to encapture movement from level to level, further enriched by waterfalls and fountains.

The water paradise at the rear of the Villa d'Este, with its multiple stairs and cascades, must surely be the quintessence of the Italian Baroque. This garden serves an outdoor room of size equal to Trafalgar Square, London, but with changes of level giving rise to ramps and steps which tumble down 20 m from the palace to the furthest terrace. Each step and turn is water-embellished, each fountain considered as a musical accompaniment, each movement down the multiple-turn stairs compared, say, to a minuet. Figures 2.06a−c capture the concept and should be studied in conjunction with Figures 2.06d−f.

The comparison of Italian garden stairs to 'dancing steps' is not far-fetched. The plans of the Spanish Steps, Rome, convey in their arabesques and curves the notion of a musical cadence. A similar theme is present in the outdoor spaces of the Villa Garzoni, where spatial effects are employed to create a veritable palace of garden rooms graced by some of the grandest external stairs ever constructed. Italianate staircases can also be envisaged as scenery, to help frame views upwards or downwards, with diagonal or curving balustrade patterns providing essential clues as

2.06 Italianate stairs

to directions to follow. Shallow landscape steps are shown in Figure 2.06e, leading in turn to gentle slopes for balustrading.

Perspective effects can be increased by tapering the flights, making them appear longer, or by reducing the balustrade in distant views, thereby giving the impression of greater distance. Stairs can also be seen as 'pinch points' in garden circulation — places where the visitor is slowed down, made to change direction or to appreciate the expanding prospect. The shape of steps assists these devices: platform or semi-circular forms anticipate expansion into the adjacent space, while reverse stairs constructed as a reduced pyramid or cone can concentrate the vista, a device popular with Lutyens. Figures 2.06f–k indicate some possibilities along these lines.

g 'Pinch points'

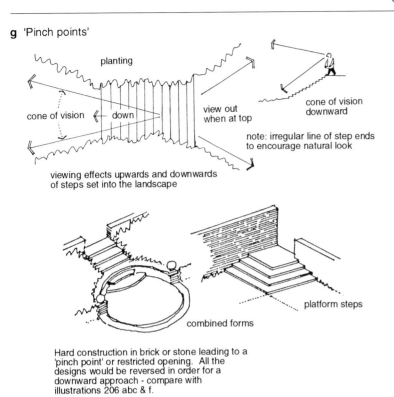

planting

cone of vision | down

view out when at top

cone of vision downward

note: irregular line of step ends to encourage natural look

viewing effects upwards and downwards of steps set into the landscape

combined forms

platform steps

Hard construction in brick or stone leading to a 'pinch point' or restricted opening. All the designs would be reversed in order for a downward approach - compare with illustrations 206 abc & f.

i Curved nosing Renishaw

h Perspective steps

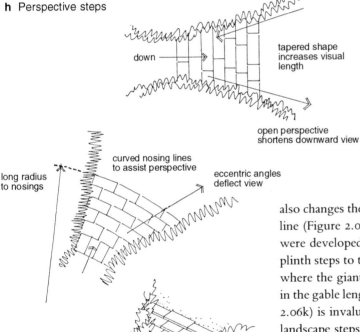

down

tapered shape increases visual length

open perspective shortens downward view

curved nosing lines to assist perspective

long radius to nosings

eccentric angles deflect view

widened steps opening to the view

Very wide stairs appear dull and over-powering, (see Figure 2.01a), and refinements such as a slightly curved nosing line improve visual impact, a point of detail observed by Sir George Sitwell in his treatise 'On the Making of Gardens' and demonstrated at Renishaw (Figure 2.06i). Creating a cross-camber helps with drainage of stormwater but

j Camber to steps

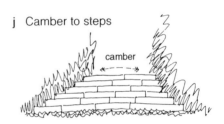

camber

Note: camber arranged on plan as figure 206h or by cambering the levels. This also helps drainage of wide steps.

also changes the geometry into a more pleasing line (Figure 2.06j). These visual distortions were developed in the construction of the plinth steps to the Parthenon on the Acropolis, where the giant 500 mm steps camber 66 mm in the gable length of 31 m. A footspace (Figure 2.06k) is invaluable at the top and bottom of landscape steps as it facilitates the collection and disposal of traffic, and on a practical level it reduces wear and tear on soft materials like gravel and grass.

The technical solution depends upon use. Simple garden steps can be laid on compacted ground, but public stairs will need consolidated foundations − in times past a packing of broken stone, but today a reinforced concrete armature cast as a slab to the required slope, with the surface stepped to receive the finished material for treads and risers − for example, brick, precast elements, stonework (natural or artificial) or tile facings.

2.06k Footspace to garden steps

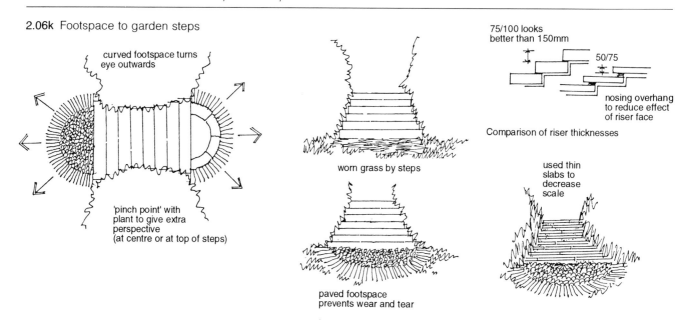

curved footspace turns eye outwards

'pinch point' with plant to give extra perspective
(at centre or at top of steps)

worn grass by steps

paved footspace prevents wear and tear

75/100 looks better than 150mm

50/75

nosing overhang to reduce effect of riser face

Comparison of riser thicknesses

used thin slabs to decrease scale

2.07 Present day construction

a Basic reinforced concrete stairs and temporary formwork

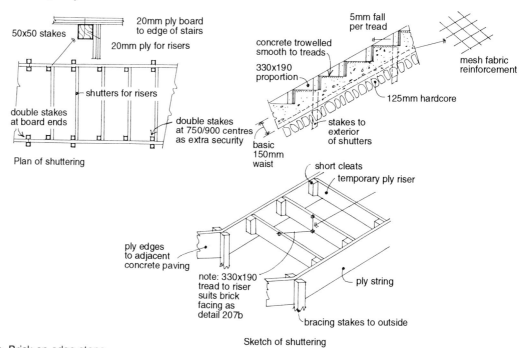

50x50 stakes

20mm ply board to edge of stairs

20mm ply for risers

shutters for risers

double stakes at board ends

double stakes at 750/900 centres as extra security

Plan of shuttering

5mm fall per tread

concrete trowelled smooth to treads

330x190 proportion

mesh fabric reinforcement

125mm hardcore

stakes to exterior of shutters

basic 150mm waist

short cleats

temporary ply riser

ply edges to adjacent concrete paving

note: 330x190 tread to riser suits brick facing as detail 207b

ply string

bracing stakes to outside

Sketch of shuttering

b Brick on edge steps

brick mowing edge carried past steps

path   1 2 3 4 5   path

Simple flight in lawn/grass

precast mowing edges

1 2 3 4 5 6 7 8

Simple flight in lawn/grass

grass

brick on edge paving and steps

330mm

headspace

190

footspace

course of bricks laid frog up in normal way

mesh reinforced concrete

150

125-150

concrete 1:2:4 mix

hardcore or leanmix concrete

Cast in-situ steps do not wear well, spalling of nosings and difficulties with trowel finishing of treads being part of the problem. It is much easier to overlay the concrete work, and this also permits the finished steps to be completed at a late stage, contractors' damage being therefore limited to the rough concrete armature. Once again a footspace will assist traffic use and also strengthen the stair slab by providing an extended bearing at the top and bottom of the flight. Similar measures are needed when reconstructing traditional garden steps to cope with the demands of present-day tourism (see Figure 2.01b). Typical details for reinforced concrete base and overlay materials are given in Figures 2.07a–f. The edge trim to stairs depends upon the setting. It is more

sympathetic to run sloping kerbs where lawns or planting adjoin the construction. Extending the riser feature into the landscape can provide a soft verge to steps and enable planting to overlap the harsh geometry, as in Figure 2.07f. A wise designer would provide a guardrail as a safety measure.

Steps placed in conjunction with retaining walls can be supported at their edges by cantilevering individual slabs from the masonry, as in Figure 2.08. This is a form of building associated with terraced vineyards, where quartz or slate blocks are built into stonework. Retaining walls built as projecting buttresses or as return walls can carry stair treads formed as slabs spanning from wall to wall up to 1.8 m span. Reinforced concrete

c Stone or artificial stone treads

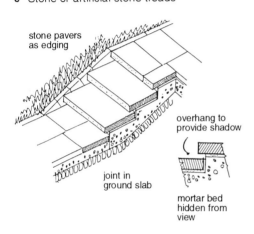

stone pavers as edging

overhang to provide shadow

joint in ground slab

mortar bed hidden from view

e Precast concrete steps

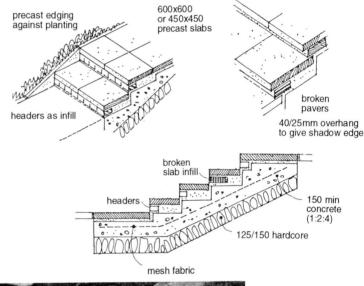

precast edging against planting

600x600 or 450x450 precast slabs

headers as infill

broken pavers

40/25mm overhang to give shadow edge

broken slab infill

headers

150 min concrete (1:2:4)

125/150 hardcore

mesh fabric

d Stone, rubble or slate creasings

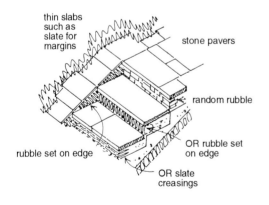

thin slabs such as slate for margins

stone pavers

random rubble

rubble set on edge

OR rubble set on edge

OR slate creasings

f Use of extended risers to form plant pockets. Zurich Botanic Garden (1986)

2.08 Stairs related to
retaining walls

a Cantilevered stone
steps to a vineyard
b Reinforced concrete
cantilevered treads

c Direct flights

guard rails

direct flight

retaining wall
returned at stairs

external buttress walls

retaining wall
as parapet
to upper level

stone/precast
treads built
into walls

Typical section

2.08d Quarter turn steps

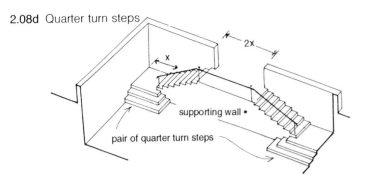

2x

x

supporting wall •

pair of quarter turn steps

e Cross wall supports

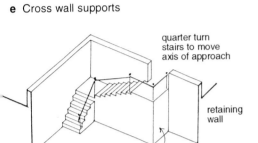

quarter turn
stairs to move
axis of approach

retaining
wall

supporting wall

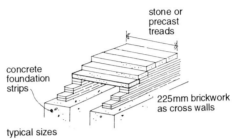

stone or
precast
treads

concrete
foundation
strips

225mm brickwork
as cross walls

typical sizes
stone: 150mm thick for spans up to 1.500
precast: 150mm thick for spans of 3.500 to 4.000

planks or slabs can also be employed, and this increases the possible spans to 6 m, the finishing for concrete being as shown in Figures 2.07a–e.

Guardrails and handrails for public stairs need to be agreed with the licensing authority for places of public assembly.[3] In essence, safety requirements stipulate handrails at 1.8 m

2.09 Guarding and handrails

a Building Regulations for external public stairs

Single family dwelling	External balconies, edge of roof	0.74kN/m	1.100mm
residential institutional educational office & public buildings	all locations	0.74 kN/m	900mm flights of stairs, but 1.100 otherwise
assembly	530mm in front of fixed seats	refer to BS6399 part 1	800mm
	all other locations	ditto	900mm for flights of stairs but 1100 otherwise

Extract from AD K2/3 Section 3 on 'Guarding design in the National Building Regulations'

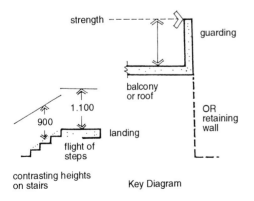

strength

guarding

balcony
or roof

1.100

900

landing

flight of
steps

OR
retaining
wall

contrasting heights
on stairs

Key Diagram

b Handrails fixed to walls
(brackets at 1.200 to 1.800 c/c)

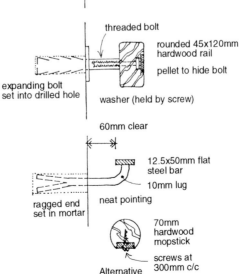

60mm clear

tube
(stainless steel
galvanised steel
or bronze)

ragged end set
in mortar

fixing plate

20mm rod

spot weld   washer

threaded bolt

rounded 45x120mm
hardwood rail

pellet to hide bolt

expanding bolt
set into drilled hole

washer (held by screw)

60mm clear

12.5x50mm flat
steel bar

10mm lug

ragged end
set in mortar

neat pointing

70mm
hardwood
mopstick

screws at
300mm c/c

Alternative
detail

c Guard rails

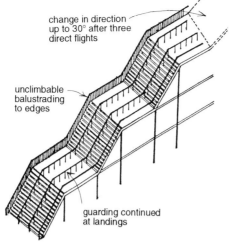

change in direction up to 30° after three direct flights

unclimbable balustrading to edges

guard rails between flights

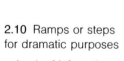

1.000 min
1.800 max

guarding continued at landings

intervals, with supports which will withstand 3.0 kN/m applied as a sideways force to the top of the railing. Outline details are given in Figures 2.09a–c, but specialist engineering

advice will be needed from railing fabricators to comply with safety codes for places of public assembly. See Chapter 9 for a description of railings that could be used at landings or to surmount retailing walls. Such construction also relates to external staircases where the vertical drop at the side of steps exceeds 380 mm (see Section 2.1 for general advice).

General consideration of safety in designing public stairs includes lighting for emergency escape routes and devices such as inset electric heating cables to dispose of ice and snow in winter conditions. Lighting can be supplied by conventional column lights, but it is often more relevant to illuminate the treads at a low level using inset wall lights or by means of strip lights mounted within the handrail elements.

2.10 Ramps or steps for dramatic purposes

a Lack of inferred movement, hence 'This Way' sign on left-hand wall
b Grass steps to theatre space at Claremont, Surrey (1728, restored by National Trust in 1980). Designer: Charles Bridgeman
c Portmeirion, North Wales (1920s to 1980s). General view of Battery Square
d Sequential view of Palatial House: view from square
e View from steps
f View from close up

g Dramatic landscaping at Powys Castle
h Water parapets and water channels to steps, Generalife Gardens, Alhambra, Granada (circa AD 1460)
i Water steps and tank in the temple at Chidambaram, India. (Tim Blanc slide)
j Submerged steps 'Botanic Gardens' Nîmes
k Submerged slab, serving as a spacious bird bath. Pond at Sir Peter Shepheard's garden, Hampstead, London

2.4 Conclusion

A primary role of steps introduced into landscape is to lead the eye and to direct movement – it would be a symbol of failure if a sign had to be painted bearing the message 'This Way', coupled with a direction arrow or finger, as in Figure 2.10a. The sequence should appear inevitable, and the spatial unfolding from level to level should have a logical arrangement (see Figures 2.06a,d and f).

Sunken layouts have the advantage of drawing the eye downwards, as to an arena or stage, a concept adapted for external theatre spaces such as Claremont (Figure 2.10b), or to townscape as at Portmeirion, North Wales (an Italianate village designed by Sir Clough Williams-Ellis) (Figures 2.10c–f). Here the main square is irregular in shape and bounded by a variety of façades of differing scale.
The connecting vistas of openings, ramps and steps leading up from the space create

perspective effects which enhance distance and spaciousness. The sequence of Figures 2.10d—f takes one nearer and nearer the eye-catcher, which happens to be a single-storey cottage, though its increased perspective and the stairs make it appear palatial. It is this magic from the play of levels, oblique vistas and steps which brings delight to sequential vision in landscape and which represents an aesthetic endeavour which links the architectural achievement of the Acropolis to the present day.[4] An essential element at the Acropolis is the use of reverse proportions of 2:5 between the minor temples at the entry compared with the principle edifice, the Parthenon. The reverse geometry means that the plinth of the Nike Apteros is 200 mm while the massive steps of the Parthenon are 500 mm high.

Water and cascade steps have already been alluded to in the study of Italianate gardens. Their origins probably stem from the Moorish layouts in Andalusia, where stairs and their parapet walls were enlivened by waterways within the copings or as a 'spring of life' within the paving (Figure 2.10h).

A differing response occurs with steps which lead down into sunken chambers or disappear below water. The psychology of descent into shade or into the depths of water is a total opposite to the scene of enjoyment seen at Villa d'Este or the Generalife. The most significant examples are the cistern temples in India, where the architectural ensemble is a preparation for the ceremonial cleansing within the water. The pattern derives from the holy *ghats* seen at Benares, where four miles of river terraces line the Ganges for Hindu pilgrims. The cisterns and water steps which feature in many temple complexes are designed for large crowds of worshippers within a sacred enclosure (see Figure 2.10i). The mystery of steps below water is often used to increase the drama of water in landscape, apart from serving more mundane needs such as pond maintenance (see Figures 2.10j—k). Sir Peter Shepeard's pond has a below water slab which also serves as a spacious bird bath and is a suitable introduction to Chapter 4 titled 'Water in Landscape'.

2.11 Stair proportions

a Practical limits for rise and going - private stairways

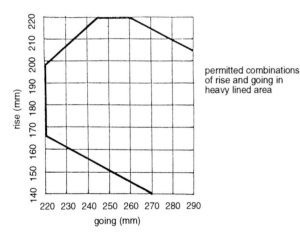

permitted combinations of rise and going in heavy lined area

b Practical limits for rising and going - institutional and assembly buildings

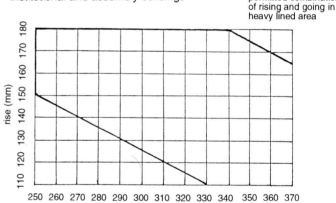

permitted combinations of rising and going in heavy lined area

c Practical limits for rise and going - other buildings

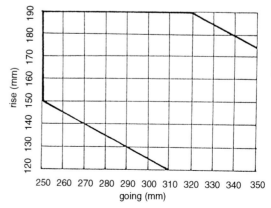

permitted combination of rise and going in heavy lined area

3   EDGE TREATMENT

The practical reason for margins between grass and walls or between grass and some forms of planting is ease of maintenance, for example, to avoid the need for hand-cutting of lawn edges. By contrast the quads and courts at Oxford and Cambridge colleges have steel 'flats' installed so that a selvage edge can be maintained by hand-trimming to a firm line at all margins (see Figures 3.01–3.02). The vertical faces of tall walls can shade vegetation, and roof overhangs will create extremely dry conditions at the base of low-rise buildings. In such circumstances surfacing alternatives to grass or planting have to be considered, *Hedera* being the only 'green' possibility.

The opposite problem occurs at the foot of curtain wall façades, where the run-off will have to be contained by drainage measures. Another consideration with fenestration related to landscape is the problem of window

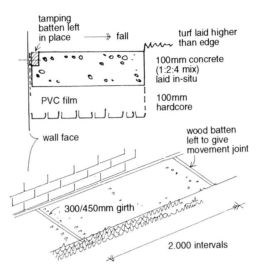

3.03 Typical in-situ concrete margin in local authority work

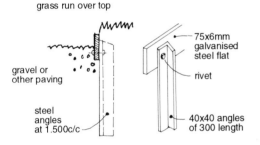

3.01 Steel flat as mowing edge

3.02 Lawns with steel flat at Trinity Hall, Cambridge. Architect: Sir Denys Lasdun

cleaning. In single or two-storey buildings this is commonly carried out from ladders placed against the façade, a ladder or access space being needed parallel to the glazing.

A plinth or shingle base is frequently used for timber buildings such as Japanese temples, to prevent splash from garden soil staining the wood facing. Similar protective devices also help where vulnerable cladding such as marble or painted surfaces come close to ground level.

The problems of grass mowing in cemetery and churchyard design are discussed in Section 3.3, and proposals are given for margins and stone-setting where an open-lawn effect is desired.

3.1   Mowing Edges

The love and care factor in grass-cutting can reach obsessive lengths, and many suburban gardeners set their mowers to run up and down in parallel lines, followed by close shear work to trim the edges. At Kew Gardens this level of perfection is achieved using steel edging, as shown in Figure 3.01, which permits the mower to trim clear above the steel once the turf thickness has firmed to roughly 20 mm higher than the metal trim. One of the problems with lawn growth is that the tilth below the grass will increase at roughly 12.5 mm per 50 years, therefore any mowing edge will eventually have to be relaid at a higher level to fulfil its original function.

Steel edging as shown in Figure 3.02 will preserve the self-contained or selvage effect along grass verges but is vulnerable to damage by tractors or heavy pedestrian traffic.
The situation in college quads is special since walking on the 'sacred' grass at Oxford and Cambridge, for example, is forbidden to the majority and the equipment used is not as heavy as that employed by public parks departments, which favour self-driven or tractor-towed mowers, involving wheel loadings that would disrupt steel edging. In these situations a flat, paved surface is needed, and one that is sufficiently firm so as not to be broken or disturbed under use. Many public

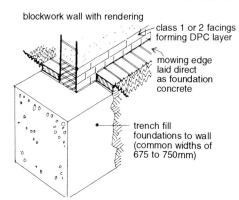

3.07 Mowing edge supported by trench fill

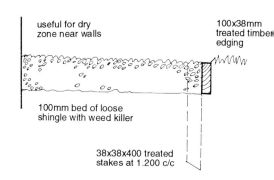

3.08 Shingle margin and wood batten kerb

authorities insist on concrete paving, either in-situ or precast (see Figures 3.03–3.04), a sub-base of all-in concrete mix being specified to prevent the settlement found with hardcore or gravel. However, movement of earth fill above traditional footings will probably mean relaying mowing edges abutting walls within a few years of completion.

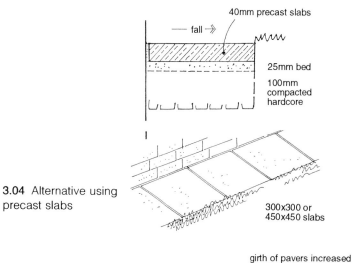

3.04 Alternative using precast slabs

3.2 Trim Near Buildings

The type of material used depends upon the budget and the form of labour available towards the end of the contract. A simple solution consists of brick facings (laid frog-down) or brick pavers (see Figure 3.05) since these blend with building textures and are easier to adapt to levels and curving shapes than precast concrete (Figure 3.06).

The current use of trench fill for wall footings means that foundation concrete is within 150 mm of the ground level, and therefore settlement is unlikely; in such locations in-situ work or long precast units could be used since a stable base is guaranteed (Figure 3.07).

The compaction and filling of planting or

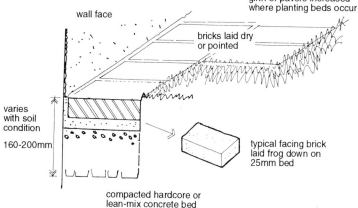

3.05 Brick mowing edge

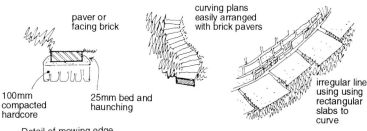

3.06 Difficulty with square compared brick units laid to curves

turf areas next to such edges needs attention, and soiling ought to be 50 to 75 mm higher and turfing 20 to 25 mm higher than the finished edge when landscaping new building sites. The fault of higher 'made levels' is easy to correct by punning/tamping but too low a level is expensive to put right.

Private clients often ask for options so that the standard of work can be upgraded as more cash and time become available for gardening activity. Shingle is a cheap margin material and can be contained by wooden kerbs against grass or planting, the 450 mm zone created being infilled with paving at a later time (Figure 3.08). Shingle and pebble paving is also invaluable for dry areas below overhangs or canopies, and acts as a good foil if *Hedera* is trailed in from wetter ground. Difficult wet areas can also be improved with shingle surfacing as a short-term measure, or while land drains are assessed for performance. Thatched buildings require French drains or paved channels run below the eaves overhang, as conventional gutters do not function for thatch. In the USA gutters are by no means universal in heavy snowfall areas, and a common practice is to employ extensive overhangs with a pebble-filled trench run-off downhill away from the building (Figure 3.09). The American solution could cause problems in the UK as reinforced concrete cellars and berming are not usual in house construction. The UK building regulations also state that rainwater has to be shed by gutters and pipes.[1]

The use of alternative surfacing to grass or plants near walls not only assists with keeping vegetation trimmed but adds an extra dimension to the wall, the 'toe' effect giving an additional periphery line rather like the US Prairie Houses with their Wrightean plinths. The transition from building to ground in traditional Chinese and Japanese designs is never abrupt. One practical reason for the use of shingle is to avoid splash and staining affecting the timber framing or plaster infill, but a further advantage is that it allows gardeners access to plants without having to walk through the foliage. Shingle or gravel is itself vulnerable to root penetration, and the edge towards the lawn or shrubs needs to be firmed up with setts (Figure 3.10), a line of pavers, or at least a timber batten.

The remarks on gardeners' access need to be borne in mind with dense ground cover,

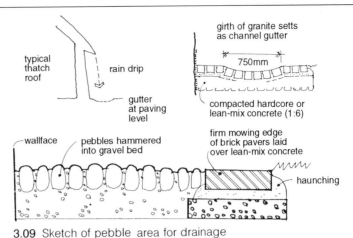

3.09 Sketch of pebble area for drainage

3.10 Sketch showing extensive shungle margin with setts to edge

3.11 Logs set in ground to form separation to ground cover

3.12 Stones used for similar purpose and for gardener's path

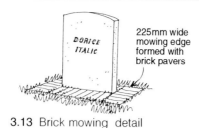

225mm wide mowing edge formed with brick pavers

3.13 Brick mowing detail

3.16 Steel cradling to support old gravestones

minimal stone slab

3.14 Pre-cast 'slotted' paving unit to form mowing edge

where a run of pavers or logs can be used to separate differing types of plant material or to provide a maintenance path (Figures 3.11–3.12).

3.3 Gravestones

The pleasantly overgrown country churchyard with the parson's sheep gently grazing on grass between the graves is no longer a common sight – in some cases the gravestones may have been lifted and laid flat to form entry paths, or simply propped up against the surrounding walls. This is particularly the case where churchyards have ceased to be used for interment and the existing graves are no longer tended by relatives.

If old gravestones are to be used for pavers photographs should first be taken for record purposes, then the stones should be laid with the inscriptious face-down so that details are

3.15 Typical German graves with paving trim

not lost to posterity. If the lettering is left as the wearing face it quickly becomes defaced.

Gravestones are sometimes rearranged to allow the economical use of a mower, but there is no reason why sound vertical stones should not be left in place. A mowing edge can be formed with a brick margin, which gives an anchorage to the gravestone (Figure 3.13).

In new cemeteries where traditional interment occurs the open-lawn effect is only too common, and there are many areas where

3.17 Short-term solution with shingle

3.18 Long-term solution with water catchment area for roof garden

vertical stones are forbidden, horizontal-bedded pavers being used instead, in which case the lettering quickly disappears. Combining the open-lawn treatment and vertical stones is perfectly feasible, and standard precast 'slots' are made to suit standard headstones (Figure 3.14). The 'casket trade' in Germany is very sophisticated, and one commonly sees a family grave already set up with granite setts as kerbs plus 'his and hers' inscriptions, with only the death dates missing! (Figure 3.15). Stones like limestone eventually deteriorate at the point of contact with the soil, and in old German cemeteries one sees metal frames used as supports, set above gravel areas to obviate grass trimming or subsequent damage (Figure 3.16).

Margins or edging can enhance the setting of buildings and planting in various ways. Figure 3.17 shows a short-term solution to prevent the pale yellow facing bricks being

splashed and discoloured (the timber margin between grass and shingle is to be replaced by brick pavers when funds permit). Figure 3.18 shows a long-term solution, a ground gutter below overhanging roofs. The water catchment serves as irrigation to the adjacent garden, this in turn forming ground cover to a basement garage. Figure 3.19 depicts a conventional mowing edge which separates lawns from borders at Bodnant, North Wales. Pavers or stone slabs are used, in widths varying from 450—900 mm according to the scale of adjacent planting. Figure 3.20 is a method used to organize an old churchyard, where brick pavers are employed to demark memorial roses, to protect standing stones from mowers, or to subdivide close-mown sections from wilderness areas.

3.20 Brick edges to demark memorial roses

4.01 Edges to water
a Moat created in 14 days for a restaurant at the Festival of Britain (1951). Architect: Sir Peter Shepheard
b Vertical abutment in concrete. Note double-depth appearance due to reflection. Artificial lake at York University shown in summer at low water (1964). Designer: Maurice Pickering

a

b

4 WATER IN LANDSCAPE

4.1 Design Principles

Water is one of the most evocative elements in landscape. It brings life and reflection, and gives movement and sparkle to the dullest of scenes. To many, water is a symbol of life, and this is not unnatural since our living world is 70% water.

The interplay of light and water is the key to success, so an open sky and access to sunlight have to accompany water in landscape design, not simply to promote mirror qualities, but to keep the water healthy and capable of supporting its flora and fauna, usually birds, fish and their insect food.

Designers often seek to extend natural water features into lakes or streams, and therefore need to understand the way nature shapes banks and edges in wet landscapes. The other introductions made are artificial constructions, such as formal pools and fountains. The water edge in all cases is the critical point in design, and the following factors are crucial to success.

Natural edges

A beach or riverbank demonstrates the forces at work, where the erosion pattern often leaves moraine or rock standing above, the ground, sand or silty mud. A saucer pattern is common, with the 'lip' formed around the high-water mark. The scale of erosion will depend upon the flow pattern: steepest at inner bends and headlands and shallowest on the opposite banks. This point was nicely observed in Sir Peter Shepheard's water garden for the Festival of Britain (Figure 4.01a). Note the firm edge towards hard landscape and the natural eroded appearance by the 'shore' line. The water is 300 mm deep and reflective due to clay filling over concrete.

Depth at edge

Vertical abutments are the most difficult details to handle. They occur in nature where ice or water have cut a channel through rock, but are seldom appropriate for the natural setting or scale of gardens. The scale of a vertical face is increased by reflections, so that a concrete embankment of 300 mm height appears to be 600 mm high (see Figure 4.01b). Filling ponds to the brim will obviate the problem, but a shelving water edge will also hide the clumsy intersection between waterscape and the bank. Shelving or curving surfaces will also mask changes due to evaporation. Designs for recreational pools recognize this problem, and have shelving margins with a scum tray provided below gratings. An emerald green or blue green band of tiling will add sparkle to fountain pools if a vertical abutment cannot be avoided. This is often found in surrounds to decorative pools in Islamic architecture, as in Figure 4.01d. The greatest pleasure obtained from water edges is the sense of fullness and the way ripples and moving water give the impression of 'winking at the brim'. Tidal rivers at full tide have the essence of this character, and one worth emulating when making artificial embankments. Figure 4.01c shows fullness compared with the restriction of water surface in Figure 4.01b. To be fair to the design at York University, it should be remembered that the water system is part of a series of balancing lakes and that the levels vary.[1]

Another solution consists of using curved blocks. Radius edging has little shadow and allows for a range of depths to hide evaporation. The mirror effect in the formal pond in Figure 4.01e is barely infringed by shadow. Similar edge blocks have been used at Rousham, Oxfordshire, and Figure 4.01f shows the difficulties in construction where the waterproofing needs to be carried in a continuous plane. The stone joints will also need effective water sealing to keep the levels up to the brim.

Reflectivity

Flush water edges carry the full mirror effect, and in bright sunlight give the effect of a glass-like intrusion within the same plane as the adjacent lawn or paving. Sunken water against vertical abutments has a dark rim and a reduced mirror effect.

Light-coloured concrete bases, tiles or grey

6.01c The Thames at full tide, with ramped causeway to emphasize character

d Blue and white tiled pool with poor refectivity. Merchant's house, Tangiers (nineteenth century)

e Reflective pool with radius edging to hide shadow. Botanic Garden, Munich (nineteeth century)

f Rounded copings used for a pool edge, showing problems with waterproofing. Rousham, Oxfordshire (1700s)

g A mirror pool created by the River Stort, in the garden at The House, Harlow, Essex (1970s). Architect: Sir Frederick Gibberd.

h Pool at Oxford Botanic Garden with hard and soft edges

plastic liners can be seen through water up to 3 m depth, and seriously compromise the reflective aspect of still water. Black plastic, asphalt or mud bottoming give the best mirror background for water, even with depths as shallow as 300 mm. The pools shown in Figures 4.01d and 4.01a show the difference between tile bases and clay bottoms in terms of mirror-like effects.

Water movement

Pools inserted into watercourses or placed as a sequence of spillways are likely to be self-maintaining. The flow keeps the edges wet and helps to clear silt as well as bringing aeration. The pool at Gibberd's garden in Harlow, Essex was created by scooping out a basin in the River Stort, with a small waterfall created downstream to give a mirror surface (Figure 4.01g). Another pool, at Oxford Botanic Garden (Figure 4.01h) is fed by the River Cherwell. The edge shaping has been sympathetically formed with shelving surfaces. These are reinforced by occasional logs and waterside plants to give hard and soft margins.

4.2 Construction of Water Features

This section covers the construction of simple water features and offers strategic advice where the garden might be served by an existing river in the way that Jellicoe's layout was enhanced at Shute House, Wiltshire (see Figures 4.04a−c).

There are four major elements in design with water:

- The pool − either a formal pool, or informal in outline and isolated;
- The cascade − a series of linked pools connected by a canal or underground pipes;
- The stream − usually linked to waterfalls, either spring-fed or using recycled water;
- The 'river lake' − an artificial form promoted by William Kent. It usually involves a lake graced by islands or a peninsula of land. It can also be made by enlarging a small river (see Figure 4.01g). Another form of 'river lake' occurs where a valley is blocked, with a series of flooded areas set behind earth berms, such as at Stourhead, Wiltshire (Figures 4.03b−c).

The pool

The natural pool with a mud bottom and dug into a level part of the garden is the ideal. The traditional bottoming with puddled clay of 150 to 225 mm thickness is easy to achieve but difficult to keep intact in dry summers. A pool without aeration will quickly form a green scum, so a balance needs to be struck with plants, fish and mechanical aeration using a battery-powered fountain unit worked by a time switch.[2]

Pool maintenance normally dictates a firmer construction and one that can be drained more readily. A bituthene (bitumen polymer)

4.02 Pond construction

a Hand dug pond with simple recycling system

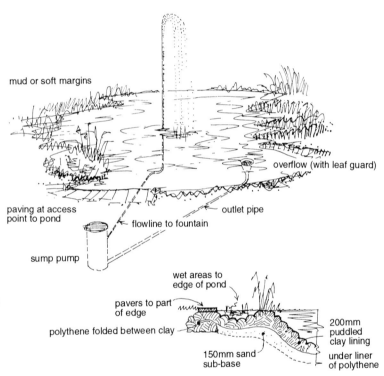

mud or soft margins

overflow (with leaf guard)

paving at access point to pond

outlet pipe

flowline to fountain

sump pump

wet areas to edge of pond

pavers to part of edge

polythene folded between clay

200mm puddled clay lining

150mm sand sub-base

under liner of polythene

b Small pond with hard margins

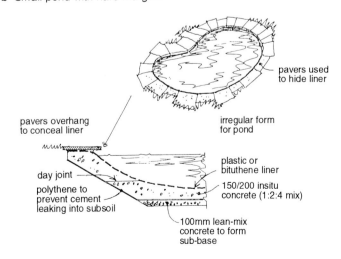

pavers used to hide liner

pavers overhang to conceal liner

irregular form for pond

day joint

plastic or bituthene liner

polythene to prevent cement leaking into subsoil

150/200 insitu concrete (1:2:4 mix)

100mm lean-mix concrete to form sub-base

4.02c Various edge details

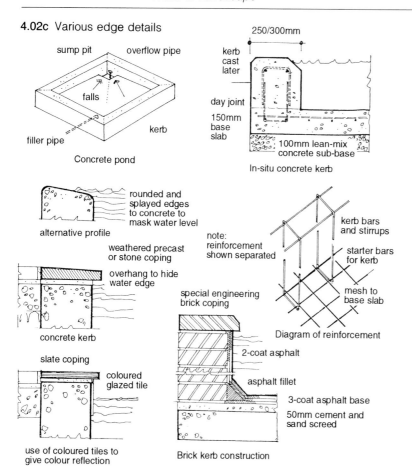

sump pit   overflow pipe

falls

filler pipe   kerb

Concrete pond

250/300mm

kerb cast later

day joint

150mm base slab

100mm lean-mix concrete sub-base

In-situ concrete kerb

rounded and splayed edges to concrete to mask water level

alternative profile

weathered precast or stone coping

overhang to hide water edge

concrete kerb

slate coping

coloured glazed tile

use of coloured tiles to give colour reflection

note: reinforcement shown separated

kerb bars and stirrups

starter bars for kerb

mesh to base slab

Diagram of reinforcement

special engineering brick coping

2-coat asphalt

asphalt fillet

3-coat asphalt base

50mm cement and sand screed

Brick kerb construction

f

d Plain concrete pool, made with unreinforced concrete base slab and kerb. (1982). Architect: Sir Peter Shepheard. Note iron bowl in foreground to top up pool in dry periods
e Town centre pools, Farsta, Stockholm (1960). Architects: Backstrom & Reinius. Note the way dark granite gives better relectivity under water
f Sunk level of water diminishing apparent pond size

d

lining or black polythene liner will prove more durable than puddled clay, and can be made firmer by laying over a sand base. The sand base needs to be 100 mm thick and could benefit from a lean mix of cement, say 1:7, to give support for the construction team and/or plant containers. Scaffold boards will be needed over the excavation in order to lay the sand/cement bedding. Lean-mix concrete is another possibility, but a rendering of cement and sand will be required to isolate the liner from the roughness of concrete aggregates. The inclusion of aerated concrete or stone

blocks (with softened edges to prevent cutting the liner) will give stepping stones for maintenance as well as providing resting points for lily containers. A convenient arrangement is to use blocks in lines, with chequer-plate panels as pot rests spanning from block to block.

A puddled clay bottom will assist the ecological balance and support plant life at the edges. Humping the liner to the periphery will create 'wet garden areas', while paving slabs laid on rounded shingle will give a paved margin where needed. Depths of pond will vary according to requirements, 600 mm for plants, but with areas 900 mm deep if fish need to overwinter. Both these figures allow 150 mm for clay bottoming. Child safety is a problem. In the USA such ponds will have to be fenced and gated. Bringing the depth down to 300 mm will not prevent legal claims, as young children can drown in a puddle.

Plastic, usually glass-reinforced polyester (GRP), is the usual material for proprietary pool construction. The modelling serves the natural requirements, with a deeper overwintering section, shelving edges and ledges for plant containers. The plastic upper edge of these liners looks as poor as black polythene, and needs to be covered with paving or pebble. Lining partly with clay will help the health of the pond (Figure 4.02b). It is worth checking the shape and size in context with the site, using perhaps a pad of news-papers cut to simulate the pool's geometry.

Concrete-lined pools combine the advantages of plastic with the freehand quality of hand-dug work. It is important that the concrete mix should not be diluted by groundwater and contaminated with clay and mud as impurities will weaken the mix. The construction should proceed by covering the bottom with a 100 mm layer of lean-mix concrete. When set, this sub-base gives a firm foothold and provides a bonding surface for bituthene or polythene. The sloping edges could also be surfaced in lean-mix concrete or simply strengthened with soil and cement to mould the surround. The concrete lining must be of structural grade (nominally 1:2:4 mix – see Section 1.4 on cast in-situ concrete) and be at least 150 mm thick. Steel mesh cast with the concrete will limit shrinkage cracking. The slumping of wet concrete on sloping surfaces governs the working joint in the casting process – the edges or enclosing elements of the pool will be cast as a second or third phase, and will need water stops within the working joint. It is possible to use a plastic liner on top of the concrete to prevent lime from leaching into the water, or to provide a cleanable surface in public parks. Draining can be arranged by housing a sump pump in the deepest section of the pond. The pump can double as a circulating device, with the water returned to a fountain jet.

Concrete tank or formal pool

This concept usually relates to a paved terrace and is seen as a reflective surface in the context of buildings or as a setting for fountains. See Figure 4.05i for an example of this application. The construction of the base and sub-base with structural and lean-mix concrete is as described above. The vertical kerb can be concrete but will need water stops at the junctions with the horizontal slabs. Connecting bars to the base slab will improve anchorage and limit cracking. The small pool made in Sir Peter Shepheard's garden has no reinforcement and has survived without leaks occurring (see Figure 4.02d).

Concrete forms an excellent background material for over-cladding. The large series of town centre pools at Farsta, Stockholm (Figure 4.02e) are floored with dark grey granite and kerbed by purple granite blocks laid flush with sett paving. The water depth is 200 mm, and they serve as ice rinks in winter.

Another treatment is to tank the pool with asphalt, which serves as a totally inert material and is suitably dark in colour to give a mirror effect under water. Water set nearly flush with the kerbs will increase the apparent size of the pool, in contrast to the example in Figure 4.02f where the sunk level of water diminishes the pond.

4.03 Lake construction

a Lake created as a bypass for a stream

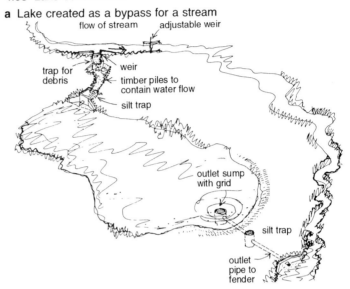

b Lakes created by dams in a river valley (as at Stourhead)

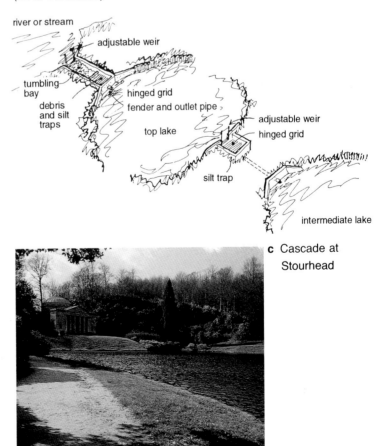

c Cascade at Stourhead

4.3 Lake Construction

The enlargement of the River Stort and the creation of a waterscape at Oxford Botanic Garden have already been shown in Figures 4.01g−h. The problems with river-fed lakes (Figure 4.03a) include the precipitation of silt and the need to control water levels, either to prevent flooding or drying out in drought. The usual solution is to provide an adjustable weir at the water entry point, with a trap for river wrack and silt. The exit point needs a further silt trap and fender to prevent damage downstream. (The construction of silt traps and fenders is discussed in Section 16.7; see Figures 16.07a−d.)

The cascade constructed at Stourhead, Wiltshire (Figures 4.03b−c) depends upon a series of earth berms which break up the valley into a series of lakes, each equipped with silt traps at water entry and exit points.

4.04 Shute House Water Garden, Wiltshire (1970s). Architect: Sir Geoffrey Jellicoe
a 'River lake', shape adapted to curving form
b Formal pool, treatment changed with bogus canal arches and overlooked by balconies

a

b

c Cascade with fountains fed by underground pipes from next pool above each water jet
d Detail of copper-faced chutes at each waterfall
e Stone-dressed outlet stream

4.4 Shute House Water Garden, Wiltshire

Spring-fed lakes provide a unique source of life-giving water, and the success of Shute House Water Garden is partly due to the continuous flow available from underground sources at the head of the waterways. The original source is directed to a 'river lake' (Figure 4.04a) and to a formal pool (Figure 4.04b) the latter feeds a cascade of small fountains (Figure 4.04c) which are interlinked on the Kashmir pattern by underground pipes.[3] This enables the fluctuations caused by gravity flow to enliven the whole sequence of pools, in addition to the descending waterfalls. The revetments were formed in elm, now replaced by elm-faced concrete with water chutes made in natural copper (Figure 4.04d). The burnished colour will last forever due to the continuous flow of spring water over the metal surfaces. A new relief stream has been cut at the lowest point and dressed in pebble to provide a lively ripple (Figure 4.04e).

4.5 Technical Details
Concealed weir

Overflows can be formed by means of a pipe placed horizontally through the pool side, but damage may destroy the pipe or break open the kerb. A vertical pipe connected to a pump is helpful, but this can also be disturbed, and is difficult to repair. A weir formed in concrete is more effective and can be constructed to the edge of ponds or on the downstream side (Figure 4.05a).

A formal pond with a regular line of kerbs can be cast with a gutter portion, either as slots or as a continuous feature with pads of mortar to give paving edge support. It can be drained by substantial pipes, such as 75 mm diameter plastic. A wire guard is useful at the inlet to prevent debris blocking the drains. Precast or stone paving can span 300 mm when not under wheel load and can serve as a simple bridge for the space over outlets.

Overflow weir

Large pools, particularly those fed by springs or streams, will need open weirs, constructed in concrete with a silt trap on the rear face (Figure 4.05b). If the flow is substantial, the waterfall face will be improved by inserting a length of metal edging in the crest of the wall. This needs to be set level so that the water falls in an even cascade (see Figure 4.05c).

4.05 Technical details   **a** Section through cleaning trench and sump

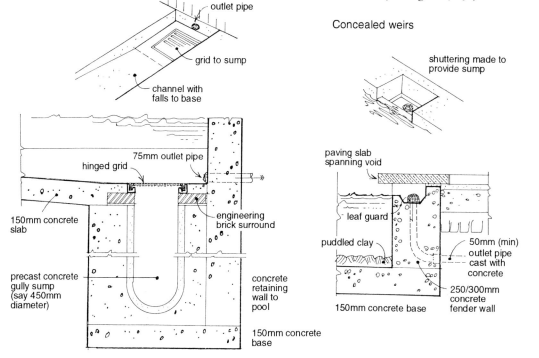

Concealed weirs

b Timber facing to water channel

Section thro' concrete weir
(reinforcement not shown)

concrete extended as fender to si   of waterfall/weir

c Metal edging set level to give even cascade. Nymphenburg Gardens, Munich

d Single-jet fountains. Generalife Gardens, Grenada, Spain (fifteenth century, restored in the 1920s). Note full basin in foreground, with overflowing rim and secondary pool

e Multiple-jet fountain. Theme garden, Liverpool International Garden Show (1984)

f Water veils. Theme garden at Bonn International Garden Show (1979)

g Trickle flow over stone block. Bonn International Garden Show (1979)

h Revolving sphere of granite carried on high-pressure jet. (Designers: Michael Branch & Gabrielle von Pape

d

f

g

e

h

4.05i Combination of floodlighting, fountains and sculpture. Garden at Museum of Modern Art, New York (1975). This garden is designed for day and night use, with underwater floodlights for the fountains and sculpture. Architect: Philip Johnson

Fountains

Battery-powered units have already been mentioned, but permanent installations have to be wired for mains electricity, unless gravity-fed as at Shute House. The patterns of fountain include ascending or angled jets, and the more interesting forms rely on geometric forms with multiple jets to create a water veil (Figures 4.05d–f). The other imaginative solutions are 'trickle flows' which envelope concrete or stone blocks, conveying the notion that the surface is barely wet (Figure 4.05g). High-pressure versions can be used to support a granite sphere (Figure 4.05h). A combination of water jets, sculpture and floodlighting is perhaps the most decorative (Figure 4.05i).

Timber revetments

The construction shown resembles the cascades formed at Shute House. The original work was formed with elm boards back-filled with clay (Figure 4.05b). Erosion has meant replacement with concrete back-filling cast integral with the base slab.

Cleaning channel

Sump pumps can be housed in deep recesses in the pool, but there is always the risk of trapping feet in such pockets, apart from the restricted space when cleaning larger ponds. A trench constructed like a monsoon drain (Figure 4.05a) but with a removable grid will be easy to flush out and enables a mobile sump pump to be used if required. Sumps should be treated in the same way as access chambers (commonly called manholes in the UK) and be at least 900 × 900 mm in plan area and fitted with hinged grid covers as a safety measure.

Water requirements

The ideal water pH value for pond life is 8.0; values below 6.5 and above 8.5 will be a problem for fish. Spring water is obviously the ideal, as found at Shute House Water Garden (see Figures 4.04a–e). Local river sources should be checked for toxicity before feeding into newly-made water features. Good-quality river water can be conveyed by tanker, and most UK water authorities are willing to advise on this matter. Extensive land drainage systems can serve as an alternative supply, and have been employed to maintain a mile-long lake created at Sutton Place, Surrey. Silt traps are essential, and phosphates and other chemicals should not be allowed to enter the waterways.

5 MARKERS

Markers such as stone cairns or stakes are invaluable as indicators in landscape to establish pathways or to define safety limits, as found on ski slopes and glaciers. Bollards (see Section 5.2) can be equally definitive in townscape to demark pedestrian from wheeled traffic areas or to provide guarding at turning points to protect building features from wheel damage. The materials utilized need to be durable, while roadside markers or bollards have to be sufficiently robust to protect pedestrians from the onslaught of the motorist.

5.1 Trail Markers

These are the simplest pattern, often a larch pole or stake with a colour band or tag, tall enough to show above snowfall levels where this is a relevant problem (Figure 5.01a). Similar methods can be used at riverfords or causeways to demark a safe crossing route, once again with a pole tall enough to show above flood or high tide level. A sensible safety measure is the provision of a calibrated marker to show the water depth at a critical point (Figure 5.01b). Ski slopes have coloured stakes to indicate the categories of ski run and also to signify boundaries to the piste. Walking trails in Alpine areas are often defined in detail with a number reference system that relates to trail maps. There are additional features such as signposts, showing the destination and the estimated time and/or distance for the journey. (The advice on time should be treated with caution since, in the author's opinion, in many cases the estimated speed must be that of mountain goats!) Figures 5.01c−e show examples from the Peak National Park in the UK. There is an excellent tourist traffic management scheme in the Peak District whereby the visitor car parks have a payment system for walking maps. Leaflets set out a number of walks, each route being colour-coded on markers or trees.

In rocky areas it is often easier to build a stone cairn than to find purchase for wooden stakes. Cementing the stones together will give extra security, and a capstone with direction

arrows would be a welcome luxury.

Signing gardens with stakes often produces a plethora of unsightly posts, not to mention the vexed question of graphics − often, today, a plastic vulgarity inspired by labelling machines. Boulders with a sawn or polished face make a more attractive low-level marker, leaving the eye undisturbed by obstructive woodwork. Figure 5.01f is taken from the Keukenhof, Holland, where the various bulb displays are subdivided by large stones set in the border edges. A plaque formed of clear

a Trail stakes as found in Alpine areas

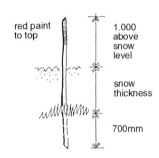

red paint to top

1.000 above snow level

snow thickness

700mm

b Causeway stakes

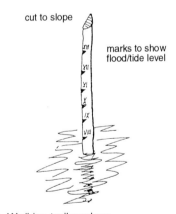

cut to slope

marks to show flood/tide level

c Walking trail markers used in Peak National Park, UK

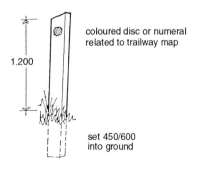

1.200

coloured disc or numeral related to trailway map

set 450/600 into ground

5.01 Trail markers and signs

5.01d Markers on the moors above Goyt Valley, Staffordshire
e Footpath sign showing distances. Peak National Park, UK
f Boulder marker
g Stained timber bulk with engraved signs. Bonn International Garden Show

d perspex with back engraving will look better than coloured labels, while metal plaques or carved letters will be best of all.

Significant signing for public gardens could be made from railway sleepers or timber bulks set vertically. Engraved letter and timber stains permit a robust quality of design, as shown in Figure 5.01g.

5.2 Road Bollards

A London tradition dating back to the eighteenth century is for pavement areas to be protected from wheeled traffic by wooden bollards.[1] These posts were placed behind the kerb line to prevent carriages and wagons from mounting the footpath and endangering pedestrians. Horses could also be conveniently tied up to these bollard posts when the carriages were stationed along the roadside. These details were also used in the colonial capital of Williamsburg, Virginia (Figure 5.02a). There has been a revival of this design theme in the traffic-free areas surrounding Covent Garden, London. The UK Ministry of Transport specifies distances between obstructions and raised kerbs according to vehicle speed − 450 mm up to 30 mph and 600 mm over 30 mph. Flush surfaces for road and walking areas will obviously save space in residential areas where a 20 mph limit exists. There are many circumstances where road bollards need a reflective finish which can be illuminated at night and where the impact strength will have to meet required standards. Proprietary items include precast concrete and steel tubular posts, coated with fluorescent paint or incorporating glass 'cat's-eye' reflectors. Other patterns feature inset electric fittings for illumination, and these are useful as an adjunct to street lighting, particularly in pedestrian areas. Figures 5.02b−e show typical products.

There are other locations where a simple boulder or granite block will provide a sufficient hazard to deter vehicles. Such measures are still used on mountain roads, where a line of rocks, set as 'dragon's teeth' is used to protect verges. Figures 5.02f−h are taken from examples seen in Switzerland. Variations of these designs would be appropriate for private roads in the UK; it should be noted, however, that landowners should maintain accident insurance in case traffic collides with unusual hazards.

5.02 Road bollards

a Traditional pavement bollard posts used at Williamsburg, Virginia (circa 1770s)
b Precast concrete bollard with hostile harsh edges
c Artificial stone bollard with integral reflective finish. Note rounded profile to provide cushioning on impact
d Illuminated steel bollard with shielded lens light on cap
e Precast concrete with painted reflective finish. C-shaped markers on right-hand side shield light fittings

f 'Dragon's teeth' using granite blocks set in soft verge

450mm clearance for estate roads

painted white at crucial corners

set 600mm into ground

g Similar design to 'f' but set in concrete with connecting steel tube

2.000 to 2.500 centres

900 to 1000mm

50mm diam tube

granite bollards 300 to 450mm square

300mm

sleeve through stone

road side

turned end for safety

concrete retaining wall

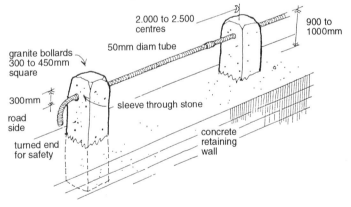

h Granite or sandstone blocks/kerbs set on end to form robust bollard

white paint to top

1200mm

clearance according to traffic regs
450mm up to 30mph
600mm over 30mph

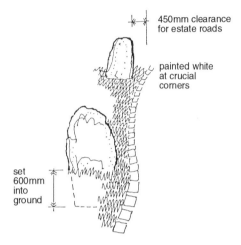

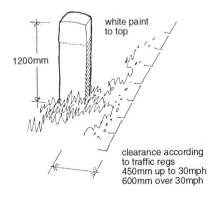

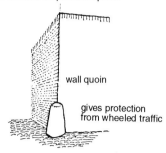

j Inset bollard to protect quoin

wall quoin

gives protection
from wheeled traffic

5.02i Granite bollards
to protect wrought
iron gates

Bollards have another traditional role in
guarding buildings and gateways against wheel
damage. A rounded stone block inset into a
pier or quoin will protect the main wall
face from scuffing or may be placed at a
distance from wrought iron gates, as shown in
Figures 5.02i–j.

5.3   Maritime Bollards

Bollards have always been part of the maritime
scene, often in concave or forked shapes to
facilitate securing vessels. Durability and
strength calls for cast iron – or today, cast
steel. Cast iron bollards are often retained as
historic landmarks on docksides and quays.
Discarded cannons, with cannonballs sealing
the open ends are another common aspect of
maritime landscape, and so popular that many
designs are cast in replica as street furniture.
The progression from naval cannon and inset
ball to functional dockland bollards and the

current replica designs is portrayed in Figures
5.03a–d. Chains are often added to waterside
bollards to give a measure of protection to the
landlubber. The advantage of chains over
railings is that it is quicker to gain access to the
water if someone falls in, and they also provide
flexibility by permitting full use of the dock or
quay with the chains removed. Such devices
are an essential element in the waterside
environment of docks and harbours. Bollards
and chains also serve as a warning, indicating
that there may be a sheer drop into deep water
(see Figures 5.03f for clarification).

5.03 Maritime bollards

a Naval cannon and
inset ball
b Replica cast iron
form of cannon bollard

c Functional form in cast iron used as landmarks at Liverpool Garden Festival Docks
d Cast steel hawser bollards, Millwall Docks' London
e Bollards and chains, Arc de Triomphe, Paris
f Waterside environment in Liverpool

5.4 Other Forms

The adaptability of chains in their contour and shape also makes them useful markers at other boundaries. Common applications are village greens where public and private domains can be signified, as shown in Figure 5.04a. The use of hook plates enables chains to be removed for mowing or for vehicle access, the latter being an asset in pedestrian streets where emergency or service traffic needs to be catered for.

Lockable bollards are preferred in traffic management schemes, enabling parking spaces to be reserved for property owners, or closing streets to all except licensed keyholders. Figures 5.04b–d feature varying forms of traffic arrangements employing hinged and other forms of lock-in-place bollards. Vandalism can be a serious problem in urban areas and public car parks, and here hinged wheel traps provide greater security. Release can be key-controlled and shared by public services (Figure 5.04e).

5.04 Posts and chains, and lockable devices used in traffic management

a Adaptability of posts and chains, demarking public and private domains. The Common at Appleby, Cumbria

5.04b Lockable
bollards controlling
access to seaside
village
c Individual bollards to
protect car spaces

b

c

d Removeable and lockable bollard

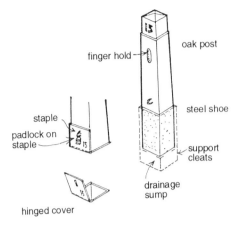

oak post

finger hold

staple

padlock on
staple

steel shoe

support
cleats

drainage
sump

hinged cover

e Hinged steel flap

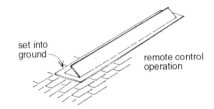

set into
ground

remote control
operation

Granite

Boulders or sawn blocks of granite are not
expensive when purchased at the quarry yard,
the major factor being transport costs.
Working granite is expensive in the UK, and
many finished products, such as shaped blocks
or rounded bollards, are worked abroad and
imported. Inset blocks or bollards should be
placed on a concrete bed of 150 mm thickness
and be encased to a depth equal to one-third of
the total height. Cost index 5 for worked
granite or index 1 for blocks obtained at a
quarry.

Sandstone

Similar remarks apply as for boulders or
blocks. Second-hand sandstone kerbs make a
cheap form of bollard if set on end, but will
need dressing to remove sharp corners. They
are not as durable as granite, with a tendency to
flake on natural bedding planes. Cost index 1
for second-hand material.

Artificial stone

The standard material for all precast forms, the
quality depends upon the selection of aggregate
and cement (crushed granite/other stones/
gravel, with sand and cement, either plain
or coloured, as for precast paving).
Manufacturers provide a cage of reinforcement

5.5   Materials

The key qualities of durability and strength
have already been mentioned. The
approximate sizes and cost indices of the
various patterns, graded 1 to 5 in ascending
order, are indicated below.

bars to improve impact strength, comprising U-shape vertical rods with circular stirrups (Figure 5.05a). The casting work can accord with British Standards, which govern product quality (types of concrete mix, curing, compressive strength, finishes, moulds and tolerances).[2] The patterns simulate masonry forms (see Figure 5.05b) and provide a close match where crushed stone and coloured cements are used in casting. Tooling or grit-blasting the finished work will expose the stone aggregate and improve appearance under weathering. The cost index at works will be dependent upon size, and varies between 1−3. It should be recalled that concrete weighs 1921 kg per cubic metre (120 lbs per cubic foot)

and that a substantial precast bollard of 1.5 m overall length could weigh 226 kg (500 lbs). Concrete is often painted to increase visibility, and if this finish is intended then plain concrete with gravel aggregate and grey cement should be specified, which will save one-third of the cost on artificial stonework.

Cast iron

This traditional material has been in use since the Industrial Revolution. The crystalline nature of cast iron and its material qualities leads to low corrosion risks. Finishes are often bitumen paint with perhaps oil-based paints for decorative installations. The sand-casting technique is still employed, using a hollow-cast method so the walls of bollards can be as thin as 12.5 mm. Bollards that require structural engineering, for example dockside or highway work, will need greater wall thicknesses and certification concerning proven strength. Guarantees should be sought concerning the durability and strength of replica designs that are now made for decorative purposes. The cost index will be 2−3 depending upon the weight of cast iron employed. Cast iron bollards are either set into concrete surrounds as for granite and precast work, or else made with a wide flanged base for bolting down to a foundation stone or concrete pad.

a Simple 'peg' form of precast bollard (450mm diam)

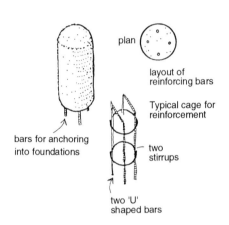

plan

layout of reinforcing bars

Typical cage for reinforcement

bars for anchoring into foundations

two stirrups

two 'U' shaped bars

b Concrete bollard types

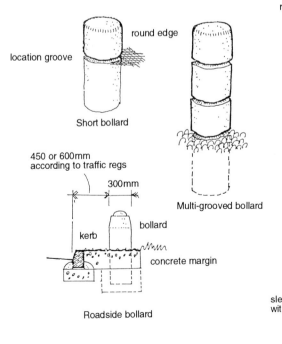

location groove

round edge

Short bollard

450 or 600mm according to traffic regs

Multi-grooved bollard

300mm

kerb

bollard

concrete margin

Roadside bollard

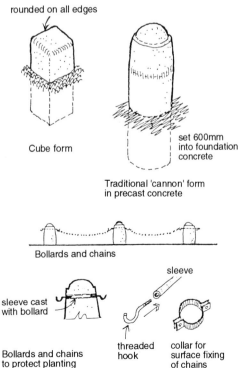

rounded on all edges

Cube form

set 600mm into foundation concrete

Traditional 'cannon' form in precast concrete

Bollards and chains

sleeve cast with bollard

sleeve

threaded hook

collar for surface fixing of chains

Bollards and chains to protect planting

5.05 Precast bollards

5.05c Layout patterns

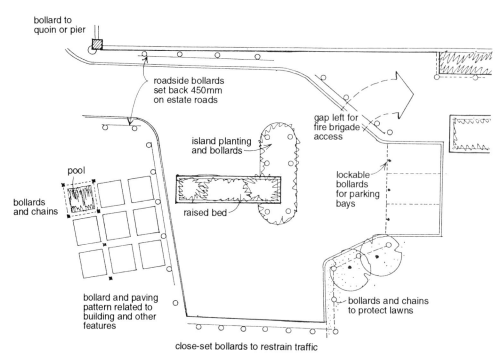

bollard to quoin or pier

roadside bollards set back 450mm on estate roads

island planting and bollards

gap left for fire brigade access

pool

bollards and chains

lockable bollards for parking bays

raised bed

bollard and paving pattern related to building and other features

bollards and chains to protect lawns

close-set bollards to restrain traffic

d Pattern of bollards and street lighting, Barbican, City of London. Architects: Chamberlain, Powell & Bon

Cast or rolled steel

Cast steel has replaced cast iron where structural qualities are required for dock and road works. Corrosion risks are much higher due to the high carbon content of modern steels, and protection will therefore have to rely on galvanized coatings (either zinc dipping or electrolytic deposition) and subsequent painting. The cost index is equal to cast iron with similar fixings (2–3). The cheapest solution is to utilize standard steel products, such as tubular sections (square or circular) or offcuts of rolled structural I-beams set into concrete pockets. In the case of tubes, the exposed ends will need to be weather-capped with a welded steel plate, or else filled with concrete. The cost index could be as low as 1 for these utilitarian solutions. Fabrication of steel tube for lockable bollards will double costs, and the details will have to allow for drainage to sockets, as well as bolt fixings suitable for replacement when damaged.

Cast aluminium

Aluminium is used for replicas since modern processes allow moulds to be prepared from cast iron work and thence cast in aluminium using electric furnaces. The material has a low corrosion risk but has to be painted to give protection against road salt and marine environments. Aluminium's strength is poor compared to cast iron, and it has to be cast in greater thicknesses.

e

Timber

This is probably the easiest material to employ for fixed or movable bollards. The selection of timber should take account of ecological issues – for example, choosing species from managed forests and woodlands. Suitable home-grown timbers in the UK are chestnut, larch and oak, whilst iroku and jarrah from tropical forests might be considered. Manufacturers offer standard lengths and patterns but it is not expensive to vary the designs or simply to invite estimates from local joinery manufacturers for the cost of making up post bollards according to detailed drawings. Finishes may prove to be a problem since durable timbers like oak and iroku contain natural tannins which destroy paint or varnish. A cycle of oiling with linseed or teak oil will restore the finish but will need regular maintenance at six to twelve-month intervals. Varnishes last two years externally, while paint may last five to six years under full weather exposure. Preservative stains are more promising for softwoods like larch, but are not suitable for dense hardwoods such as oak. The price index will be 2−3 depending upon the timbers chosen, but it should be remembered that the life span of wood buried in the ground is limited to around 25−40 years. Tar-coating the embedded wood will enhance the durability of all timbers.

f

e Bollards used to demark space. 'De Zonnehof', Amersfoort, Holland
f Boulders used as sitting-stones or bollards. Munich, Germany

5.05g Idealized townscape from Gordon Cullen's sketches (reprinted from The Concise Townscape by Gordon Cullen. Publisher Architectural Press, London, 1971)

5.6 Bollards and Townscape

The use of bollards to demark space has a prominent place in the art of townscape in marking salient zones or subdivisions in the spatial arrangement of buildings. At the simplest level a ring of embellished stones can delineate the outer limits of a memorial — for example, the setting of the Arc de Triomphe in Paris (see Figure 5.03e). Alternatively, the spatial subdivisions of the building can be captured in the paving design and be further marked by stone blocks at the periphery of the total composition. This is the purpose of Rietveld's use of bollards in the surrounding to the Arts Museum, De Zonnehof, Amersfoort, as shown in Figure 5.05e.

Bollard patterns in townscape are therefore not simply functional devices to divide cars from people or to separate watersides from pavements, but can be seen as indicators of urban spaces and markers which give scale to the surroundings of buildings (see Figures 5.05c–f). Some years ago the *Architectural Review* carried a theme month-by-month dedicated to 'townscape' illustrated by the lively pen of Gordon Cullen.[3] Bollards and setts abounded, as in Figure 5.05g to such an extent that a group of designers involved with the Festival of Britain sent barrowloads of granite setts to the editor's office in Queen Anne's Gate, London. It made no difference to the *Architectural Review's* policy, and one supposes that the setts and a bollard or two simply graced editor J. M. Richard's back yard!

6 SIMPLE RAIL FENCING

The simple post and rail fence is the cheapest boundary solution where continuous demarkation is needed. In building development, post and wire is even cheaper and is used widely in agricultural work or as a temporary measure in housing layouts until hedges and planting screens are established. In this chapter temporary solutions are considered in detail since landscape designers are usually involved with the initial protection needed for planting schemes in urban environments. Limitations upon capital expenditure may mean fencing initially intended to be temporary may become permanent — many local authority housing schemes from the late 1970s in the UK still have the original chestnut palings in place! (See Section 7.3.)

6.1 Temporary Details

One of the most vexed problems with maintaining grassed areas in public spaces is the question of corner-cutting or tracking independent of a footpath system. It might be possible to adopt the users' preferences, as occurred at Massachusetts Institute of Technology, Boston, where the surroundings to new halls of residence were topsoiled and turfed, with the desired lines macadamized/tar coated at the end of term one. The result is short on visual delights, judging by Figure 6.01a. Desires are often codified in the USA, so that a humble footpath becomes, by demand, a jogging and cycling route, each user having a mandatory space which transforms a metre-wide path into a 3.6 m wide 'black-topped' trail to accommodate the users. It is often easier to separate the different categories of users to keep the scale down to reasonable levels, implying that temporary fencing will have to be used to keep the soft landscape intact.

Public places such as the Royal Botanic Gardens at Kew, London face this problem every summer due to the pressure of visitors. Temporary iron hoops have been used from time immemorial — they comprise 10 mm rods bent to a semi-circular form and spiked in the

6.01 Temporary details

a Footpaths at New halls of residence, MIT, Boston use of desire lines that were macadamised

b Bent metal hoops used as temporary protection of lawns

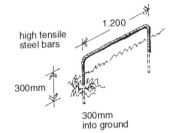

high tensile steel bars

1.200

300mm

300mm into ground

bamboo or hoops of 12mm painted steel rods

c Bent bamboo canes used for a similar purpose
d Rose cuttings entwined to give a more aggressive defence. Botanic Garden, Leiden, Netherlands
e Post and wire fence to protect new planting

6.01f Various forms of temporary fencing in wire

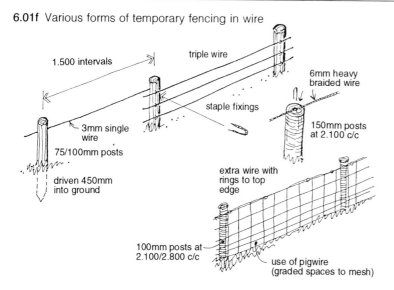

g and **h** The 'Garden City' ideal, early view and contemporary scene at Eastwick, York, with 'green' solution to boundaries

ground, interlocking together to form a low palisade which easily adapts to site geometry. The barrier is moved according to which routes need to be thwarted. The other advantage with this flexibility is that abused grass areas can be reseeded while protected, and likewise vulnerable lawns with spring bulbs and meadow flowers can be excluded from trampling crowds. Bent bamboo canes could also be used. Figures 6.01b−f develop these ideas and reveal how gardeners have perfected more aggressive protection.

Entwined rose cuttings form the inspired fence deployed at the Botanic Gardens in Leiden, a kinder notion than the rusting barbed wire of Topkapi, Istanbul. Post and non-barbed wire is more civilized and has the advantage of being lost to view when the planted areas mature. The agricultural pattern with multi-strand wires or mesh is effective against children and pets, and will form an adequate enclosure around private gardens where hedgerow planting is provided.

It is worth recalling the ideals of the 'Garden City' movement inaugurated by Raymond Unwin and Barry Parker at Eastwick, York, and Hampstead Garden Suburb, London.[1] The intent was a 'green' solution to the enclosure of building plots between houses and as the boundary to the street. Hedging supported by post and wire may look untidy for a few years, but the long-term effect is immensely superior to the tatty 'larchlap' beloved by developers today (see Figure 9.06a). By comparison, Figures 6.01g−h show the inception and the resultant 'green' boundaries at Eastwick.

6.2 Permanent Details

Triprails are one of the permanent details chosen by gardeners to protect soft landscape, whether lawns or plant material at risk from trampling. The height can be as low as 250 mm, which is not obtrusive. Knee height, say 450 mm, may be more effective in areas of heavy use. Grass-cutting round the supporting posts is labour-intensive, so designers place triprails within the curtilage of paths or terraces or within a gravel margin to the soft landscape which is being protected. Metalwork will give a more robust construction than timber, with no risk from splintering by mowers. A framework of steel flats and tubular horizontals is also very resistant to vandalism.

The Royal Parks, advised by Sir Hugh Casson, selected a range of standard furniture at the period of the Coronation in 1953. These included triprails, similar to those shown in Figure 6.02a, used for the Aston Campus, Birmingham University, UK. The materials are mild steel flats and bars, the standards having forged ends to secure the solid bar rail. Turning the square section through 45° increases the strength under vertical load and

d Steel tube barriers

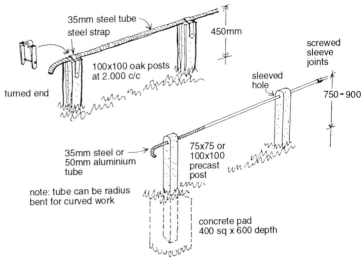

35mm steel tube
steel strap
450mm
screwed sleeve joints
100x100 oak posts at 2.000 c/c
sleeved hole
750 - 900
turned end

35mm steel or 50mm aluminium tube
75x75 or 100x100 precast post

note: tube can be radius bent for curved work

concrete pad 400 sq x 600 depth

e Metal post and tube construction.

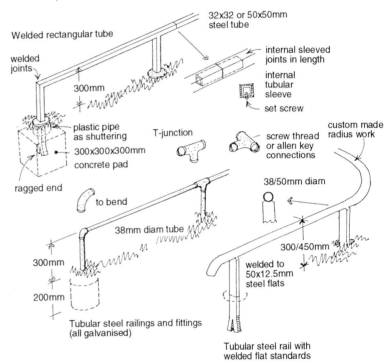

Welded rectangular tube
32x32 or 50x50mm steel tube
internal sleeved joints in length
internal tubular sleeve
set screw
welded joints
300mm
plastic pipe as shuttering
300x300x300mm concrete pad
T-junction
screw thread or allen key connections
custom made radius work
ragged end
to bend
38/50mm diam
38mm diam tube
300/450mm
300mm
welded to 50x12.5mm steel flats
200mm

Tubular steel railings and fittings (all galvanised)

Tubular steel rail with welded flat standards

makes a difficult toehold for budding acrobats. Variations on this principle could be made using tubular sections. A design of elegant simplicity was produced by Schinkel for the gardens at Potsdam, Germany, where cast iron posts in the form of plant stems secure the wrought iron triprails (Figure 6.02b).

High-tensile steel reinforcing bars give a very robust barrier and, if obtained in a galvanized finish, provide a long-term solution — 20 mm bars will be sufficiently strong to span 1.8 m and could be made as U-shaped elements, staked into the ground in the same manner as the Kew hoops. Concreting the ends would give permanence,

while curves could be arranged by having the bars bent to the required radii (see Figure 6.02c for details and a sample application). Taller versions require stout uprights to withstand torque, and typical examples have tubular steel pipes threaded through oak or precast concrete posts.

Galvanized steel water pipe serves as an economic railing element, since it can be readily bent or curved and can be coupled by threaded sleeves or by threaded ends in straight runs. More sophisticated patterns are manufactured for industrial applications and are often adopted for road and riverside railings. The elements include cast iron or steel

6.02 Permanent details

a Triprail at Aston Campus, Birmingham University' UK. Architects: Casson & Conder (similar design to Royal Parks London)
b Elegant simplicity: triprails at Potsdam, Germany, by Schinkel (1830s)
c High-tensile steel triprails by the Louvre, Paris

6.02f Timber construction using strap connectors

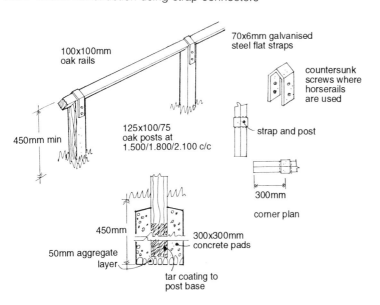

100x100mm oak rails

70x6mm galvanised steel flat straps

countersunk screws where horserails are used

450mm min

125x100/75 oak posts at 1.500/1.800/2.100 c/c

strap and post

300mm

corner plan

450mm

50mm aggregate layer

300x300mm concrete pads

tar coating to post base

g Timber post and galvanized steel tube. Alexandra Road Estate, Camden, London (1979) Note illuminated bollards to side of path
h Timber post and triprail at service road, Blenheim Gardens, Lambeth, London (1974)
i Rustic triprail seen in Danish housing (temporary construction until garden is fully developed)

g

h

i

standards with socket holes to receive tubular guardrails, the standards having flanged bases which are bolted down to concrete, either the paving deck or the margin. There is a demountable form assembled from aluminium or steel tube with cast sockets which is sleeved together and secured by inset Allen screws at

every socket. It can be adapted to curved and raking alignments and designs with single, double or treble rails, and it is commonly used in traffic management for pedestrian guardrails or for crowd control. The industrial finish and character may look inappropriate in a garden setting. A neater finish can be obtained by using internal sleeves with steel tubular sections adapted from balustrade railing used in staircase design.

The timber version relies on a square-profile rail, turned through 45° (for the same reason as given for the triprails in Figure 6.02f) and birdsmouthed over a rectangular post. The rail-to-post joint is secured by a U-shaped metal strap bolted to the post. The construction is ideal for inclined and straight runs, providing a robust and visible triprail. It is often used around planting areas and tree guards or in car parks. A rustic and simple triprail can be made from tree stakes, with a sawn stake used as a capping or side rail, an effective detail often seen in newly-landscaped areas in Scandinavia. Figures 6.02d–i provide constructional details and examples for concrete, metal and timber assemblies.

6.3 Multi-rail Fencing

The industrial patterns of guard rail featured in Section 6.2 have already shown the possibilities with tall multi-rail fencing in crowd control. Garden boundaries may need defining by framework higher than a trip rail, and where mesh protection or wind screening may be used. Timber post and multi-rail fencing is a cheaper solution than close boarding and permits a variety of detail and finish. Figures 6.03a–f feature typical products available.

A circular post and rail furnishes a comfortable handhold and is essential where the fencing is to form a contact point for the public. The same considerations apply to animal enclosures, where fencing should be splinter-free and have smooth surfaces which will not harbour parasites. Fence suppliers offer home-grown hardwoods and softwoods in prepared sections, cut to standard lengths, with the tenons between post and rail already prepared. Assembly relies upon ensuring a loose fit of all members and the prepared post holes, followed by plumbing, temporary staying, then filling and compaction at post holes, and finally pegging the tenon joints.

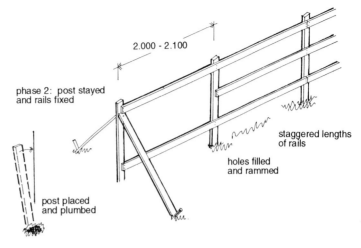

b Typical assembly method for post and rail fence

2.000 - 2.100

phase 2: post stayed and rails fixed

staggered lengths of rails

holes filled and rammed

post placed and plumbed

phase 1: posthole made by auger

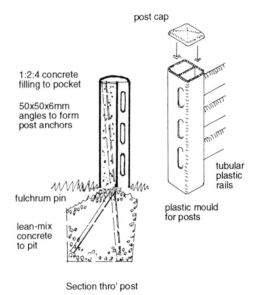

f Plastic form using recycled uPVC
details provided by kind permission of Duralock (UK) Ltd

post cap

1:2:4 concrete filling to pocket

50x50x6mm angles to form post anchors

fulchrum pin

lean-mix concrete to pit

tubular plastic rails

plastic mould for posts

Section thro' post

6.03 Multi-rail fencing

a Standard post and rail assemblies in timber (round profile on left-hand side and rectangular on the right)
c Rectangular post and rail (applied to one face)
d Use of half-round profiles cut from larch poles to form a robust rail fence in Copenhagen
e Application using interwoven larch boards in Copenhagen

Typical diameters for components are 100 mm posts with 75 mm rails assuming 1.8 m centres for posts with a height of 1.2 m above ground.

The rectangular form is related to agricultural patterns and has the advantage that wire mesh or plastic windscreening can be stapled over the face of the framing from the side where horizontal battens or boards occur. A tighter fit will ensue if the mesh or plastic is stapled directly to the posts before overlaying with the horizontal members, the bottom edge of the mesh or plastic being heeled into the ground or fixed to a gravel board.[2]

Using stouter rails or interleaving the posts with thin planks of larch or plywood will stiffen the framing. Round poles are prepared from woodland thinnings and have many uses in landscape construction, as tree stakes,

6.04 Elm board
fencing

a

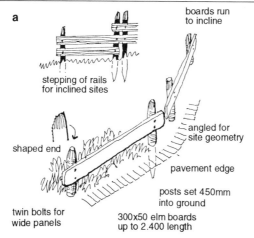

boards run
to incline

stepping of rails
for inclined sites

shaped end

angled for
site geometry

pavement edge

posts set 450mm
into ground

twin bolts for
wide panels

300x50 elm boards
up to 2.400 length

b 'Waney' edged elm
used for a front garden
triprail. Haarlem,
Netherlands

b

timber revetments for embankments and
fencing. Poles cut lengthwise provide a robust
fencing rail. These D–shaped timbers are
spiked with their flat side to one face of the
posts. Lengths up to 4.5 m are readily
available, while green timber can be bent for
curved work. Close spacing will provide a
stockproof fence where animal enclosures are
required, and will make a very sturdy structure
in public spaces. This form of fencing is much
heavier than close-boarded or interwoven
panel fencing and requires closely-spaced
posts – say 100/125 mm diameter or 125 × 75
rectangular members at 2.1 m centres.
The interwoven design is often used for wind
protection. The posts are usually rectangular
and placed parallel to the fence line, with long
lengths of larch boarding or cut strips of
external-grade ply woven between the
verticals. Diagonal cross-stakes could be added
to give extra security in exposed locations.

The ravages of Dutch elm disease still
produce a glut of that valuable timber. Wide
planks cut with a band saw will provide

'waney'-edged boards that make an interesting
form of wide-railed fencing. The usual
preparation is to sand and stain the boards,
allowing the natural shape to be utilized. Elm
distorts and twists with weathering, so discrete
lengths should be used rather than continuous
rails. Figures 6.04a–b show the effective use of
this form in the Netherlands. The low-level
form makes a sturdy triprail, and is often seen
as an edging to Dutch suburban front gardens.

Recycled plastic is another source of
fencing material. In this case offcuts of uPVC
from the window and cladding industries are
chemically modified and extruded as durable
and resilient profiles for posts and rails. The
strength under torque is given by galvanized
steel T-sections housed within the hollow post
section, and the bonding of steel and plastic
is achieved by filling with concrete on site.
The assembly is completed by fitting the rails
into preformed post sockets and applying
adhesives. The post caps are also glued in place
after the concrete filling is in place (see Figure
6.03f). For the relevant materials employed
in all types of post and rail fences, refer to
(Figure 7.01 in Chapter 7).

The briefest arrangement of post and rail is
often sufficient to indicate the boundary
between the private and public domains.
Figure 6.02i shows the way a temporary
framework can be used to define the private
space until such time as the gardenscape has
grown in.

The concluding anecdote for this chapter
concerns the open garden created between our
garden and our American neighbours when we
moved into a new housing development in
Kingston. It was mutually agreed that the lawn
ran through. There was, however, the
question of children, who know nothing about
private space. That problem was solved by a
triprail formed of two roofing battens about
450 mm high (not unlike that shown in Figure
6.02i) which kept the young Blancs in place on
their side of the boundary. All went well until
we had new neighbours, and we employed a
new babysitter in our house, who spent the
evening surveying the scene like a dedicated
voyeur. A brick wall was built by the new
comers next door within a month, whereas the
triprail had worked perfectly well between
neighbours who respected each other's
privacy.

The details described for simple post and rail fences in the previous chapter are mainly derived from agricultural fencing. Such construction gives the cheapest form of enclosure, often as low as £3.00 per metre run per metre height for wire mesh or barbed wire stapled to timber posts. Barbed wired can be said to be one of the basic inventions which made it possible to domesticate the prairie wilderness of North America.[1] Lines of posts with barbed wire strands re-drew the domestic boundaries of a large part of North America in little more than 30 years, from the end of the Civil War to the 1890s. It is significant today that motorways (highways) are increasingly bounded by wire fencing due to the high replacement costs of the timber rail fences put in place in the late 1950s when the motorway programme began in the UK.

7.1   Comparative Data for Post and Wire Fencing

Materials and methods of assembly for various forms of fencing are given in Table 7.1. The actual strengths and recommended construction methods may be found in British Standards documents or from the equivalent documentation in the USA.[2] (For specific advice regarding timber selection and preservatives refer to Chapter 8.) The sections which follow give details of the various fencing materials and applications, including types of agricultural gates, gate ironmongery, vernacular finishes and examples of types of stiles.

Table 7.2 (p. 89) provides guidance on height and number of wires required for various applications.

Table 7.1   Materials and assembly for various forms of wire, rail and chestnut fencing

Type	Duty	Wire Ocrails	Posts	Heights above ground	Post centres		Straining posts		Foundations
					plain	with droppers	plain	with droppers	
Post and wire	Light	Barbed Plain Mesh (all galv)	**Timber** 75 100 150	1000 to 1200 1800 2100	3.000 to 3.500	12.000 with droppers @ 2.0	150 metres	300 metres	driven into ground up to 1200 ht otherwise post holes formed and rammed with soil
Post strained wire	Medium	Plain or high tensile (galu)	**Timber** 100 150	1800 2100	3.000 to 3.500	12.000 with droppers @ 2.0	150 metres	300 metres	Post holes rammed or concrete filled
Post and wire	Medium	Plain or high tensile (galv)	**Precast concrete** 75 × 75 100 × 100	1200 2100	3.000 to 3.500	12.000 with droppers @ 2.0	150 metres	300 metres	Post holes enlarged with concrete pad and surround
Post and wire	Light– medium	Barbed plain or mesh, (all galv)	**Steel L/Ts** 50 × 50	up to 1800	3.000 to 3.500	12.000 with droppers @ 2.0	150 metres	300 metres	Post holes, concrete filled
Cleft rail	Light– medium	Rails Ex 100 × 100 oak	100 × 100 125 × 125 (oak or softwood)	900 1200	3000				Post holes formed and rammed with soil

Table 7.1 continued

Face rail	Light–medium	100 × 50 or 38 (softwood)	100 × 100 (oak or softwood)	up to 1800	3000		Post holes formed and rammed with soil
Morticed rail	Medium	550 × 50 in 6000 lengths (softwood)	100 × 100 (oak or softwood)	up to 1800	3000		Post holes formed and rammed with soil
Chestnut paling pales @ 75 mm spaces	Light	1.9 mm stranded wire (galv)	75 mm Chestnut	up to 1200	2.000 to 2.500	45 mm	Post holes formed and rammed with soil
Chestnut spile spiles @ 50.75 or 100 mm spaces	Medium	4 mm stranded wire (galv)	75 mm Chestnut	up to 1800	3.000		ditto with spiles driven into ground

The wire spacing or type of mesh used is critical to the functioning of farm fencing. The wire is usually plain mild steel (carbon steel) and galvanized, in thicknesses of 1.6, 2.0, 2.5, 3.15, 4.0 and 5.0 mm; 2.5 and 3.15 mm are the most common sizes, with 3.15 mm thickness reserved for the top wire; 4.0 and 5.0 mm will be needed for cattle, horses and where vandalism may be a problem. The wire spacing is closer at the base – say 100 mm, increasing to 300 mm at the top. Special precautions will be needed for rabbit and deer fencing. In the former case, 31 mm galvanized wire netting will be required, of at least 900 mm height, heeled in below the ground for 150 mm towards the rabbit paws. Deer cause far more damage and are far more troublesome, so the fencing needs to be 1.8 m high with wire mesh for small fauna, and at least 2.0 m for larger species like Highland deer. The wiring pattern used by the Forestry Commission in the UK has alternate, lines of barbed wire and plain 2.5 mm galvanized wire, as in Figure 7.01a. Droppers are essential to keep wires taut and to prevent antlers becoming trapped. Straining posts are placed 150 m apart and at positions where the fence line changes direction.

Stock fencing is used for field enclosure where livestock needs to be contained or displayed, as in the case of zoos or farm parks. Security is given by woven or welded mesh galvanized wire stretched from stretcher bars as shown in Figures 7.01a–e, the height

limitations following those given in Table 7.2. The mesh is made in square or rectangular patterns, the latter having the advantage of graded spacing so that close meshing can be placed near ground level to deter children and pets. This is a point of concern where open farmland adjoins habitation or public rights of way. It is also a factor to bear in mind if mesh fencing is employed in housing estate development (see Section 6.1).

A significant visual advantage of post and wire fencing is the ability to blend with the landscape (see Figure 7.01d). The use of mesh is particularly helpful for climbing plants or for hedge support. The weathering of the timber elements further assists naturalization, and is preferable to the harsh appearance of concrete or steel framing. Plastic colour-coated wire appears out of place in any rural setting. Camouflage-effect wire is not manufactured to date, but black or brown wire seen against green sports fields looks more congruous than the vitriolic greens preferred by many borough surveyors in the UK.

The use of tensioning to increase stiffness has been mentioned in connection with mesh work for stock fencing (Figures 7.01b–c). Similar advantages can be obtained with line wire designs where the straining posts and struts are placed centrally to the thrust. Figure 7.01e provides typical details, and ground conditions clearly dictate the type of foundation to use – soft ground will require

a Forestry Commission fencing for protection against red deer

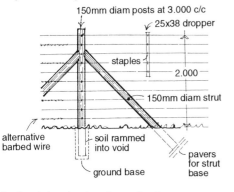

b Stock fencing for pigs or lambs

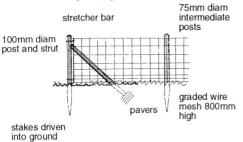

c Stock fencing for cattle

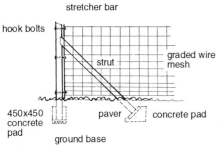

note: concrete pads for end/corner posts and for struts

Table 7.2 Height and scale of wiring for post and wire fences

Situation	Type	No. of wires	Height (mm)
High security for stock	Dropper	16	2100
		11	1800
Light security & highways	Plain wire or dropper	9	1350
		8	1350
		7	1350
Large stock & highways	Plain wire or dropper	6	1200
Field and forestry fences	Plain wire or dropper	6	1050
For medium & small stock		5	1050
Garden fences	Plain wire or dropper	3	900

Source: BS 1722: Part 3 (1986).

e Line wire fencing using straining eyebolts, struts and droppers

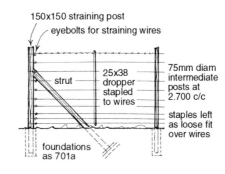

7.01 Details of wire fencing

d The ability of post and wire fencing to blend into the landscape

hardcore bottoming and concrete encasement, while firm ground will need the post hole to be consolidated with rammed earth. Light fencing or hedge protection can simply be supported by post stakes driven into the ground.

7.2 Post and Rail Fencing

The sturdiest form relies on cleft oak rails which are mortised into chestnut or oak posts. The rails are made from forestry thinnings, either barked or left clean, and cleft into triangular lengths. The ends are reduced with an adze on site to complete the tenon joints at post positions. Posts may be 100 mm square or round in section and placed at 2.4–3 m centres. It is labour-intensive and difficult to repair, but looks attractive (see Figure 7.02a for constructional detail). Cleft oak fencing is

7.02 Post and rail fencing

b Primitive form of rail fence, using split pine poles

f Early motorway fencing in the UK (M6 near Knutsford, Cheshire)

a Cleft oak fencing

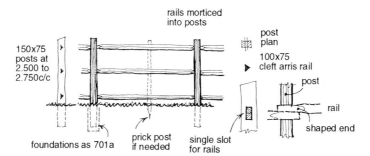

rails morticed into posts

150x75 posts at 2.500 to 2.750c/c

post plan

100x75 cleft arris rail

post

rail

shaped end

foundations as 701a

prick post if needed

single slot for rails

e Post and rail fence

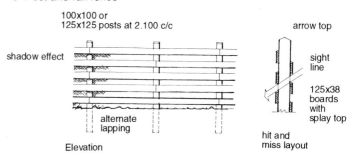

100x100 or 125x125 posts at 2.100 c/c

shadow effect

arrow top

sight line

125x38 boards with splay top

alternate lapping

Elevation

hit and miss layout

c Post, rail and mesh fencing, using larch poles

shaped end to posts

900mm

pig wire

larch stakes 75mm diam up to 1.500 c/c 100mm diam up to 2.500 c/c

kerb and path

adaption for stock fencing

d Post and rail using mortised joints

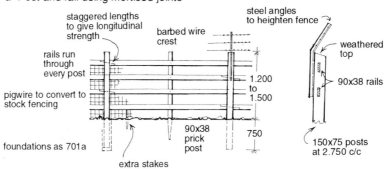

staggered lengths to give longitudinal strength

barbed wire crest

steel angles to heighten fence

rails run through every post

weathered top

pigwire to convert to stock fencing

90x38 rails

1.200 to 1.500

90x38 prick post

750

foundations as 701a

extra stakes

150x75 posts at 2.750 c/c

popular in estate work and with organizations like the National Trust, where forest managers have both materials and a skilled workforce at hand. There are regional variations in the style of design, and it is worth taking note of these where a vernacular character is required. More primitive forms exist where coniferous timber abounds, the construction relying on split pine poles stacked between twin posts, with briar or hazel ties forming ladder supports, as in Figure 7.02b.

Face-nailed rails use less timber and are less labour-intensive. Larch poles or stakes cut to a D profile have already been shown in Figure 6.03c. This pattern, if reinforced with mesh wiring, gives a robust stockproof fence, though not covered by British Standards. Figure 7.02c shows typical details. Sawn timber enables a larger girth of log to be converted to fencing material, with rails cut as 38 × 100, 125 or 150 mm boards and supplied up to 6 m lengths. Posts are commonly of rectangular profile, and ideally cut from the heart timber to minimize defects. The usual sizes are 100 and 123 mm square, or at least 100 × 150 mm where mortised rails are installed.

Sawn rail fencing is associated with motorway (highway) enclosure in the UK, where reliance has been placed upon pressure-impregnated Douglas fir or larch for the total assembly. Longitudinal strength is improved by staggering the rail joints, as in Figures 7.02e−f. Nowadays, construction with face-fitted rails is preferred to the mortised version, owing to the cost of dismantling fences where built-in rails and mortising have to be repaired. However, a considerable amount of British motorway fencing of this construction (Figure 7.02f) has survived 35 years in open country, away from urban vandalism. Stockproofing can be achieved by the addition of mesh wiring, while guarding against deer will need greater height, using steel angles and barbed wire to elevate the posts. Some years ago a fox hunt from Badminton, Gloucestershire, caused chaos on the M4 when horses and hounds cleared motorway fencing, the fox getting clean away. That stretch of the M4 is now protected by 3 m high wire. The post foundations follow the construction given in Section 7.1. Straining posts are not required since the integral construction of posts, nailed rails and vertical cross-members (called 'prick posts') gives overall stability. Bracing is given by curving or angular geometry on plan, and

larger posts of 200 × 100 cross-section will be needed every 30 m or so on long, straight runs.

The life of exposed timber posts and rails can be improved by taking the following precautions. First, specify the appropriate British Standards or equivalents and upgrade those standards where maximum durability is needed − for example, use chestnut or oak posts instead of Douglas fir or larch and specify stainless steel nails. Second, insist on hot tar dipping of all buried post material, whether hardwood or softwood. Third, profile members so as to shed rainwater, using bevelled tops on posts or vertical members and bevelled rail tops to be weathered away from the posts. Rebating rails into post sides may increase the bearing capacity but runs the risk of rot pockets in the trapped end grain of every post. Post holes that have broken stone bases will give better drainage than full concreting under and around timber (see the notes accompanying Figures 7.01a−c).

7.3   Cleft Chestnut Paling

Cleft chestnut paling is commonly employed for temporary protection on building sites and for guarding new lawns and plantings from damage. The customary pattern is 1.2 m high with chestnut pales set 75 mm apart and held by three lines of four-stranded 1.9 mm wire to form a continuous bale of fencing, each bale giving a run of 40 m. The method of erection is to unwind the bale and to hand-stretch the pre-wired pales along a line of posts at 2−2.5 m centres with intermediate fixings by nail and/or staple. Eye bolts are used on straining posts placed at the ends of bale runs. It is wise to add an extra top wire to stiffen the assembly where crowds are involved.

The ragged and untidy appearance can be improved by reverting to the traditional agricultural form of chestnut paling. It is termed 'spile' fencing and is formed like a palisade, with each pale driven into the ground at 150 mm centres. The pales are 50 mm chestnut stakes connected by 4 mm seven-ply line wires which in turn are stapled to 75 mm chestnut posts at 3 m intervals. Variations exist, including a closed palisade, which is virtually a wall of timber stakes. Refer to Figures 7.03a−c for comparisons.

A compromise can be made by using the

7.03 Cleft chestnut paling

b Use of chestnut spiles. Left: continuous palisade, right: placed at 150 mm centres

c Rail and chestnut spile

d Untidy appearance of temporary fencing in public housing, London

a Temporary form used for site protection

end post and stay

other posts at 2.000/2.500 c/c

900/ 1.200/ 1.500

roll of chestnut paling

c

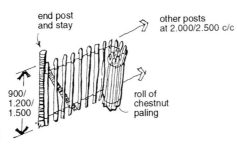

b

d

spiles as vertical pales nailed to a rail fence. Once again, the strength will be increased by driving each spile into the ground before completing the assembly. The more permanent forms of chestnut paling are barked and pointed at both ends. They make a durable and tough form of palisade with a life span of 30 or more years, the extra care taken with the sizing of timbers and subframing being preferable to the untidiness of temporary chestnut paling, as shown in Figure 7.03d.

7.4 Stake Pile Construction

The close palisade referred to in Figure 7.03b has its origins in the defensive staked walls erected in times past. There is archaeological evidence that Celtic settlements constructed

such defences, while North America is littered with timber forts, or rather the 'stake and pile' remains from the epoch 'when the West was won'. Figures 7.04a–d show reconstructions of defensive structures using stakes or spiles today. Such contemporary construction uses steel cables stapled to the back of the timber piles, or else screw bolts driven through cross-rails to give cohesion to the structure.

b

7.04 Stake pile walls

a Traditional sea defences at Walcheren, Holland

b Replica village built at the site of the landing of the Pilgrim Fathers, Plymouth, Massachusetts

a

d Construction details of stake pile walls

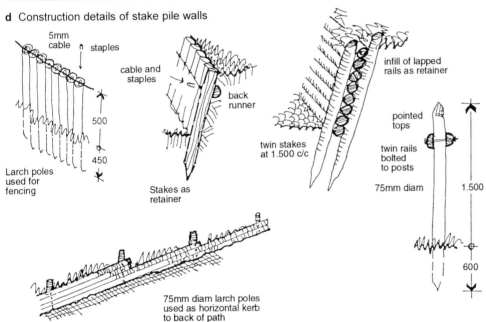

5mm cable

staples

cable and staples

back runner

Larch poles used for fencing

500

450

Stakes as retainer

infill of lapped rails as retainer

twin stakes at 1.500 c/c

pointed tops

twin rails bolted to posts

75mm diam

1.500

600

75mm diam larch poles used as horizontal kerb to back of path

7.5 Agricultural Gates

The basic designs in steel or timber are for utilitarian applications such as driveway or field gates. British Standards recognize two forms.[2] Many fencing contractors make up gates in styles complementary to fence patterns. The standard widths for agricultural purposes run from 2.4–4.2 m in 300 mm steps, with 1.1 or 1.3 m heights. A wide gate is always an advantage in turning vehicles through an opening, and similarly a gate swing which operates two ways is easier to operate,

particularly where the swing can reach 110° to 120° each way. It is worth recalling that emergency vehicles in the UK require 2.7 m clear width for access.

Standard metal and timber gate designs rely on lattice timber bracing, which implies hanging from either side. In reality, wood framing takes into account the need to lighten the construction away from the hinge side with tapered or reduced members to the closing edge of the gate. Refer to Figures 7.05a–b for examples of standard and custom-made gates. Gates designed for regular use should be made

7.05 Agricultural gates

a Standard metal gate. Note equal-sized members and lattice of diamond framing to allow hanging from either side

b Custom made and standard timber gates

typical size 3.000x 1.500
members:
hanging stile 125x75
closing stile 75x75
rails 75x25

pointed posts

8mm diam bolts

pivot hinges and strap plates

posts 250x250 on hanging side
200x200 closing side

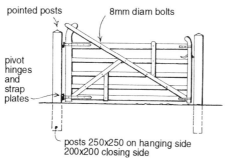

c Combined entry and wicket gate

members as 705b

typical size 4.800 opening

loop-over latch

swing stiles

lead cappings

hinge held by stile plates

200x200 or
250x250 posts both sides

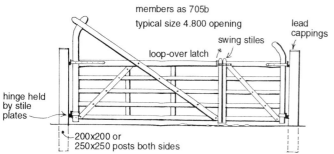

from hardwood with a planed and sanded finish, and the top rails and edges of bolt posts and closing stiles should have the arises rounded to prevent splintering. The latter can be designed to suit various functions which are summarized below.

d Horse gates

round top posts

125-75x75 top rail

175x175 posts

spring catch

125x75 hanging stile

75x25 braces

75x75 swinging stile

75x75 bottom rail

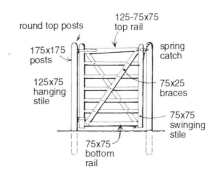

e Hunting gates

sizes similar to 705b

loop-over latch

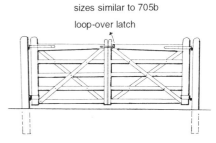

f Kissing gates

typical size 1.200 high
by 900/1000 width

post and rail fencing design

top rail - rounded 125x75

100x75 swinging stile

125x75 hanging stile

rails 75x38

bottom rail 100x50

175x175

gate

175x175

hard paving

200x150

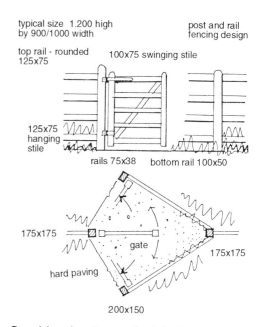

Combined entry and wicket gates

These are common on estate drives or entries in rural areas (Figure 7.05c). The gates are arranged in proportions of 1:2 or 1:2.5, with swinging stiles secured by a cross-over bracket. The narrower wicket gate is reserved or pedestrian use, additionally secured by a drop bolt.

Horse gates

These are single seven-bar gates of 1.65 m height with a width of 1.1–1.2 m

(Figure 7.05d). The closer is usually a vertical spring rod which is mounted at the head of the closing stile to facilitate use by riders.

Hunting gates

These are double versions of horse gates with total widths (for twin leaves) of 1.8, 2.4, 3.0, 3.6 and 4.2 m, secured by a cross-bracket to avoid the need to dismount. See Figure 7.05e.

Kissing gates

These are covered by BS 5709 (1979) but sizes need to be checked against potential users. Pushchairs/strollers or wheelchairs or for that matter stout persons with large backpacks, will need different layouts.

There is much to be said for a swinging gate designed for single-way working and laid out with an adequate turning bay. See Figure 7.05f.

Cattle grids

Cattle grids are placed as stock barriers to control access to open land, and are also used on farms to overcome the problems of opening and shutting gates on private roads. In the UK one refers to BS 4008 (1973); this describes a construction which will support vehicles up to 10.16 tonnes. The road deck is formed with steel channels or rectangular tubes spanning at right-angles to the road and set 75−100 mm apart. Support is given by 100 or 150 mm reinforced concrete fender walls carried on a base slab. The pit below the 'steels' needs to be at least 300 mm deep to be self-draining, and arranged with a removable deck bay for cleansing. Refinements include an overhead beam to prevent caravan access, and a post and rail fence mounted on the fender walls to deter stock from attempting to force past the barrier. The addition of a kissing gate alongside will facilitate use by walkers, etc., while bridle gates would solve the problems for horse riders. Small mammals such as hedgehogs should also be considered, and land drains installed to serve as escape tunnels from the pit trap.

a Hook and band hinges with pivots.

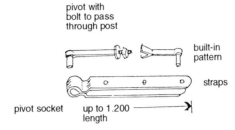

pivot with bolt to pass through post

built-in pattern

straps

pivot socket   up to 1.200 length

b Double band hinges with twin sockets and rocker action to lower pivot.

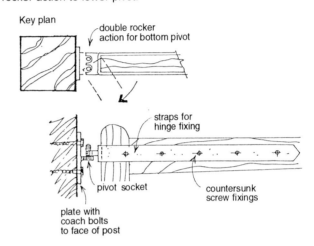

Key plan

double rocker action for bottom pivot

straps for hinge fixing

pivot socket

countersunk screw fixings

plate with coach bolts to face of post

c Loop-over latch.

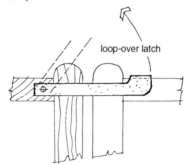

loop-over latch

7.6 Gate Ironmongery

The selection of the appropriate ironmongery is as important as the design of the gate. Catalogues from leading manufacturers provide detailed illustrations and guidance regarding the girth and size of hinge in relation to the weight of gate carried. Figures 7.06a−f show typical fittings for agricultural gates. T-hinges are not shown as these are only appropriate for light use on shed doors and similar duties. Hook and band hinges should be used generally, with the hinge pins firmly bolted to wooden posts or built into masonry piers. Double-band hinges are installed for two-way opening gates. Pivots will last longer if washered, and suffer less wear and tear when

7.06d Spring catch.

Key plan

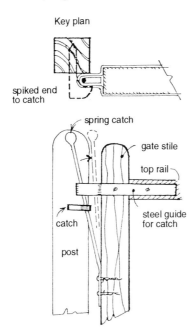

spiked end
to catch

spring catch

gate stile

top rail

catch

steel guide
for catch

post

e Counter-balance latches.

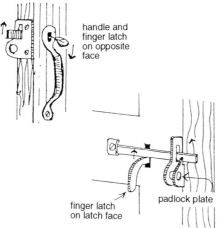

handle and
finger latch
on opposite
face

finger latch
on latch face

padlock plate

f Barrel bolts

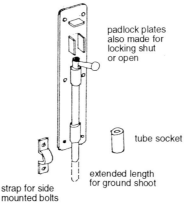

padlock plates
also made for
locking shut
or open

tube socket

extended length
for ground shoot

strap for side
mounted bolts

provided with twin sockets at the top and
bottom of the hinge pin. Simple pivots placed
'pin upwards' enable gates to be lifted for
maintenance, and the use of twin pins on the
lower rail imparts a rocking action which
renders the gate self-closing.

Gate latches need to be chosen from patterns
which allow for settlement of gates and/
or posts.

Loop-over latches

A popular form which loops over the stiles of
double gates. These are not self-closing, but
are sturdy in use.

Spring catches

Also called hunting latches, these consist of a
spring rod mounted vertically on the gate stile.

Counter-balance latches

These resemble 'Suffolk' latches, and consist of
a hinged bar which engages with a strike plate
on the gate post. They can be self-latching, but
are vulnerable to settlement.

Barrel bolts

These are often preferred due to ease of
padlocking in place. They are better set
horizontally from the top rail, with the bolt
end received into a socket fixed to the side of
the post or into a mortised hole within the post
and pier.

7.7 Vernacular Character and Finishes

Regional differences in materials and craftwork
have already been noted in relation to hand-
made cleft-rail fencing. Similar points arise in
gate design where the woodwork is locally-
made. White-painted joinery is often preferred
for visibility with road gates, and is certainly
traditional for equestrian property.
The availability of working quarries will affect
the choice of materials for gate piers or posts.
Granite posts are as cheap as precast concrete at
the quarry yard and look better in a moorland
setting than industrialized products.

Hand-made ironwork is seldom specified
since catalogue items are available for hinges,
bolts and spring catches. The functional quality
of well-made ironmongery does not require
embellishment with bogus hammered textures
or 'antique' finishes. It is important to specify
the soundest rustproofing available — either

galvanizing (hot dipping is preferred to electrolytic deposition of zinc) or hot zinc spraying. The fastenings should be of similar quality, or stainless steel. Paint or black japan coatings last a year or so under full external exposure, while zinc coatings (depending upon thickness of deposition) can last 15 years without being painted. Waiting a year before priming and painting galvanized steel will improve the bond between paint and the zinc coating.

Durable hardwoods like chestnut, iroku, jarrah, oak or teak do not require painting.

Oak and teak contain tannins and resins which render overpainting a failure. Regular oiling with linseed oil will darken the timber but preserves the grain. Under natural weathering most timbers turn silver grey.

7.8 Stiles

Reference could be made in the UK to BS 5709 (1979) for recommendations concerning assembly and sizes for timber stiles. The salient

7.07 Stiles and kissing gates
a Oak-framed stile, Kennedy Memorial, Runnymede. Architect: Sir Geoffrey Jellicoe
b Walk with stiles, Gateshead International Garden Show, County Dash. Designer: Hamilton Finlay
c Field gate left in place with log stiles placed either side. Scotney Castle, Kent. Designer: The National Trust

dimensions should be as follows to be safe in use: height to rail 900 mm, each step 300 mm rise, clear width 1200 mm. Consolidated broken stone or paving should be placed as a threshold for the stile to give a non-slip surround. Figures 7.07a–c show differing solutions from various districts of the UK.

Kennedy Memorial, Runnymede

The walking route commences with a kissing gate with well-finished oak posts and rails, the latter being square timbers turned through 45° with pegged tenon ends. The post and rails are rounded to be splinter-free. The turning bay, although accommodating a tree, has sufficient space for the heavily-laden.

Walk with Stiles, Gateshead International Garden Show

This nature trail was created as a permanent feature at Gateshead. Each stile is constructed as a unique feature in contrasting materials. The entry point is signed by an oak mast, with the stile set astride a post and rail fence. The heights of rail do not follow British Standards, but the design provides adequate space, good handholds and proper provision of hard paving.

Scotney Park

A former bridleway has been converted to a footpath. The existing field gate has been left in place but made more climbable by log stiles. The lift-off hinge lugs mean that the gate can be lifted clear if necessary in an emergency.

In areas where field stone walling is traditional it is not necessary to construct timber stiles. The usual solutions are cantilever steps formed by projecting slabs built into the walling; the other solutions are V gaps left between stone posts or slabs set on edge. See Section 11.2 for illustrations.

8 SECURITY FENCING

The design considerations for this type of fencing depend on the degree of security required. A minimal level may be called for by insurers, who may specify heights and a type of wire mesh which is unclimbable. Security fencing can also serve as protective fencing where ball games are played, or in the case of adventure playgrounds or educational facilities which need to be secure from trespass after closing time. High-security fencing is required for prisons, mental health facilities and military establishments. Detailed design advice from government departments is available through official publication such as the HMSO in the UK.[1] BS 1722: Parts 1 & 2 are most useful references in the UK since they contain details for specifying wire and coatings as well as qualitative requirements for posts (concrete, steel and timber). Standardized heights and weights of mesh are given, with reference numbers which simplify specification writing.

A common parameter for all security fencing is the provision of chain link or welded mesh enclosure, the differing types being summarized below.

8.1 Chain Link Fencing

A 'market leader' as trade journals would say, its common use is perhaps the main reason why the twentieth-century urban environment in the UK appears spoilt in comparison with the nineteenth century, when railings or walls were erected which related to the built fabric. Chain link is relatively unclimbable, difficult to damage and cheap. Timber posts soften the appearance, but the dictates of durability imply precast concrete or steel posts (angles or tubes). The interlocking mesh of steel wires can be made as follows:

- Galvanized steel link in 50 mm mesh, or 25 mm and 40 mm for high-security, with gauges varying from 2.0–3.55 mm.
- The same specification but with the addition of plastic coating.
- Light-gauge mesh (2.0 mm diameter) with plastic coating.

- Stainless steel mesh. The most expensive, and used for industrial plants with high corrosion risks in the locality.

Plain galvanized wire has a life span of around 30 years, the breakdown of the galvanizing being caused by chafing at the links. Plastic coating prolongs the galvanized finish and enables the mesh to be coloured, black or dark brown looking best in a landscape setting. Plastic-coated steel (ungalvanized) is a short-lived product, since breakdown of the coating within five years leads to severe corrosion of the exposed steel wire.

The posts appear less conspicuous in dark colours, and precast concrete can be self-coloured green with copper-based salts. It is more effective to use external emulsion paint in brown or slate greys. In the USA, enlivening of drab runs of chain link is achieved by interleaving with coloured aluminium blades derived from the Venetian blind market, a decorative feature of 'Main Street', USA, that thankfully has not crossed the Atlantic in force. Russian vine and convolvulus thrive on chain link support but will not grow freely until the zinc coat is weathered. This is due to the corrosive run-off from freshly-made zinc surfaces, perhaps another reason to specify plastic-coated wire, which has no effect upon flora.

Successful screening can be obtained on one face immediately by running plastic wind-screening to the smooth side of the fencing; the fixings can be made with additional straining wires interweaving through the plastic mesh. Once again, dark brown or black colouring will give better camouflage to a new chain link fence and the ranks of concrete posts. For further consideration of colours relative to landscape refer to Section 9.8.

Stability depends upon firmly-held posts set into concrete-filled holes. Straining posts are needed to secure the stretcher bars and anchor eye bolts for line wires. Wire ties or hog rings will effectively tie the mesh to the line wires, and both mesh and line work are stretched to ensure a well-secured fence. Heights up to 4.5 m are feasible. Additional security can be furnished by extended posts

a General construction

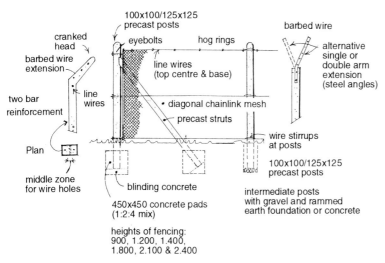

cranked head

barbed wire extension

two bar reinforcement

line wires

Plan

middle zone for wire holes

100x100/125x125 precast posts

eyebolts

line wires (top centre & base)

diagonal chainlink mesh

precast struts

blinding concrete

450x450 concrete pads (1:2:4 mix)

heights of fencing: 900, 1.200, 1.400, 1.800, 2.100 & 2.400

hog rings

barbed wire

alternative single or double arm extension (steel angles)

wire stirrups at posts

100x100/125x125 precast posts

intermediate posts with gravel and rammed earth foundation or concrete

b

8.01 Chain link fencing surmounted with barbed wire, and the defences can be reinforced by electrical current and surveillance devices. Barbed wire needs to be placed towards the owner's side of the fence and should not project beyond the boundary line. Advice must be taken from insurers before using razor wire and other forms associated with military defence. Figure 8.01a gives the basic constructional detail for chain link fencing, and Figure 8.02b reminds the reader of the ugly reality.

8.2 Other Mesh Fencing

Open-mesh designs have already been described for agricultural work (see Section 7.1 and Figures 7.01a–e). Expanded metal (steel or other metal mesh formed by slotting a metal sheet and then stretching the material so that the slots extend to a diamond shape) or close-welded mesh are reserved for security fences or enclosures for ball game areas. High-tensile wire mesh will give high strength and resilience. Metal tubular posts permit heights up to 9 m, and the architectural appearance of square or rectangular mesh is superior to chain link, while the smaller profiles which pertain to structural steel framing avoid the clumsy proportions of precast concrete. Many fabricators have developed assemblies which conform to complex site geometry, such as sloping ground or cranked and curved boundaries.

The appropriate type of fencing needs to be chosen, and it is usually assumed that 25 mm meshes are impossible to climb. This is not the case – athletically-inclined people can scale 3 m chain link fencing without difficulty, and those wearing boots equipped with toe spikes can scale any form of mesh fencing.[2] The security aspect can be enhanced using the extra defences mentioned for chain link in Section 8.1, namely barbed wire extensions and electrical devices.

Welded mesh

This is constructed from steel mesh electrically welded at every junction and hot-dip galvanized, with the edges either trimmed flush or projecting. The pattern can be square mesh (50 × 50 mm) or rectangular (25 × 75 mm). There is a wide range of fabricators, and other sizes are available. Common wire gauges are 2.6 mm and 3.3 mm, but it is also made in stouter sections, as well as high-tensile wire. Coating with plastic is feasible in a wide colour range. Some makers provide a heavier rod welded to the periphery of mesh sheets so that fencing can be formed in a series of panels. This technique is also applied where mesh is cut on the rake to bind together the free ends of wires. High-tension mesh is stretched between strainer posts similar to chain link, and is often employed in play areas to lend extra resilience to the enclosure.

a General construction of welded mesh
using tubular steel posts

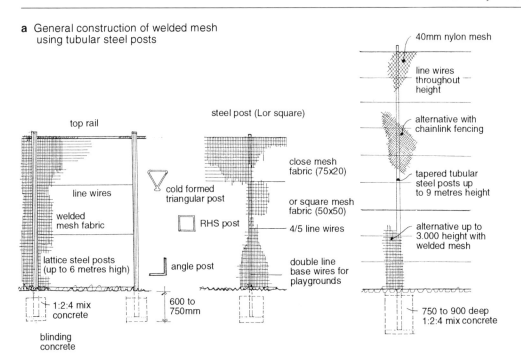

top rail

steel post (Lor square)

line wires

welded
mesh fabric

lattice steel posts
(up to 6 metres high)

cold formed
triangular post

RHS post

angle post

close mesh
fabric (75x20)

or square mesh
fabric (50x50)

4/5 line wires

double line
base wires for
playgrounds

1:2:4 mix
concrete

600 to
750mm

blinding
concrete

40mm nylon mesh

line wires
throughout
height

alternative with
chainlink fencing

tapered tubular
steel posts up
to 9 metres height

alternative up to
3.000 height with
welded mesh

750 to 900 deep
1:2:4 mix concrete

8.02 Other mesh
fencing

b Typical installation for
an adventure play-
ground (reprinted by
kind permission of
Binns Fencing Ltd)
c High-tensile wire
screens at a sports area

b

c

d Stainless steel crimped wire fence

e Industrialised system using serial
production of balustrade panels

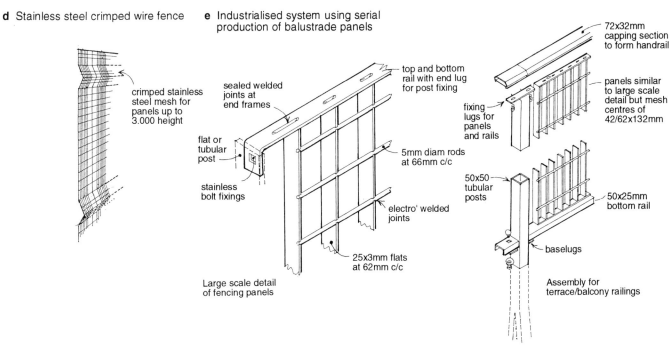

crimped stainless
steel mesh for
panels up to
3.000 height

sealed welded
joints at
end frames

flat or
tubular
post

stainless
bolt fixings

top and bottom
rail with end lug
for post fixing

5mm diam rods
at 66mm c/c

electro' welded
joints

25x3mm flats
at 62mm c/c

Large scale detail
of fencing panels

72x32mm
capping section
to form handrail

panels similar
to large scale
detail but mesh
centres of
42/62x132mm

fixing
lugs for
panels
and rails

50x50
tubular
posts

50x25mm
bottom rail

baselugs

Assembly for
terrace/balcony railings

8.01f Fencing screen adapted to sloping site **g** Enclosure including pergola. (Illustrations 802 e–g reprinted by kind permission of Orsogril Sarl (UK Department c/o McArthur Group Ltd, Gedding Road, Hoddesdon, Herts, EN 11 OW2)

Other forms of mesh use crimped wires to give extra stiffness in relation to height, and are available in stainless steel, which has high strength combined with considerable durability.

Finally there are structural steel meshes which involve 3, 5 and 6 mm bars which are made up as balustrade panels. A fully industrialized system exists for serial production of fencing features, enclosures and pergolas, and is a patented form of fabrication called 'Orsogril'[3] available in a wide range of coatings. Refer to Figures 8.02a–g for general details and views of various installations.

9 PALISADE FENCES, RAILINGS AND GATES

The term palisade is derived from the French verb *palisser*, meaning 'to enclose with pales or stakes driven into the ground'. The defensive image has been explained in Section 7.4 and historic reconstructions are shown in Figure 7.04a–d.

9.1 Traditional Patterns

Traditional farm enclosures in Scandinavia use a lighter form of palisade with sharpened stakes secured to rails and larger posts. Hand-made versions are still manufactured, the Figures in 9.01a–b showing the Open Air Museum fencing at Lillehammer, Norway, and the constructional detail involved. The spare profile of Scandinavian examples is the inspiration for decorative painted palisades that are such a feature of urban gardens in Scandinavian towns. The patterns rely on prepared timber (sawn and planed), the convention of arrow- or round-headed timber follows the principle of finishing exposed end grain with weathered surfaces. Typical details are given in Figures 9.02a–e, which include views of traditional painted palisading seen in the USA.

A noteworthy point is the way present-day microporous finishes have taken over from labour-intensive brush-applied oil paints where five operations were initially required (knotting, priming, undercoat and two gloss finishing coats).[1] Coatings with the new alkyd/acrylic paints require two to three coatings and are applied quickly by roller. The US examples have been selected from the refurbished areas in the colonial capital of Williamsburg, Virginia, and reveal the elegant patterns that can be obtained. A successful design depends as much on the shape of the pale as upon the space between. White or light coloured paint enhances the contrast, while brown or darker tints merge the woodwork with the landscape. The most economic form relies on pales fixed to horizontal rails mortised and dowelled into posts. Careful detailing with timbers of equal girth can hide the posts from the 'fair' side.

9.01 Farm enclosures in Scandinavia

a Open Air Museum, Lillehammer, Norway (eighteenth century)

b

a

9.02 Decorative palisading

a Face-nailed palisade to cross-rails, supported on gravel board. Note sawn finish, with pale placed in front of post to preserve pattern. Reconstruction at Williamsburg, Virginia

Plastic components with concrete-filled plastic moulds serve as the posts (see Figure 6.03f for the principles involved). The wooden framework can also be assembled like wrought ironwork, with vertical bars threaded through rails with a capping and base timber.

The slenderness of the wooden bars can be countered visually by turning the square profile through 45° to present a wider girth to the eye, as in Figure 9.02c.

9.02b Palisade formed as railings, with rails drilled to receive verticals.
Raleigh Tavern, Williamsburg, Virginia (reconstruction)
c Decorative palisade with spearheads. Note 45° turn in verticals. Williamsburg, USA (reconstruction)
d Fencing and gates at Mount Vernon, Washington, DC (circa 1780)

b

c

d

e Details of assembly of pales and framing

100/75x25/20mm pales
material: pressure impregnated and stained larch, douglas fir or oak

finishes: stain or paint

square cut with bevelled surface

Alternative designs for paling tops

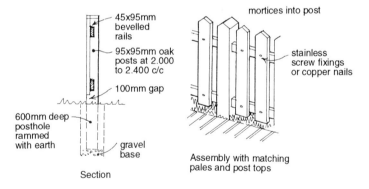

45x95mm bevelled rails

95x95mm oak posts at 2.000 to 2.400 c/c

100mm gap

600mm deep posthole rammed with earth

gravel base

Section

mortices into post

stainless screw fixings or copper nails

Assembly with matching pales and post tops

9.2 Hit-and-Miss Fencing

The arrangement of plain boards and rails is also retained for hit-and-miss fencing, where a degree of shade is needed in screen designs. The weight of the boards needs to be carefully considered since this affects the strength required in rails and posts. Figure 9.03a gives sizes for specific heights. Hit-and-miss boards provide greater openness but increase the weight due to the closer spacing. Horizontal battens or planks may relate better to terraces or nearby buildings, and will ensure a more varied appearance due to shadow lines. Arranging standard boards as an abstract pattern avoids the repetitive style resembling a pallet crate turned on edge, as in Figure 9.03c. The creative design shown in Figure 9.03d occurs between adjoining terrace gardens and acts as a privacy barrier and as a sturdy framework for climbing plants. Compare this with the more open character of trellises (shown in Figures 12.04a–b).

a Vertical board design and typical sizing

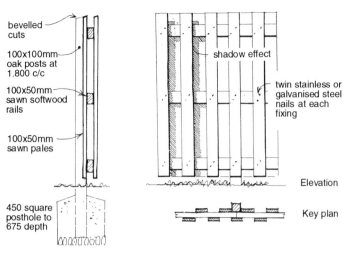

- bevelled cuts
- 100x100mm oak posts at 1.800 c/c
- 100x50mm sawn softwood rails
- 100x50mm sawn pales
- shadow effect
- twin stainless or galvanised steel nails at each fixing
- Elevation
- Key plan
- 450 square posthole to 675 depth
- hardcore/shingle bottom

d

e Diagonal or star shaped panels

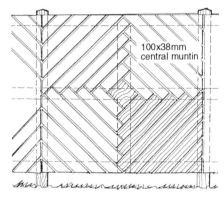

- 100x38mm central muntin
- 125x125 or 100x100mm oak posts
- 75x38 or 25mm sawn softwood boards (impregnated larch or douglas fir)

f

g

9.03 Hit-and-miss palisading, including diagonal forms

b Hit-and-miss fencing on a site boundary in Coombe Hill, Kingston upon Thames
c Sample fencing of the 'pallet-crate' pattern. Speculative housing estate, Toronto, Ontario
d Horizontal-board pattern with abstract design. Terrace screen at Pertenhall, Bedfordshire (1964). Architect: Ian Hill
f Roadside fencing in Hampshire
g Lift-off panels of diagonally-framed larch fencing. Terrace garden wall, Bodnant, North Wales

9.3 Diagonal Fencing

The decorative aspect can be enhanced by securing diagonal boards or star patterns placed at angles to one another, as in Figure 9.03e. Snow loading requires greater strength, particularly where snowploughs may throw a considerable weight of ice against the fence during clearing operations. A diagonal trellis of stout pales or chestnut spiles driven into the ground gives lateral strength to roadside fencing where this is a problem. Figure 9.03f shows a British example, though this type of fencing is more commonly found in central Europe. A diagonally-braced fence is used at Bodnant terrace gardens as a removable barrier. Lift-off panels occur along the top of a retaining wall, enabling large-scale material such as planters to be moved around without having to negotiate curving steps. The larch framing in Figure 9.03g dates from the 1900s, the same period as the trellised pergolas discussed in Section 13.7 (see Figure 13.07c).

9.4 Close-boarded Fencing

The close-boarded form of palisade has overtaken the other patterns for garden enclosure, to the detriment of visual delight. Insurers will advance arguments about the additional security afforded by a close-boarded fence of 1.8 m height and the ease of repair in

9.04 Close-boarded fencing

a Close-boarded oak fence with pales set alternately bay-by-bay
c Erection work in progress, using precast posts and wooden rails

b Constructional detail of close boarded work

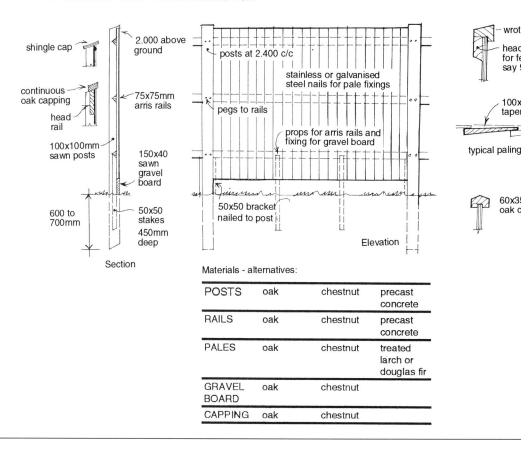

Materials - alternatives:			
POSTS	oak	chestnut	precast concrete
RAILS	oak	chestnut	precast concrete
PALES	oak	chestnut	treated larch or douglas fir
GRAVEL BOARD	oak	chestnut	
CAPPING	oak	chestnut	

comparison with more decorative forms. It is also true that close boarding coupled with back-up panels will form an effective barrier where protection is needed from exhaust and noise pollution alongside a motorway/ highway. The dull appearance of long runs of boarding can be improved by turning the feather-edged cladding in alternate directions, as in Figure 9.04a.

Standardized close-boarded fencing kits involve less weight of timber per metre run than traditional palisades or hit-and- miss screening, and therefore involve the lowest unit cost for boundary work. This is another reason for its popularity with building developers. A properly-made fence with oak or precast posts, oak rails and impregnated larch boards will have a life span in excess of 40 years. Detailing with oak boards and cappings will prolong matters to 60 years. The weak points are the post bases and post and rail junctions. The problems can be countered by using galvanized steel connectors, and post shoes where all-timber construction is employed. Otherwise, precast concrete replaces wood for both posts and rails, with nailable inserts cast in for fixing the paling boards. The general construction is shown in Figure 9.04b, while Figure 9.04c shows assembly and erection work in progress. Note that the 'fair face' or paling side faces the neighbour.

The mechanics of forming post holes depend upon the space available. Tractor- mounted augers can be used on open sites, and hand-operated augers or post-hole spades may be necessary when working in the confines of back gardens. Tolerances are needed in constructing the post holes since the posts and rails are part-assembled before plumbing, staying and pegging. It is customary to make the holes 750 mm deep and 450 mm in diameter. Setting out should allow a 20 mm tolerance between the agreed boundary line and the paling side of the fence to provide latitude for slack setting out. Such a precaution is less costly than an angry neighbour who forces the fence owner to remove and re-erect work that has strayed across the boundary. Post holes are firmed up with 50/75 mm of gravel, and wooden posts are dipped in hot tar and consolidated with lean-mix concrete (1:6) finished off with a chamfered surface which falls away from the post. Allowing 150 mm covering of soil over the concrete surround

will encourage plant growth. A gravel board helps support the lower edge of the fencing, but the board itself requires bearers to give secure fastenings to each post, while stakes (called stumps) restrain the gravel board and limit sagging.

Arris rails are either triangular or trapezoid. Cappings are grooved to fix over the pales and have weathered tops and subrails. The mortise fixings between rails and posts permit the fencing to follow inclines up to 15°, and the tops and bottoms of pales can then be chain sawn to the required slope. A well-made timber fence of this pattern has a robust appearance from the 'fair face' and provides a generous scale for situations such as urban motorways/expressways. However, the quality seen in Figure 9.04a is very impoverished on the reverse face, namely the one viewed by the building owners. The ugly proportions are exaggerated by contrasting materials such as precast concrete posts and rails, the scale appearing inappropriate in the context of small gardens. Compare Figures 9.02c and 9.03d with the crude suburban taste of Figure 9.04c, nothing need be that ill-considered. The concrete in that example could be camouflaged by painting with brown emulsion paint or even creosote. For guidance on preservation of fencing timber refer to Section 9.10.

9.5   Precast Fencing

Framing with precast posts and rails has already been mentioned where permanence is a factor. Manufacturers also offer precast ribs to serve as a palisade or plank infilling which is held between H-shaped posts. Reinforcement is cast with the elements, with mesh fabric for panels and single steel rods in ribs. Stainless mesh improves durability and is found in motorway/highway screens, where reinforced framed panel walls can be achieved on a 6−9 m module spanning horizontally between structural columns. Standard patterns are shown in Figure 9.05a, and typical examples of noise-absorbent barriers are shown in Figures 9.05b−d. The finishes can be self-coloured plain grey (buff, blue grey, red or black cement) and textured on one side to represent brick or stonework. More sophisticated patterns include an overlay of wooden rails with vertical battens or tongued and grooved

9.05 Precast fencing   **a** Standard patterns

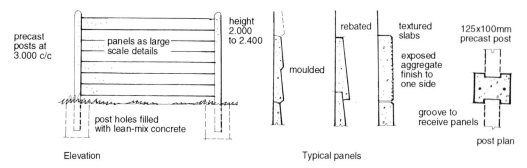

precast posts at 3.000 c/c

panels as large scale details

height 2.000 to 2.400

post holes filled with lean-mix concrete

Elevation

moulded

rebated

textured slabs

exposed aggregate finish to one side

Typical panels

125x100mm precast post

groove to receive panels

post plan

b Combined acoustic screens with precast panels and palisade fencing

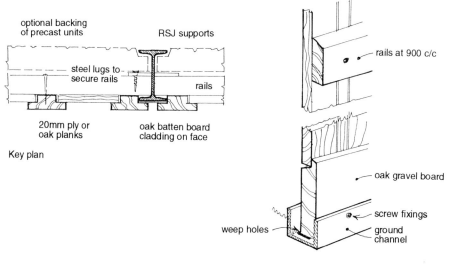

optional backing of precast units

RSJ supports

steel lugs to secure rails

rails

20mm ply or oak planks

oak batten board cladding on face

Key plan

rails at 900 c/c

oak gravel board

screw fixings

weep holes

ground channel

Assembly detail (rear view)

c Motorway screens with long precast panels held by steel columns

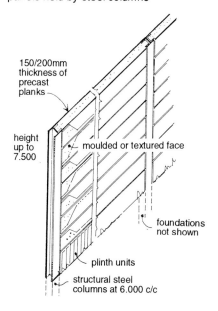

150/200mm thickness of precast planks

height up to 7.500

moulded or textured face

foundations not shown

plinth units

structural steel columns at 6.000 c/c

d Exposed aggregate panels
bevelled corners to feature joints

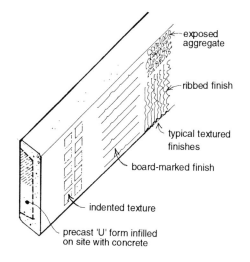

exposed aggregate

ribbed finish

typical textured finishes

board-marked finish

indented texture

precast 'U' form infilled on site with concrete

boards to resemble close boarding. The concrete panels can be grit-blasted to expose the aggregate on all visible faces, which looks superior to colour treatment or paintwork.

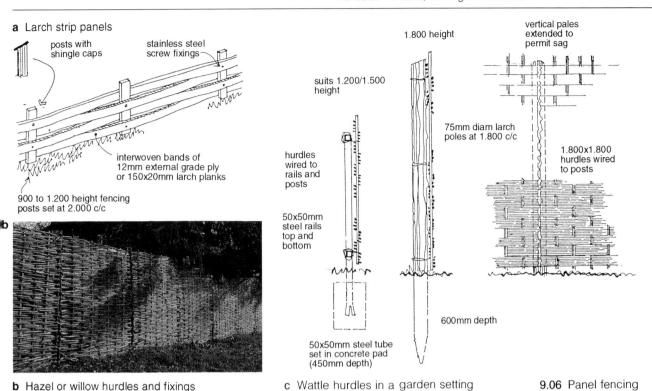

a Larch strip panels

posts with
shingle caps

stainless steel
screw fixings

interwoven bands of
12mm external grade ply
or 150x20mm larch planks

900 to 1.200 height fencing
posts set at 2.000 c/c

b Hazel or willow hurdles and fixings

1.800 height

suits 1.200/1.500
height

hurdles
wired to
rails and
posts

50x50mm
steel rails
top and
bottom

50x50mm steel tube
set in concrete pad
(450mm depth)

vertical pales
extended to
permit sag

75mm diam larch
poles at 1.800 c/c

1.800x1.800
hurdles wired
to posts

600mm depth

c Wattle hurdles in a garden setting

9.06 Panel fencing

9.6 Panel Fencing

Light-weight panels of interwoven larch strip are cheap, and are associated with short-term fencing. The light weight causes problems with security. Ideally, the fixings should be to four sides, as in Figure 9.06a. A better appearance is given by hazel or willow hurdles, formerly used for sheep enclosures. The 'basket' pattern of woven branches suits a garden setting well, though frame fixing needs care.

Steel tubular framing with black-coated metal makes a tough post and rail framework, but fixings between the wattle and the tube will need to be flexible metal connectors (Figures 9.06b–c). The major shortcoming of panel fencing is that the assembly does not suit sloping sites, unless the posts are angled to give a raking line. Most erectors prefer a stepped line to the panels, which looks unsightly and unduly fussy in gardens.

a Primary patterns

9.07 Railings

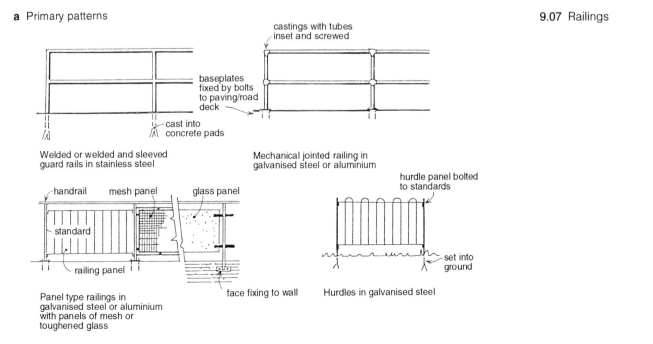

castings with tubes
inset and screwed

baseplates
fixed by bolts
to paving/road
deck

cast into
concrete pads

Welded or welded and sleeved
guard rails in stainless steel

Mechanical jointed railing in
galvanised steel or aluminium

handrail   mesh panel   glass panel

standard

railing panel

face fixing to wall

Panel type railings in
galvanised steel or aluminium
with panels of mesh or
toughened glass

hurdle panel bolted
to standards

set into
ground

Hurdles in galvanised steel

9.07b Railing hurdles

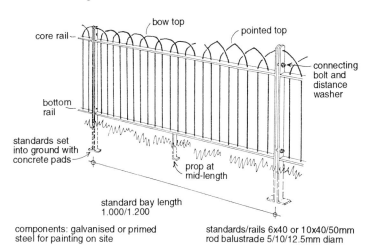

core rail
bow top
pointed top
connecting bolt and distance washer
bottom rail
standards set into ground with concrete pads
prop at mid-length
standard bay length 1.000/1.200

components: galvanised or primed steel for painting on site

standards/rails 6x40 or 10x40/50mm
rod balustrade 5/10/12.5mm diam

c Application of hurdles to forecourts in public housing
d Gameproof hurdles adapted to provide childproof screen

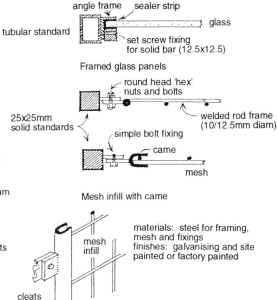

angle frame   sealer strip
glass
tubular standard
set screw fixing for solid bar (12.5x12.5)

Framed glass panels

round head 'hex' nuts and bolts
welded rod frame (10/12.5mm diam)
25x25mm solid standards
simple bolt fixing
came
mesh

Mesh infill with came

e Standard vertical bar railings, and mesh/glass panel designs
(refer to elevations in 907a)

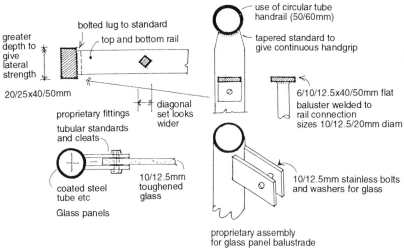

greater depth to give lateral strength
bolted lug to standard
top and bottom rail
20/25x40/50mm
diagonal set looks wider
proprietary fittings
tubular standards and cleats
coated steel tube etc
10/12.5mm toughened glass
Glass panels

use of circular tube handrail (50/60mm)
tapered standard to give continuous handgrip
6/10/12.5x40/50mm flat baluster welded to rail connection sizes 10/12.5/20mm diam
10/12.5mm stainless bolts and washers for glass
proprietary assembly for glass panel balustrade

mesh infill
cleats
12.5x20mm came

materials: steel for framing, mesh and fixings
finishes: galvanising and site painted or factory painted

9.7 Railings

Railings fall into three categories:

- Triprails (already dealt with in Section 6.2 and shown in Figures 6.02a–e).
- Guarding to stairs (the functional requirements were covered in Chapter 2 and shown in Figures 2.09a–c).
- Balustrading – a term usually used to describe a complete railing screen, as used to protect the edges of stairs or landings or enclosures to the head of retaining walls.

This section covers balustrading and railings in landscape construction. Figure 9.07a outlines the primary patterns, which can be chosen from fabricators' catalogues and specified to British Standards like other metal fencing. It may be helpful to summarize the advantages and disadvantages of metalwork in landscape enclosures at this stage.

Railing hurdles

Refer to Figures 9.07b–d for details and examples of applications. These hurdles are associated with estate work, where standard 2 m lengths of railing frames are spiked into the ground using coupled bolts for lateral strength. The fabrication is covered in BS 1722: Part 12 (1979), where component sizes and heights are specified. The heads of the railing bars are bent over to form 'hairpin' tops, either as pairs or interwoven. Hurdles for estate work are often assembled from welded mesh to make gameproof enclosures. Figure 9.07d demonstrates the adaptation of this principle to childproof screens adjoining a floodwater brook. Low-level versions on this principle are run as triprails at 600 mm height to protect planting in public areas, and can be moved if the spiked verticals are driven into the ground rather than concreted in place. The 'hairpin' crest is safe to use where the public might fall against railings or in playground layouts. Heights are usually 900 to 1200 mm where young children are involved. In those circumstances the space between verticals should not permit the passage of a 100 mm sphere, to prevent heads being trapped. Fabricators offer standard-radius work and have jigs to enable raking work to be made for sloping sites. This is to be preferred visually to stepped hurdles. Extra strength can be imparted using stays or by inserting tubular standards between hurdle frames at 4 or 6 m intervals.

Vertical-bar railings

Full guidance is given in BS 1722: Part 12 (1979), where heights, spacing and sizes are specified. The intention is a permanent installation with comprehensive framing. Standards are 40 × 10 mm and placed at 2.7 m centres, with welded lugs for bolting to panels of factory-welded railing panels. The railing bars are 12.5 mm diameter, and are passed through top and bottom flat rails of 40 × 10 mm profile. Extra lugs are placed at mid-span to limit sagging, while stays are used for sideways restraint. Once again fabricators offer standard-radius work and have jigs to enable raking work to be undertaken. It is wise practice to make the fabricator responsible for survey work. The railings are terminated with loops or spears. Blunt tops with 6 mm flat ends must be used for safety where public areas are enclosed – for example, footpaths, highways and space accessed by the general public. Common sense should prevail in domestic work since accidents happen within the private domain as well – for example, pointed railings in proximity to buildings or trees present potential hazards to painters or tree pruners, who may fall off ladders. It is preferable to call

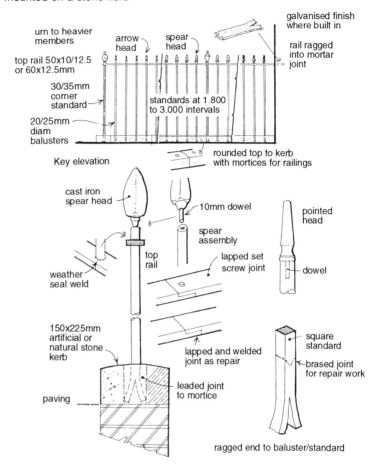

f Traditional 18th and 19th century railings mounted on a stone kerb

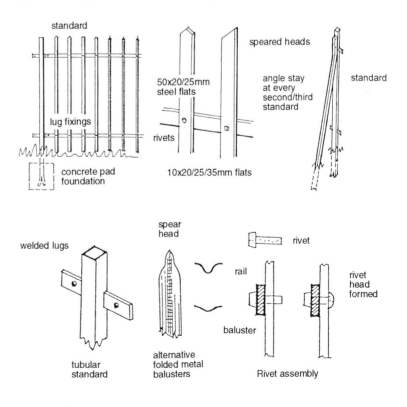

g Industrial type steel palisade fencing

9.07 Continuous metal bar fence

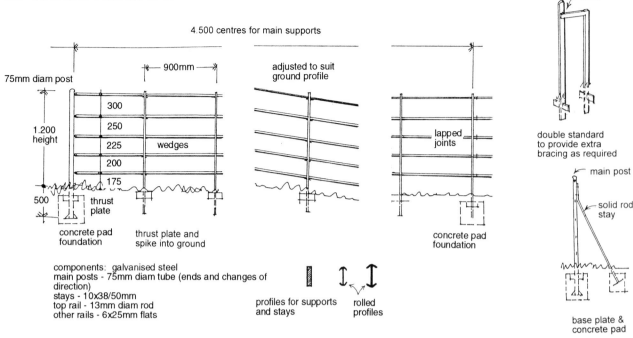

4.500 centres for main supports

75mm diam post

900mm

adjusted to suit
ground profile

weld

1.200
height

300
250
225   wedges
200
175

500   thrust
plate

lapped
joints

double standard
to provide extra
bracing as required

concrete pad
foundation

thrust plate and
spike into ground

concrete pad
foundation

main post

solid rod
stay

components: galvanised steel
main posts - 75mm diam tube (ends and changes of
direction)
stays - 10x38/50mm
top rail - 13mm diam rod
other rails - 6x25mm flats

profiles for supports
and stays

rolled
profiles

base plate &
concrete pad

i Continuous metal bar
fence
j Parkland setting
Killarny National Park,
Eire

for protective boards to be tied alongside
the railing heads when overhead work is
undertaken than to decapitate the Georgian
and Victorian heritage of railings in our urban
landscape.

Historic patterns differ from factory-
made elements in a number of details. Firstly,
the vertical members are far thicker than
present-day products, and made from 35 mm
diameter cast iron (often fluted or enriched) or
wrought iron of 25 × 25 mm cross-section.
The embellishments of spearheads and urns are
still made in cast iron, but the balustrade rods
and rails are of carbon steel nowadays, due to
the demise of the handwork furnaces in the
UK which formerly produced wrought iron.
Carbon steel can be welded to wrought iron in
repair work. Small quantities of new wrought
iron are imported from China and France, and
this has to suffice for decorative forged work.
Figure 9.07f shows traditional eighteenth
and nineteenth-century railings mounted on a
kerb. These were used to protect the gardens

of London squares and parks and to surmount
area walls to front and back gardens. The 'leaded
in' joint between the railing base and the kerb
or stone stair tread is the most significant
difference to contemporary work, and it is
costly to execute in comparison to factory-
produced panels site-bolted to standards at
2.4−2.7 m intervals. Further savings can be
made by substituting welded mesh panels, as
discussed in Section 8.2 (Figures 8.02d−g).

Steel palisade fencing

This industrial pattern is covered in the UK by
BS 1722: Part 12 (1979) and can be selected by
number reference (Figure 9.07g). It forms a
tough, resilient palisade with V- or W-shaped
vertical steel pales having forked crests and
fixed to one or both sides of steel sheeting rails
secured by cleats to tubular posts. Adjustments
in rails and cleat angles permit the palisading to
accommodate 1:6 slopes on raking ground.
This type of fencing is specified for high

security, often as a second line of defence to chain link.

A combined wood and metal palisade is available in Germany and the USA, where tubular steel posts and channel rails provide carriers or slender battens on the 'face' side. The effect is trellis-like and provides interesting shadows reminiscent of Oriental gardens. Figure 9.07h shows an example of a garden setting.

Continuous metal bar fencing

This type of estate fence has been fabricated since the early days of the Industrial Revolution. Today in the UK it is specified from BS 1722: Part 9 (1979) and termed steel (low-carbon steel). Such fences have round or square verticals and flat sections for posts and horizontals. Typical assemblies are shown in Figure 9.07i, and are suitable for heights up to 1.8 m. The arrangement of wedge fixings between rails and the slot holes in the verticals will accommodate slopes up to 1:6, while curving work can often be formed on site. The line and style of horizontal metal bar designs have much to commend them to the eye, in particular the sympathetic relation to site geometry. Figure 9.07j shows its appearance in a parkland setting.

Protective barriers

Protective barriers relate to highway work, but also include guardrails to protect pedestrians from traffic and to counter crowd surge in stadiums. The relevant British Standards are given in reference 3 and the specifier selects the assemblies for specific situations.

Railing fabricators offer ranges of standardized designs to fulfil each category required by British Standards and provide refinements such as radius and raking work to handle stairs and ramps. There is little scope for modification with special designs. Figures 9.07k–l are typical standard items of manufacture. Guard-rails used for industrial plant or to protect catwalks have a relevance as guarding devices in public gardens, though high-specification protective barriers are not needed in these situations. Some of the more useful designs are shown in Figure 6.02e. Standardized selection from catalogue designs follows a similar process in the USA.

9.07k standardized guard railing for pedestrians

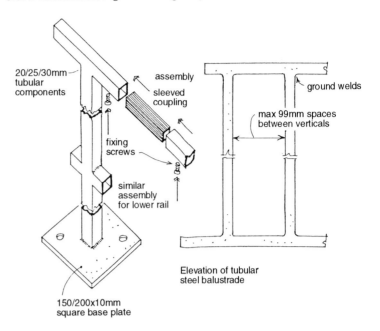

l Standardized balustrading for stadia

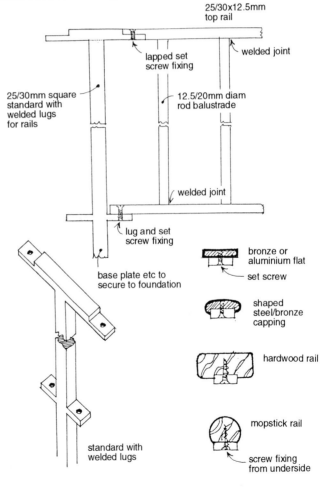

113

9.8 Metalwork in Landscape

9.08 Garden gates

a Rustic gate to rear gardens, Maastricht, Holland
b Engineered gate, Headmaster's House, Dartington, Devon (1932). Architect: William Lescaze

The benefit of dark colours as camouflage in green landscape has been described in Section 8.1, in the context of chain link fencing. Green fences or railings seen against a green background always look discordant, as the eye experiences an after-image effect when concentrating on particular accents. Looking at a blue sky against white mountain peaks produces a yellow 'corona' at the skyline. Brown or black railings seen against a green hedge will merge as sienna browns and resemble woody stems. Bright green railings have a red after-image and therefore appear strident. This argument can be extended further to the relationship between painted metalwork and buildings. Black railings will appear smaller than white — in the latter case, the space between the railings becomes the dominant pattern. Bright colours emphasize features, so emerald green, Cambridge blue or gamboge (like gold leaf) draw attention to items that may look better suppressed. Black has many tones, and it is worth experimenting with admixtures of black and dark blue to achieve slate colours that are gentler on the eye than jet black. Matt paints also appear less vulgar than shining gloss in landscape.

9.9 Gates

Estate and farm gates have clear functional requirements, but garden and house gates also serve aesthetic often emotive needs, and have to be appropriate to the setting. The practical considerations are similar to those governing farm gates, but the modesty of scale usually entails a single-leaf design. Fasteners and hinges are similar to those shown in Figures 7.06a−f. Examples of domestic gates in different materials and settings are given below.

Rustic gate, Maastricht, Holland

The rear garden of this house is designed as a safe retreat for children, hence the catch on the side towards the street (Figure 9.08a). The construction resembles the agricultural pattern, including pin hinges with chestnut spiles screwed to hinge rails at top and bottom,

braced by a diagonal tie. Opinions vary on the role of a diagonal member: one view is that it is a 'tension' tie, to prevent dropping of the gate. Alternatively it is reversed in direction to prop the top rail, close by the catch. This method at least reinforces the most abused part of a gate frame.

Engineered gate, Headmaster's House, Dartington, Devon

Engineering design has been brought to bear, with oak framing combined with galvanized steel rod (Figure 9.08b). The rectangular gate frame is braced by a diagonal steel tie rod to prevent drop, while extra stiffness is given by steel rods passed vertically through the rails. The mesh also gives security regarding both children and pets.

Traditional slatted gate, National Park Centre, Edale, Derbyshire

The traditional principles are demonstrated by a stout frame, reinforced by vertical slats and propped by a diagonal strut (Figure 9.08c). This is a heavy construction compared to the engineered solution, and relies upon painted larch instead of hardwood. However, the posts are 300 × 300 mm oak capped with code 4 lead (4 lb) for extra protection.

Lattice gate, False Creek, Vancouver

The joinery is in redwood, a very durable West Coast softwood which requires no preservative treatment. The construction employs standard wrought timbers, with an edge frame reinforced by solid battens in lattice form and propped by a brace. All fixings are in non-ferrous metal to prevent corrosion by resins in the redwood. (See Figure 9.08d.)

Steel and timber gate, Zutphen, Holland

Another engineered solution, and one that would have received planning consent under the stringent environmental laws which

govern Holland, where barriers above 300 mm in height within front gardens or between footpaths and adjoining property need consent from the local authority. Architects and designers are therefore employed for front garden fences and gates in the Netherlands, which accounts for the higher visual standards in Dutch garden design. The gates featured have a welded tubular steel frame and open in two parts, a wicket for the house entrance and a swing gate for the car (Figure 9.08e). Long drop bolts exist at the meeting stiles so that each element may open separately. The facing is clad with battens of varnished utile. The varnish failed quickly and the timber was painted over.

Steel gate, Coombe Hill, Kingston upon Thames

Another steel gate, this time the main entry to a suburban house (Figure 9.08f).

c Traditional slatted gate, National Park Centre, Edale, Derbyshire (1972)
d Lattice gate, False Creek, Vancouver (1970s)
e Steel and timber gate, Zutphen, Holland (1960s)

9.08f Steel gate, Coombe Hill, Kingston upon Thames (1949)
g Mechanical gate, School at Alexandra Road, Camden, London (1978). Architect: Neeve Brown
h Security gate, Crematorium Chapel, Alstatten, Switzerland (1968)
i Designer's gate, Île aux Moines, Brittany (1980s)

The construction is welded lattice, relying upon a continuous band of framing steel to make an integral structure. The finish is gloss paint over galvanized steel. Note the use of pin hinges with lugs welded to tubular posts. The gate dates from 1949, and is still in good working condition.

Mechanical gate, school at Alexandra Road, Camden, London

Sliding gates are increasingly specified where safety devices to prevent crushing or collision similar to those fitted to lift gates are required. The school gates shown are hand-operated with an overhead track and bottom guides (Figure 9.08g). The framing uses pressure-treated Douglas fir for rails and battens, but steelwork for the load-bearing head beam and column.

Security gate, crematorium chapel, Alstatten, Switzerland

The ultimate forms of mechanical gates are used for high security, and involve a pair of rail tracks hidden in a service trench. A guide trolley runs like a wheel between the tracks, and carries a steel framework for the gate (see Figure 9.08h). The design can match fencing, but cantilever poles or spiles are preferred as they are more difficult to climb over.

Manufacturers of security fencing have diversified into electrical gates and doors and similar mechanical forms.

Designer's gate

This is an inspirational example, where conventional timber design is transformed by a wave shape to the rails, which suggests a welcome perspective at the end of the lane and a pointer forward when both gates are open (Figure 9.08i). The designer is not known but a genius was evidently at work.

9.10 Finishes for Timbers in Fencing and Pergolas

Timbers exposed to sun and rain are affected in many ways: the wood swells in wet weather and shrinks upon drying. Such movement causes checks or splits in the surface of many timbers. Wood fibres on the edges and faces tend to become detached and form a spongy layer which holds dirt and promotes mould growth. Durable timbers such as chestnut, jarrah and oak are resistant to this problem, as are close-grained softwoods like West Coast redwood, cedar and larch. Weathering of most timbers reduces the natural colour to silver grey unless paint, stain or varnish is used as a coating.[3]

Four choices of finish are given below, with estimates of life span between applications:

- Preservative materials applied by impregnation and brush (ten years);
- Paint treatment by brush or roller (five to six years, but ten years in protected situations);
- Preservative stains applied by brush or spray coat (three to ten years);
- Varnish applied by brush (two to three years).

Varnish is only suitable for small-scale details such as sign boards or furniture, and unsuitable for general external application. Paint wears far better than varnish and has the advantage that minor defects can be touched up without total repainting being involved. Preservative impregnation and stains are the principal external finishes employed due to the high initial cost of paintwork.

Preservative materials

There are three main types of preservatives — tar oils, water-borne and organic solvent-based — which suit sawn lumber as well as planed and sanded material.

Tar oils Still popular due to cheapness and ease of application, tar is one of the best treatments for post bases. The normal process is to stand posts a butt of coal tar for a day before setting in the ground. It is effective for hardwoods and impregnated softwoods. Creosote is a thinner form used extensively on external timber. The most reliable method is to pressure-impregnate the timber in tanks, followed by cold steeping. The disadvantage is the smell and stickiness, coupled with the injuries that can be caused to flora and to exposed skin. It cannot be painted over.

Water-borne preservatives The commonest method today, relying on vacuum or pressure-impregnation. The types of chemical preservative needs to be checked for toxic safety where human or livestock contact is involved. Treated timbers tend take on green tints, but these disappear. Most preservatives are suitable for over-brushing with stains or paint to improve the appearance. Certificates concerning the percentage and type of impregnation achieved are available from licensed firms.

Organic solvents Organic solvents are applied by dipping or by vacuum/pressure-impregnation as with water-borne preservatives. They are generally used by window makers, when subsequent coatings are made with paint or preservative stains.

Painting external woodwork

The painting of external woodwork is a well-established process, but good materials and thorough preparation and application are essential for long-term success. Paint suppliers will give excellent written advice upon suitable specifications, both for new work and for refurbishment. It is important to realize that skimping is still a common practice. Traditional practice involved stopping cracks and crevices with white lead, priming with a lead-based primer, followed by three coats of oil-based paint (either two undercoats and one gloss finish or one undercoat and two gloss). Today the safety of lead-based materials is questionable, and they have been replaced by titanium dioxides. Modern paints (see Section 9.1) are developed from alkyd resins. These are water-based and similar in many respects to emulsion paints.

Traditional lead-based oil paints have a lot to commend them in terms of bonding to the timber and their long-term durability. Sound examples of eighteenth-century paintwork can still be found in Georgian buildings in Eire, but cleaning down and sandpapering over old lead paint presents considerable health hazards, and expert advice is needed.

For remedial work where residual lead oxides exist, the specifier needs to consider low-lead primers. These are acceptable under safety regulations and available in water-thinned (to BS 5082) or solvent-thinned forms (to BS 5358).

Exterior stains

Three forms are available: clear, natural (tinted in wood colours) and coloured (opaque and resembling paint).

Clear finishes are not recommended externally, and are intended for the internal faces of doors and sheds, etc. Natural finishes resemble wood colours and need to be selected with the character of the original timber in mind. Slightly darker tints will help mask differences in colour. All fade eventually, and recoating will be needed at three to ten year intervals. Danish examples of treated fencing are shown in Figures 6.01i and 6.03e. Enquiries revealed that the house owners expected to recoat timber every three to four years. Opaque finishes have been developed for the window market, where greater protection is needed for small joinery sections such as sashes and glazing beads. Opening of the grain in softwood causes splitting and twisting of sections. Most timber in landscape construction involves more substantial profiles. However, feather-edged boards and trellis timbers are just as vulnerable, and here the new opaque finishes may be helpful. Traditionally, such timbers were creosoted. See Figures 12.04c−e for examples of the effect of modern opaque finishes on fences and trellis panels.

9.11 Finishes for External Metalwork

The problems of rust and ferrous corrosion are mentioned elsewhere in this book. Bollards are covered in Section 5.5, ironmongery in Chapter 7, pergolas in Section 13.6, and mesh and chain link in Sections 8.1 and 8.2.

Protection with zinc coating (by the hot-dip process preferably) is explained in Section 7.6. The appearance of weathered zinc coatings is not attractive, and designers usually prefer opaque coatings which enhance the metalwork. Wire and wire mesh can be plastic-coated as described for chain link fencing in Section 8.1. Larger-scale metal components, like tubular steel, railing bars and rails, are usually painted. This process involves oil-based paints similar to those employed for woodwork, but requiring an etching primer such as acetic acid (called a mordant solution) to remove contaminants and grease from the galvanized surface. This process is followed by a coating of calcium plumbate primer. This work is difficult to carry out on site and is better undertaken by the metal fabricator at the works. Alternatively galvanized steel can be left to weather for a year and then site-primed and painted.

Today many steel components, such as garden furniture, grilles and ironmongery, are galvanized and then powder-coated and kiln-fired to provide an enamelled coating.[2] Other metals, such as aluminium, bronze or stainless steel, do not need painting, but exposure to road salt and seawater severely corrodes commercial grades of aluminium, and anodic coatings of pure aluminium will be required. There are few non-ferrous or stainless applications in landscape construction apart from standardized balustrading, guardrails and signage.

10 THE HA-HA

10.1 Historic References

The ha-ha is defined as a sunk fence or wall bounding a park or garden towards open country or woodland.[1] The removal of a visual barrier between garden and nature was seen as an asset and as a way to naturalize the settings of buildings. The writings of d'Argenville on this topic were introduced to Britain by John James in his treatise *Theory and Practice of Gardening* first published in 1712. Charles Bridgeman was the first garden designer to translate the concept into reality with his works at Rousham Park (1721) and Stowe, Buckinghamshire (1730s). The original ha-ha at Rousham still separates the paddock from the garden promenade, giving the illusion of spaciousness where none exists (Figure 10.01a). At Stowe, the grass podium below the main façade has no visible boundary against the parkland scenery (Figure 10.01b). William Kent claimed most of the credit since his landscape sketches illustrated the potential where visual barriers were removed. Horace Walpole wrote with enthusiasm of Kent's abilities: 'he leaped the fence and saw that all nature was a garden.' Kent sometimes used watery ditches for ha-ha features, as shown in Figure 10.01c.

10.2 Historic Details

The original purposes of ha-has were to prevent cattle and deer from defacing the surroundings of buildings, and, later in history, from devouring Humphrey Repton's flower beds. Differing treatments were devised according to the security required, and Figures 10.02a−e demonstrate various designs employed to keep cattle, deer or people from passing the 'invisible' barrier. A fence at the bottom of a ditch is the simplest construction, but it creates a wider gash in the landscape than a masonry-faced ditch. The top of the retaining wall can be splayed back to encourage overgrowth, or have coping stones laid flush like pavers. Wide coping stones provide a suitable base for a light balustrade or triprail

a Layout plan of Rousham Park, Oxfordshire, showing Charles Bridgeman's Ha-ha (1721)

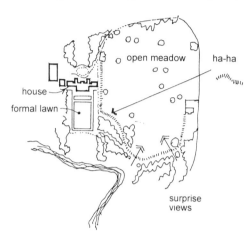

10.01 The ha-ha in history

b Stowe, Buckinghamshire. Fusion of grass podium to house with landscaped park (1730s). Architects: Charles Bridgeman and others

c Water-filled ha-ha at Claremont (1730s). Designer: William Kent

b

c

10.02 Differing treatments for ha-ha features

f Urns to demark top of ha-ha. Renishaw, Derbyshire
g Railings to surmount wall. Keddleston, Derbyshire
h View of Keddleston ha-ha from house

a Railing in base of ditch.

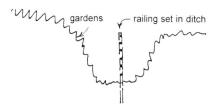

gardens — railing set in ditch

b Defensive stakes at side of ditch.

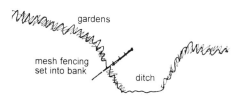

gardens

mesh fencing set into bank

ditch

c Secret retaining wall.

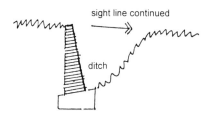

sight line continued

ditch

d Differing coping treatments.

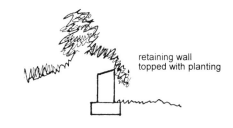

retaining wall topped with planting

ornaments to edge of garden

ditch

land drain at wall base

Traditional stone built Ha-ha.

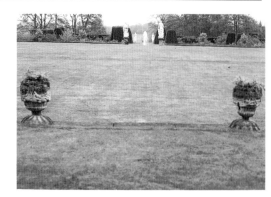

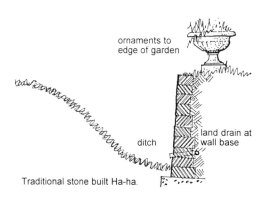

(Figure 10.02g), but the traditional solution would be garden urns set at intervals along the wall (Figure 10.02f). One of the finest examples is the ha-ha combined with flood defences installed along the Thames at Kew Gardens, London (Figure 10.02e). Here the façade of Syon House successfully terminates the Capability Brown vista from the ornamental lake without the intervention of ornamentation. However, today there is a triprail and a range of memorial benches alerting visitors to the dangers of the sheer drops. The detailing of the discreet ha-ha at Kedleston, Derbyshire holds the secret to success where an effective and secure boundary is made towards the open parkland while the view from the house reveals an elegant triprail to edge the sward (Figures 10.02g–h).

10.3 Current-day Examples

The open ditch or grass mound is often seen in traffic management schemes for common land. A dry trench with a gravel base, like a French drain, prevents vehicles from crossing but presents no hazard to pedestrians. The disabled will need a small footbridge but this can be scaled down to prevent cars crossing over. A mounded bank, say 450 mm height and 1200 mm girth, will stop most drivers and obviate the need for more conspicuous barriers such as bollards or posts (see Figures 10.03a–b).

The ditch and fence solution effectively hides the ugliness of chain link except at close range, and is an arrangement suitable for

a Open ditch dug to protect common land from vehicles

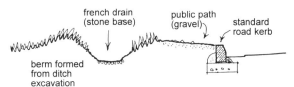

10.03 Current examples

b Mounded bank to contain cars. Nature park at Lepe, Hampshire (circa 1960s)
c Chain link fence hidden in ditch.
d View of Crescent Wing, Sainsburys Visual Art Centre, University of East Anglia, Norwich Architects: Foster Associates

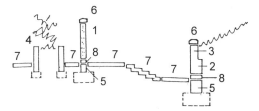

Diagram to identify the different exposure conditions in landscape brickwork. The minimum standards for bricks and mortar in each numbered location relate to table 11.1

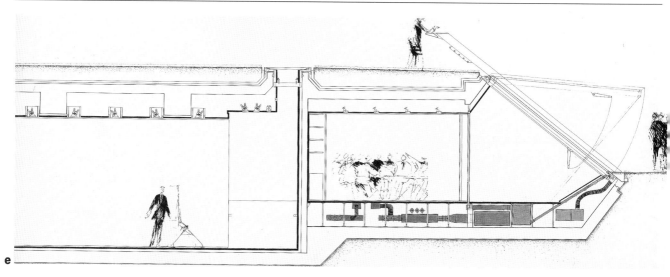

e

f

10.03e Section through Crescent Wing, UEA, Norwich

f Ha-ha on western boundary at Hidcote, Gloucestershire (1920s). Designer: Lawrence Johnston

g Reverse side of Ha-ha at Hidcote

g

h House at Wantage, detail of newly built ha-ha, with end returned against fence and planting. Architect Michael Branch

the short term until a retaining wall can be afforded. The example shown in Figure 10.03c is taken from the earliest boundary treatment at the University of East Anglia in the 1960s. The campus was on the fringe of open farmland, and the ha-ha was seen as the natural way of preserving the vistas from the built-up areas to the open landscape beyond. The latest extension to the Sainsbury Visual Arts Centre occurs below ground, and the enclosing façade is contained within a glass-walled ditch (Figures 10.03d−e). This twentieth-century ha-ha provides fenestration for underground accommodation while permitting the green sward to appear as a continuous podium for the main gallery. The thickness of conventional roof soiling has been reduced from 450 mm to 75 mm by installing prepared trays of fertilized peat and sand for the rooftop lawn.

The surprise view is still a popular concept in garden layout, and the traditional masonry-faced ha-ha continues to perform this function. The western edges of Hidcote, Gloucestershire, have a magic quality, with the line of ditch and wall rising and falling with the contours to blend land and gardenscape into one entirety (Figure 10.03f). A level plane is easier to handle but needs camouflage at the extremities to hide the ends of the 'window' cut into the landscape. Figure 10.03h shows the way

10.04 The Ha-ha and town planning concepts
a Path at Hampstead Garden Suburb

Michael Branch relates the surprise view and ha-ha to the terrace of a house at Wantage, Oxfordshire, with hedges to contain the view.

The edge between country and town has long fascinated urban designers. Raymond Unwin took pains with the boundary of Hampstead Garden Suburb and the fringe of Hampstead Heath, London where a hard edge was required.[2]

A long retaining wall was built to contain the urbanized elements, with portals spaced at intervals demarked by stairs and garden pavilions. Ernst May took Unwin's ideas a stage further at Neue Frankfurt-am-Main, where a vast flood wall was required to enclose the flood plain of the river Neider.[3] The functional concrete retaining structure becomes a visible barrier from the open land, but is an open promenade linked to gardens facing the habitation. May's 'great wall' takes on a defensive character and makes an embrasure to the housing settlement in the medieval manner preferred by Raymond Unwin.

Figures 10.04a–b demonstrate the way the ha-ha has been adapted in twentieth-century town planning.

11 WALLS

The particular character and durability of bricks, stone and concrete have bearing upon the method of putting materials together and their performance under exposure. It is important to understand these materials for building walls.

The selection of building stone for paving has been examined in Chapter 1, but the same considerations apply to wall masonry. The types of stone and their cross-references are given below:

- **Limestones and sandstones** – commonly obtained for garden walls and field boundaries in stony districts (see Section 1.4e).
- **Granite, marble and slate** – reserved for specific details such as copings, and for decorative effects (see Sections 1.2 and 1.4d). Granite blocks and slate rubble are also used for garden walls in proximity to quarries. (See Figures 11.04c–g which show vernacular work using local materials.)
- **Pebble** – utilized for flint walls and in a vernacular tradition where chalk strata are common. (See Figures 11.05b–c.)

Brick and blocks used in free-standing garden walls or as retaining structures need to be selected for the same stringent exposure rating as for paving work. The classification by method of manufacture of clay brick, silicate brick or concrete brick and block was covered in Chapter 1, under Block and Brick Paving, but paving bricks and blocks are specific to that purpose in terms of size and thickness, and are made with emphasis on the top wearing surface. Facing bricks and blocks have, as the name implies, a vertical 'face' quality appropriate to walling. Bricks of 'engineering class' will match the performance requirements needed under conditions of severe exposure – for example, retaining walls, copings, and brickwork in contact with the ground. In the UK frost-resistant bricks carry a suffix F in the maker's catalogue.

There are, however, sheltered situations in the leeway of buildings, overhangs and trees where lesser-quality facings could be chosen. Such bricks in the UK are termed moderately frost-resistant and are categorized by the suffix M. They will not withstand being soaked and then subjected to repeated cycles of freezing and thawing. See Figure 11.14e for an example of typical failure. The Brick Development Association give general advice on selection.[1] Brick suppliers will also confirm frost-resistance and compressive strengths and advise on previous applications in landscape work. See Section 11.1 for advice on mortars and the performance of brickwork and blockwork under movement stresses.

Cast in-situ concrete walling is another option, and one associated with civil engineering contracts, such as retaining structures (see Figure 10.04c). The making and casting of concrete work for paving has been discussed in Section 1.4, and has a direct relevance to the skills needed in making in-situ concrete elements, whether retaining structures or free-standing walls. Steel reinforcement is placed to distribute loading stresses, and engineering advice is needed for profile and reinforcement design. See Section 11.16–17 for details of retaining walls. In most garden construction it is probably easier to build masonry armatures for reinforced concrete than to expend time and effort constructing shuttering timber and obtaining well-finished 'faced' concrete. 'Faced' concrete is a natural finish obtained from the texture of shuttering or by machine tooling to expose concrete aggregates (see Figures 11.17a–c for examples). Figure 11.05d shows how brick or stone armatures appear more sympathetic in a garden setting.

11.1 Mortars for Wall Masonry

Mortar serves as both a glue and a gap filler between masonry elements. The gluing together is achieved by cementing together the opposing surfaces in horizontal, vertical and internal joints. The gap-filling role overcomes the irregularity of surfaces, which can produce joints which vary between 12 and 25 mm in stonework or between 8 and 12 mm in block and brickwork. The traditional proportions of lime and sand – or today, the ratios for cement, lime and sand, or cement, plasicizer and sand – depend upon

11.1 Brick and mortar selection for brickwork in landscape construction

Location	Suitable qualities of brick	Suitable mortar designations	Suitable brick classes		Suitable mortar designations
1 *Freestanding walls (excluding the coping or capping)* Freestanding walls are likely to be severely exposed, irrespective of climatic conditions, and an effective coping will protect the brickwork from saturation.	Effective coping used	Ordinary Special	(i) (ii) (iii)[1] (i) (ii) (iii)[1]	3.7	(iii)
	Flush capping used	Ordinary (frost-resistant)[2] Special	(i) (ii)[1,3] (i) (ii)[1]	3.7	(iii)
2 *Earth-retaining walls (excluding the caping or copping)* Because of the possibility of contamination from the ground and saturation by ground waters, in addition to severe climatic exposure, these walls are particularly prone to frost and sulphate attack, if not protected. It is strongly recommended that such walls are back-filled with free-draining material to prevent a build-up of water pressure.	Waterproofed retaining face; effective coping	Ordinary Special Engineering	(i) (ii) (i) (ii) (i) (ii)	3.7	(ii) (iii)
	Waterproofed retaining face; flush capping	Ordinary (frost-resistant)[2] Special Engineering[2]	(i)[4] (i) (i)	4.7	(ii)
	No waterproofing of retaining face	Special Engineering[2]	(i) (i)	4.7	(ii)[5]
3 *Facing brickwork to concrete retaining walls*	Low risk of saturation	Ordinary Special Engineering	(i)[4] (ii)[4] (i) (ii) (i) (ii)	2.7	(iii)[6]
	High risk of saturation	Ordinary (frost-resistant)[2] Special Engineering[2]	(i) (ii)[4] (i) (ii)[4] (i) (ii)[4]	2.7	(iii)
4 *Planting boxes* Planting boxes should be waterproofed on the inner face for the full depth of earth fill.		Ordinary (frost-resistant)[2] Special	(i)[4] (i)	4.7	(ii)
5 *Work below or within 150 mm above ground level* Brickwork near external ground level is vulnerable to frost action and sulphate attack, particularly one course (75 mm) below and two courses (150 mm) above ground level. In this area, brickwork will become wet and remain so for long periods. The degree of saturation will mainly depend on the climatic exposure of the building, the nature of the soil, and the site drainage. Care should be taken to ensure that paved surrounds do not channel water into the brickwork.	Brickwork near ground level: Low risk of saturation, well drained site	Ordinary Special	(i) (ii) (iii)[5,7] (i) (ii) (iii)[5,7]	3.7	(iii)[5,7]
	High risk of saturation, poorly drained site	Ordinary (frost-resistant)[2] Special	(i)[5] (i)[5]	3.7	(iii)[5,7]
	Brickwork wholly below ground level	Ordinary[8] Special	(i)[5] (i)[5]	3.7	(iii)[5,7]
6 *Copings and steps* Purpose-made sill and coping units to BS 5642 and BS 3798 may be preferred, but their specification and use are outside the scope of this note. The requirements for brick-on-edge and similar cappings of clay and calcium silicate bricks are given.	Standard format bricks and standard and purpose-made special shapes[11]	Ordinary (frost-resistant)[2] Special	(i)[9,10] (i)[9,10]	4.7	(ii)[9,10]

7 *Paving*	Interlocking pavers, paving	Ordinary		see note 13
This relates to lightly trafficked pavements (for up to 1.5 million standard axles design life).	bricks and facings	(frost-resistant) Special	(i)[12] (i)[12]	

	Suitable qualities of brick	**Maximum water absorption (per cent by mass)**[14]		Suitable mortar designation[5]
8 *Clay brick damp-proof courses* Certain low water absorption clay bricks with good frost resistance properties may be used for the construction of damp-proof courses. Such DPCs can resist rising damp, although they will not resist water percolating downwards. They are particularly appropriate in positions where the DPC is required to transmit tension, e.g., in freestanding and retaining walls. Guidance on the laying of brick damp-proof courses is given in BS 743	Damp-proof courses in external works	Ordinary (frost-resistant)[2] Special	7.0 7.0	(i) (i)

⋆ Table extracted from Brick durability by J. R. Harding and R. A. Smith.

[1] In areas of severe driving rain, designations (i) and (ii) mortars are preferred and, if designation (ii) is specified with ordinary quality bricks, the use of sulphate-resisting Portland cement should be considered.

[2] The manufacturers' recommendations as to suitability should be sought.

[3] Sulphate-resisting Portland cement is recommended with designation (ii) mortar.

[4] Sulphate-resisting Portland cement is recommended.

[5] If sulphate ground conditions exist, the use of sulphate-resisting Portland cement is recommended.

[6] For work above the DPC near to ground level, designation (iv) mortar may be used when it is known that there is no risk of frost during construction.

[7] Strict supervision of batching is particularly important to ensure that the requisite amount of cement is incorporated in designation (iii) mortars.

[8] Where brickwork is (at least 150 mm) below finished external ground level, most ordinary quality clay bricks may be suitable, although the manufacturers' recommendations should be sought.

[9] Designation (i) mortar should be used for bedding associated DPCs in clay brickwork, and designation (ii) for the same function in calcium silicate brickwork.

[10] When used in chimney cappings, sulphate-resisting Portland cement is recommended.

[11] To BS 4729.

[12] Bedding and pointing for a rigid construction, not required with flexible construction.

[13] Calcium silicate pavers stronger than 28 N/mm² should be durable but it is advisable to consult the manufacturer about suitability.

[14] Five-hour boiling method.

the workability needed by bricklayers: in other words, the speed of work and working conditions (for example, winter versus summer). The design of mortar mixes has to take into account the ultimate wall strength expressed as compressive stress values and frost-resistance. Tables 11.1–11.2 give relevant brick and related mortar mixes and are reprinted by kind permission of the Brick Development Association and the *Architect's Journal*. The cross-references in Figure 11.01 refer to brickwork used in paving and steps. Mortar mixes i and ii are most popular with bricklayers due to the ease of working. Mortar mix iii is closer to the character of older work and should be used where refurbishment is involved.

The chemistry of setting mortar triggers off irreversible stresses in built masonry. Most ceramic products expand in combination with cement mortars, requiring expansion joints within the length of wall structures to absorb movement. Cement-based products, such as concrete bricks or blocks, suffer from drying shrinkage. This process is complex and involves two-way movement upon wetting and drying, but ultimately a reduction in dimension. This necessitates closer safeguards in the design of movement joints. Refer to Figures 11.02a–b for design guidance regarding joints. Traditional lime/sand mortars avoid these problems and have provided trouble-free walls in times past. The reasons are complex and result from the decayed condition of lime mortar after many years, exposure. The bond strength is less than cement-based material and lends a flexibility to masonry. The bricks or stones stay bonded due

a Expansion and movement problems

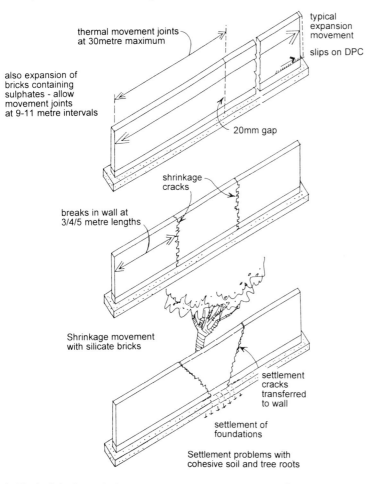

thermal movement joints at 30metre maximum

typical expansion movement

slips on DPC

also expansion of bricks containing sulphates - allow movement joints at 9-11 metre intervals

20mm gap

shrinkage cracks

breaks in wall at 3/4/5 metre lengths

Shrinkage movement with silicate bricks

settlement cracks transferred to wall

settlement of foundations

Settlement problems with cohesive soil and tree roots

b Typical design solutions

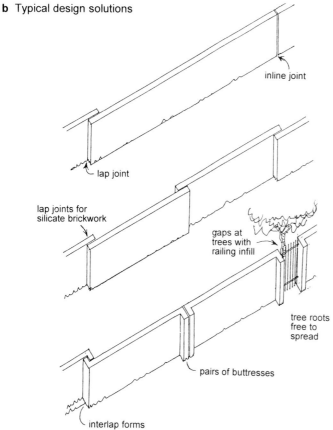

inline joint

lap joint

lap joints for silicate brickwork

gaps at trees with railing infill

tree roots free to spread

pairs of buttresses

interlap forms

11.02 Design of movement joints

11.2 Standard mortar mixes – proportions by volume[1,2]

Mortar group	Cement: lime: sand	Cement ready mixed with lime: sand	Masonry cement: sand[3]	Cement: sand with plasticiser (air entrained)
i	$1:0-\frac{1}{4}:3$	$= 1:3$	—	
ii	$1:\frac{1}{2}:4-4\frac{1}{2}$	$= 1:4-4\frac{1}{2}$	—	
iii	$1:1:5-6$	$= 1:5-6$	$1:4-5$	$1:5-6$
iv	$1:2:8-9$	$= 1:8-9$	$1:5\frac{1}{2}-6\frac{1}{2}$	$1:7-8$
v	$1:3:10-12$	$= 1:10-12$	$1:6\frac{1}{2}-7$	$1:8$

[1] Where a range of sand contents is given, the larger quantity should be used for sand that is well graded and the smaller quantity for coarse or uniformly fine sand. Investigations have shown that mortars on site often have much less cement than specified.
[2] Coloured pigments (to BS 1014) can be added to any of these mortars but are usually used with ready-mixed mortar.
[3] Masonry cement is not often used now.

to self-weight and geometry, but the relative 'softness' at the jointing permits settlement or slight movement to occur without fracture. Repointing will improve weather-resistance and hide movement joints if such repairs are required.

Repointing garden walls is a vexed problem and often causes more problems than necessary. It is often best to leave them alone unless the structure in question is part of a building and causing damp penetration, or free-standing and in danger of collapse. Repointing needs to be carried out from both sides, since the cement mortars used today will cause slight expansion and could destabilize the wall if only applied to one side. This is an important point to settle with neighbours when an old brick garden wall forms a boundary line and needs repointing. Similarly, bracing piers need to be built on both sides rather than one side only, to balance the stresses caused. For details of pointing styles refer to Figures 11.12a–f. The same problems occur in repairing old stone rubble walls, and care should be taken to retain mortar textures using stone dust and lime-based mortars. Organizations such as the specialist workshops retained by many cathedrals can supply stonemasonry mortars and advise on renovation techniques.

Mortar mixes with rich cement proportions can give rise to visual defects in completed brickwork. A common problem is the outbreak of efflorescence on facework. The discolouring is usually white and stems from the deposit of soluble salts from the combination of bricks and cement mortars. The usual culprit is sodium sulphate, found in some facing bricks and present in Portland cement. The remedy rests with selection of facings with

a low sulphate content. It is good sense to obtain advice via the brick makers on other applications where the facings have been used satisfactorily. Free-standing and retaining walls are subject to saturation and may not be suitable for facings which perform well in drier situations. The other source of sulphate polution is groundwater, and bitumen protection will be needed on walls buried in contaminated ground such as reclaimed rubbish dumps.

The problem is often temporary, and results from lack of protection while building in wet weather or soaking due to poorly-designed copings. Coping overhangs are always beneficial. Traditional recipes to counter efflorescence include regular brushing, followed by a coating of liquid cow manure. My neighbour has a gable wall built in yellow stocks with cement mortar (1:3). It has white efflorescence whenever wet spring weather arrives, which is every year for the past 20 years.

11.2 Movement Joints

Figures 11.02a–f demonstrate the problems and solutions.

Thermal movement

This is a reversible movement, and affects external structures such as paving and walls. Full southern exposure and dark-coloured materials cause larger-scale movements. In general terms a 20 mm compressible joint is needed every 30 m. In walling this is best achieved by leaving an open joint. Soft mastic filling will be needed in paving or steps.

11.02c Buttress features (opposite). 'Span' housing, Taplow, Buckinghamshire (1970). Architects: Lyons & Cunningham
d Zipper joint, Sutton House Garden, Surrey (1982). Architect: Sir Geoffrey Jellicoe
e Shrinkage of silicate bricks cracking a wall at the weakest point
f Movement stresses at the weakest point above stepped DPC in a long run of restrained wall

Expansion movement

An irreversible movement caused by the chemical interaction between cement mortars and ceramic (such as clay brick or tile). The degree of movement depends upon the sulphate content of the brick and the mortar strength. Designers should allow for movement joints at 9–11 m intervals, using either an open 20 mm joint or a soft mastic filling over a compressible filler. Bricks with high sulphate content should be avoided in full-bedded paving work.

Shrinkage joints

Skrinkage is associated with concrete, whether in-situ or precast. Walling employing precast concrete bricks or blocks or silicate (sand/lime) bricks suffers movement stresses as curing proceeds. The situation changes with the wet-to-dry cycle, but the net result can be shrinkage of up to 3 mm per 3 m length. The usual pattern in walling is the straight joint arranged at 3/4/5 m intervals. Advice should be sought from silicate brick and concrete block makers. The joint could be left open or pointed with a soft mastic.

Joint design

Clearly a wall surface which is seamed with mastic at regular intervals does not look as attractive as continuously-bonded work. Designers seek to modify matters by lapping wall lengths or by featuring the gaps at the end of buttresses. This 'zipper'-effect leaves an opening within the brick mass without breaking the bond. Compare Figures 11.02c–d, where the designers have sought to hide or emphasize the joint.

Fender walls

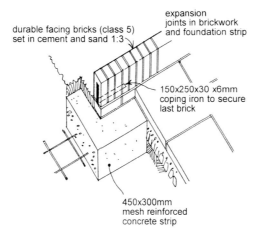

durable facing bricks (class 5) set in cement and sand 1:3

expansion joints in brickwork and foundation strip

150x250x30 x6mm coping iron to secure last brick

450x300mm mesh reinforced concrete strip

11.03 Fender walls

Care is needed with features which break up the monolithic character of walls, such as arches or doorways. Such items should be placed within a panel of brickwork contained by movement joints in close proximity. Long runs of wall broken in the middle by an arched opening will give rise to movement cracks at the weakest point — between the arch head and the crest of the wall. Figures 11.02e–f demonstrate the problems. It is relatively easy with silicate bricks or concrete blocks to arrange garden walls without arches or lintels and to treat doorways as increased gaps without the encumbrance of continuous walling (see Figure 11.02b).

11.3   Fender Walls

Dwarf or fender walls are popular garden designs for marking boundaries at public roads or as definition alongside terraces and paving. Sleepers or kerbstones have been mentioned for similar roles in Chapters 1 and 2, and in Figures 1.29a–d and 2.02a–b. However, brick provides a material which blends with buildings and is often readily available when contractors are finishing off external works. Laying bricks on shallow strips of poured concrete will lead to failure due to frost heave and the ravages of differential movement caused by clay subsoils. Wet or dry conditions can give rise to movement of 20 mm up or down, and can distress subsoil to a depth of 450 mm.

Reinforced precast plank foundations will also settle, but at least the lengths of concrete will stay intact. Figure 11.03 describes the technique which can be adopted for small-scale fender walls on clay subsoils.

11.4   Field Stone Walls

The historic association of fields enclosed by stone rubble often dates back to the original land clearance for agriculture, when stones picked out by hand were stacked or built up as dry stone walls at the edge of enclosures. In 'stone' districts of the UK such features became a permanent element in the landscape following the Land Enclosure Acts of the sixteenth century. Many of the field stone walls in the Cotswolds and in the White Peak, Derbyshire, date back 400 years.

a Constructional detail

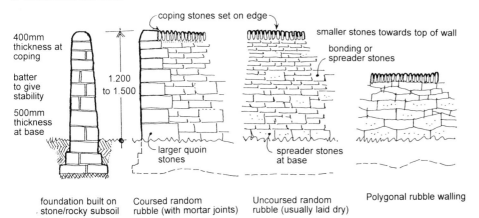

400mm thickness at coping

batter to give stability

500mm thickness at base

1.200 to 1.500

coping stones set on edge

larger quoin stones

smaller stones towards top of wall

bonding or spreader stones

spreader stones at base

foundation built on stone/rocky subsoil

Coursed random rubble (with mortar joints)

Uncoursed random rubble (usually laid dry)

Polygonal rubble walling

b Forms to give stability

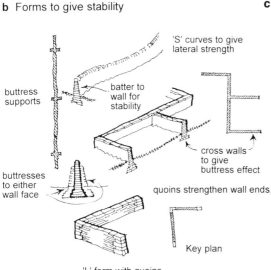

buttress supports

buttresses to either wall face

'S' curves to give lateral strength

batter to wall for stability

cross walls to give buttress effect

quoins strengthen wall ends

Key plan

'L' form with quoins at corners

c

The building or repair process differs little today. A stable, rocky subsoil is often found not deeper than 400–450 mm, and this is overlaid with larger flat stones to form a stepped foundation. The dry walling is then built up in tapered form to give greater stability, with the stones graded from large to small as the work proceeds. A timber profile board is used together with lines to ensure consistency of profile (see Figure 11.04d). The top is capped with flattish stones set on edge to secure the coping work against damage from stock climbing over the wall. Tougher measures are used today to guard against cattle, as well as careless walkers who scramble over walls, ignoring gates and stiles. Edge-set coping stones are mortared together, and another defence comprises larch poles built in horizontals 600 mm below the top and carrying barbed wire on the side towards roads or trails. Figures 11.04a–g cover varying details, and the salient points are covered below.

Constructional detail

The character of random rubble walls (Figure 11.04a) depends upon the locality and the quarry stone available. The vernacular character therefore varies from the polygonal blocks of millstone grit seen on the Pennines to the segments of flat stone found in the Cotswolds (Figure 11.04e). Prepared stone is also available, sawn into batched thicknesses for coursed rubble walls, where the stone blocks are built in regular courses, though with smaller units towards the coping. Larger stones, called quoins, are used to strengthen corners or wall ends. Building stone is either dumped loose at the site, leaving the waller to sort out the sizes (as shown in Figure 11.04d) or supplied batched and palleted according to size. It is worth making a photograph or sketch record of existing walling and to record stone sizes where conservation work is involved. Advice on quarries and walling firms can be obtained from trade associations like the Stone

11.04d Profile stakes and assembly from dry stone rubble in Cotswolds
e Cotswold stonework at Lower Slaughter, Cotswolds
f Coursed random rubble with mortar joints
g Millstone grit walling near Edale, Derbyshire

Federation in the UK (at 82 New Cavendish Street, London W1M 8AD).

Building forms

Vertical stability depends upon a tapered shape to keep the centre of gravity low. (Figures 11.04b–c) Lateral stability relies upon geometry – either curving lines or else buttressing obtained at wall junctions. L– or U-shaped wall plans also assist, and tall walls can be buttressed. Figure 11.04c shows the attractive way field stone walls fit the shape of a hill, the sinuous curves no doubt following the rough boundary, but also imparting strength through the crinkle-crankle (zig-zag) configuration (compare with Figure 11.18e).

Vernacular quality

The tragedy of mass transport and mass taste is that the vernacular identities of stonework

and locality are lost. (Figures 11.04e–g) Green Westmoreland slate garden walls in brick-built Wimbledon look as incongruous as buff Cotswold rubble in slate made Windermere. Planning restrictions help to maintain the balance, but it would help if designers could content themselves with local recycled materials or materials quarried from nearby.

11.5 Stone Boundary Walls

Greater rigidity is given by bonding stone blocks together with mortar joints. The bond relies upon the vertical joints being staggered to key the blocks together. Quarries prepare the stonework in sawn thicknesses, course by course, identified by a letter or number reference. The bedding mortar needs to be 20 mm thick to allow for tolerances (Figure 11.05a). The selection of mortar is important to ensure a good match to the stonework, with the cement content kept as low as mixes iii, iv and v in Table 11.1. Quarries will supply stone dust to supplement sand in mixes, while traditional hydraulic limes used in the past, such as Blue Lias limes, can be obtained from cathedral workshops. Raking back the mortar with a stubby paint brush will expose each stone, as found in weathered masonry. Flush mortar may be needed for soft stones, and here small particles of stone debris will improve the texture. Figure 11.05g gives a close-up view.

Stonework built with mortar can incorporate strips of damp-proof coursing (such as lead-cored bitumen felt) just above ground level to prevent rising damp from discolouring the masonry, and can incorporate bedded coping blocks placed over another damp-proof course to prevent saturation to the top of the wall.[2] Many sedimentary stones suffer from the cycle of freezing and thawing and need a measure of protection at wall base and coping level.

Very durable limestones (like Portland) or sandstones (like Yorkstone) need less protection, though rising salts (such as sulphates) from clay subsoils will cause crystallization and stone decay in most sedimentary stone. Damp-proof coursing and bitumen painting (to backs of stones) are essential in such situations, and particularly in retaining structures.

Flint nodules have been used for walling since Roman times. The laying process follows the 'armature' pattern, with the flintwork built up in mortar beds and back-filled with structural-mix concrete (1:2:4 by volume). The cross-strength depends upon lacing courses of brick or stonework, with the casting depths limited to around 900–1200 mm. The flint nodules can be natural and rounded or knapped and cut down to a rectangular shape. Figure 11.05b shows construction details, while Figure 11.05c illustrates garden walls recently built in Norwich. The Roman technique shown in

11.05 Stone boundary walls

a Coursed random rubble

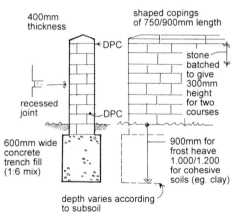

b Flint Walling

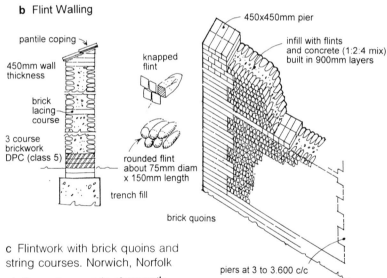

c Flintwork with brick quoins and string courses. Norwich, Norfolk

d Concrete cores to stonework

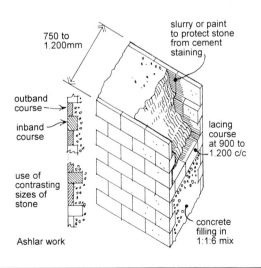

11.05e Composite stone and concrete blockwork

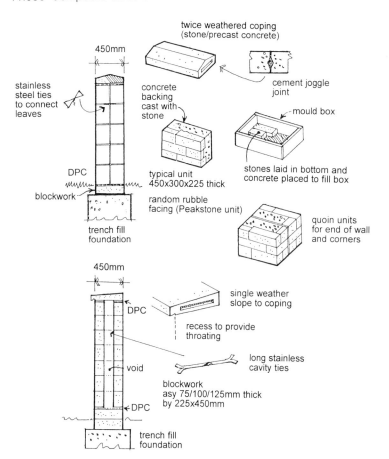

- stainless steel ties to connect leaves
- 450mm
- twice weathered coping (stone/precast concrete)
- cement joggle joint
- concrete backing cast with stone
- mould box
- stones laid in bottom and concrete placed to fill box
- DPC
- blockwork
- typical unit 450x300x225 thick
- random rubble facing (Peakstone unit)
- quoin units for end of wall and corners
- trench fill foundation

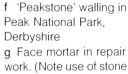

- 450mm
- DPC
- single weather slope to coping
- recess to provide throating
- void
- long stainless cavity ties
- blockwork asy 75/100/125mm thick by 225x450mm
- DPC
- trench fill foundation

f 'Peakstone' walling in Peak National Park, Derbyshire

g Face mortar in repair work. (Note use of stone debris to improve the texture.) Sir Gordon Russell's workshops, Broadway, Worcester

Figure 11.05d is still utilized in the erection of stone-built cores of walling or piers which are back-filled with lean-mix concrete (1:1:6). The relatively weak mix is to reduce shrinkage stresses, with the stonework built 'inband and outband' to form an envelope for the structure. The stones, called 'ashlars' are cut to the proportions 1:2 to 1:1.5 on elevation to assist longitudinal stability.

In the UK, National Parks and Conservation Area authorities insist upon local stone for walling in 'stone' districts of the UK. The high cost of quarried stone has encouraged the recycling of second-hand material and quarry waste. The latter can often be taken away free, and makes a valid component in the casting of stone-faced concrete blocks. Figure 11.05e shows the production process using stone-based moulds. A ribbon of sand at the base of the joints will prevent the mortar grout from staining the mould face. Cement paint to the stone backs could prevent concrete-induced efflorescence. The eventual units measure 450–600 mm and course at 300 mm heights. The wall-building technique resembles that of compound walls – either built as two skins with cavity ties or else of hollow-cavity construction. The completed walls match the coursed random walls of the Peak District closely, as shown in Figure 11.05f.

11.6 Brick Boundary Walls

Traditional form

The traditional form of brick boundary wall is built one brick thick (225 mm nominal thickness) and to a maximum 1925 mm height above the ground to fulfil the Building Research Establishment (BRE) rule-of-thumb conditions applied to free-standing walls in sheltered locations[3] (Figure 11.06a). It is customary to construct such brickwork on the ground of the building owner, with a 'fair face' and good pointing to the wall facing the neighbour. It is wise to set out the wall 20 mm clear from the boundary in case of inaccuracy. It is also best to avoid overhanging copings on the neighbour's side unless prior agreement has been obtained. Such a wall can be built to any length, subject to the movement joints referred to in Figures 11.02b–d, and providing it complies with highway regulations at exits to

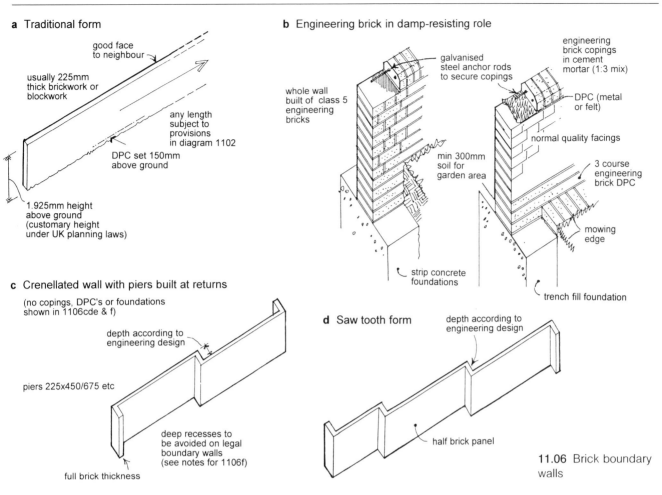

a Traditional form

good face
to neighbour

usually 225mm
thick brickwork or
blockwork

any length
subject to
provisions
in diagram 1102

DPC set 150mm
above ground

1.925mm height
above ground
(customary height
under UK planning laws)

b Engineering brick in damp-resisting role

engineering
brick copings
in cement
mortar (1:3 mix)

galvanised
steel anchor rods
to secure copings

whole wall
built of class 5
engineering
bricks

DPC (metal
or felt)

normal quality facings

min 300mm
soil for
garden area

3 course
engineering
brick DPC

mowing
edge

strip concrete
foundations

trench fill foundation

c Crenellated wall with piers built at returns

(no copings, DPC's or foundations
shown in 1106cde & f)

depth according to
engineering design

piers 225x450/675 etc

deep recesses to
be avoided on legal
boundary walls
(see notes for 1106f)

full brick thickness

d Saw tooth form

depth according to
engineering design

half brick panel

11.06 Brick boundary
walls

a road. It seldom needs planning consent, except in Conservation Areas or in proximity to Listed Buildings in the UK. The rules of thumb mentioned leave a lot to be desired, and the designer is better off using a consulting engineer or taking local authority advice on height, length and thickness schedules, if these exist. The BRE rules specify tight limits for severely-exposed walls built in continuous runs, as set out below:

- Half brick — 375 mm above ground
- One brick — 1075 mm above ground
- One-and-a-half brick — 1825 mm above ground
- 100 mm block — 325 mm above ground
- 150 mm block — 775 mm above ground
- 300 mm block — 1525 mm above ground

Engineering design will prove otherwise and show considerable savings on these figures.

A well-engineered wall will be constructed without a single-leaf damp-proof course which can form a 'hinge point' and cause overturning. The damp-proofing will be better achieved by incorporating damp-resisting engineering bricks throughout, or by using three courses just in proximity to the ground, as in Figure

11.06b. The geometry of the wall plane will be serpentine or crenellated to provide lateral strength (see Figures 11.18e and 11.06c–f). Step-back profiles will reduce the risk of overturning, and the inclusion of stainless brick reinforcement within the horizontal bed joints will strengthen the resistance to wind loads.

Pier and panel walls, as shown in Figures 11.06e–f will reduce thicknesses. The face pier is flush since it preserves a uniform face to the neighbour's side. Crenellated patterns look better but leave a strip of wall that has to be dedicated to the neighbour, or else defined as a 'hostile' strip in the property deeds, concrete-filled at ground level and deemed an area not to be cultivated. Crenellation works perfectly well with publicly-owned land and has a long history in walls constructed to provide recessed protection for pleached trees (Figure 12.02b).

The building of composite structures relies upon reinforced concrete cores to brickwork armatures. Figure 11.06g demonstrates the principles of achieving continuity of structure with foundation beams. Binding the reinforcement together converts the vertical shaft from a pier into a cantilever column.

11.06e Pier and panel wall

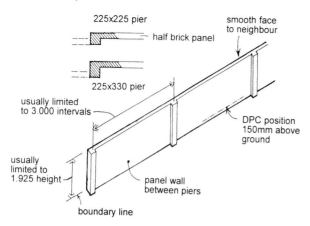

225x225 pier
half brick panel
225x330 pier
usually limited to 3.000 intervals
usually limited to 1.925 height
boundary line
panel wall between piers
smooth face to neighbour
DPC position 150mm above ground

h Detail based on architect's sketch for composite wall at Sutton Place, Surrey (1981)
Architect: Sir Geoffrey Jellicoe

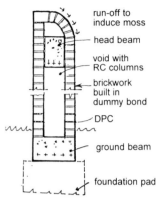

run-off to induce moss
head beam
void with RC columns
brickwork built in dummy bond
DPC
ground beam
foundation pad

f Pier and panel in crenellation

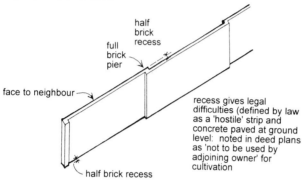

half brick recess
full brick pier
face to neighbour
half brick recess
recess gives legal difficulties (defined by law as a 'hostile' strip and concrete paved at ground level: noted in deed plans as 'not to be used by adjoining owner' for cultivation

g Composite construction with reinforced concrete columns and foundation beams

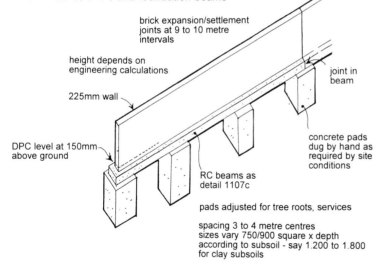

brick expansion/settlement joints at 9 to 10 metre intervals
height depends on engineering calculations
225mm wall
DPC level at 150mm above ground
RC beams as detail 1107c
joint in beam
concrete pads dug by hand as required by site conditions
pads adjusted for tree roots, services
spacing 3 to 4 metre centres sizes vary 750/900 square x depth according to subsoil - say 1.200 to 1.800 for clay subsoils

half brick pier infilled with reinforced concrete

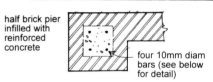

four 10mm diam bars (see below for detail)

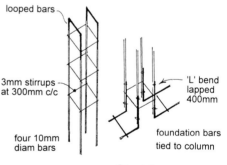

looped bars
3mm stirrups at 300mm c/c
four 10mm diam bars
'L' bend lapped 400mm
foundation bars tied to column

Foundation

The strength is enhanced for wind restraint. Brick reinforcement run horizontally in the mortar could unite the wall panels between the columns into a homogeneous structure. Composite wall structures of this form can be built 6–9 m high, and would consist of thin brickwork skins cladding a reinforced concrete frame. This technique was chosen at Sutton Place, Surrey for the enclosures to the walled gardens. Figures 11.06h–i show Sir Geoffrey Jellicoe's technical concept and the brickwork cladding built in dummy bond. The cavity wall reduces self-weight and lessens the foundation costs for beams and pads. The site at Sutton Place was level, but the design could have been adapted to sloping ground by incorporating steps in the coping. A better solution is to build the brickwork on a raking line in harmony with the ground and to sweep the bedding plane of bricks to the horizontal when meeting gate piers or wall ends. Such a solution is similar to that employed for dry stone walls following ground lines (Figure 11.04c). Walls built around country estates in brick or stone are similar.

11.7 Wall Foundations

The depth and type of foundation depends upon the substrata and the wall loads to be carried. Garden walls built one brick thick (225 mm nominal) and 2 m above the ground weigh roughly 440 kg per metre run, equal to 900 lbs per yd run. The bearing stresses permitted in subsoils have a safety factor of 2, which means that concrete strips carrying the wall described will have to be 600 mm wide. The safety factor mentioned allows for variation in subsoil bearing capacity due to varying compaction and soft pockets. The permitted bearing pressures for various subsoil characteristics are listed in Table 11.3.

There are few problems with rocky subsoils other than the actual task of excavation, often involving blasting where trenches are made. Compact and non-cohesive materials such as chalk or gravel involve no problems other than frost heave, which affects subsoils down to 900 mm depths in the UK.[4] Cohesive subsoils − such as clay, clay/sand mixtures, peat or silt − all suffer from shrinkage or swelling due to dry or wet conditions. These differential movements occur down to depths of 1200 mm. The water table also affects bearing strengths and the angle of repose.

Angle of repose

For any given granular material, the steepest angle to the horizontal at which a heap of that material will stand in stated conditions. Typical angles of repose are as follows:

	Wet	**Dry**
Sand	25°	30°
Loose rock	45°	45°
Gravel	25°	30°
Chalk	45°	70°
Brown clay	15°	30°
Loamy clays	15°	30°

Foundation depths of 1200 mm or more with clay subsoils add onerous costs to masonry wall construction, with one-third of the cost hidden below the ground. In these cases

Table 11.3 Bearing pressures permitted for various subsoils and their characteristics

Group	Soils	Allowable bearing pressures KN/m²
I	Granite	1070
	Limestone, sandstone	430
	Hardstone, soft sandstone	220
	Clayshale	110
	Solid chalk	65
	Brokenstrata, soft chalk	
II	Compact gravel	60★
	Dense gravel, sand/gravel	20−60★
	Loose gravel, sand/gravel	20★
	Compact sand	30★
	Dense sand	10−30★
	Loose sand	Less than 10★
III	Hard clay	43−65
	Stiff clay	22−43
	Firm clay	11−22
	Soft clay and silt	5.5−11
	Soft clay, soft silt	Less than 5.5
IV	Peat	Foundations taken down *below* organic soil
V	Landsilt	Make local assessment. Commonly, one uses piles or raft, dependant on the watertable

designers should question the validity of brickwork or stonework when timber construction could suffice.

Precast planks have already been mentioned in connection with fender walls (see Figure 11.03). The notion can be extended with beams spanning onto concrete pad foundations, and can show savings compared to continuous-

a Continuous foundations with trench fill

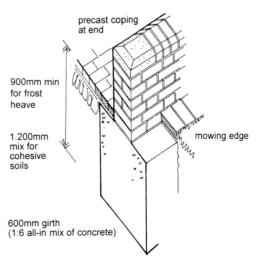

11.07 Wall foundations

11.07b Reinforced concrete columns combined with beams and ground pads

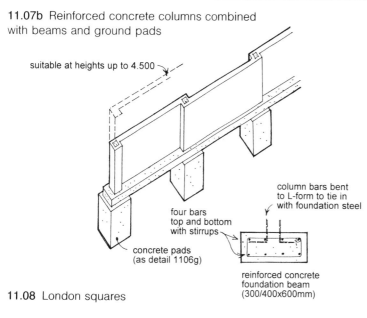

suitable at heights up to 4.500

column bars bent
to L-form to tie in
with foundation steel

four bars
top and bottom
with stirrups

concrete pads
(as detail 1106g)

reinforced concrete
foundation beam
(300/400x600mm)

11.08 London squares

a London squares from the 18th and early 19th century: enclosure of tree planted area by surrounding cellar walls

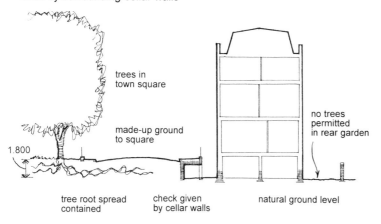

trees in
town square

made-up ground
to square

1.800

no trees
permitted
in rear garden

tree root spread
contained

check given
by cellar walls

natural ground level

b Contemporary protection from tree root damage using concrete filled trench or 'berm'

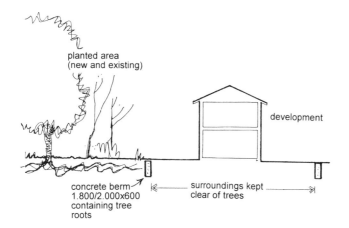

planted area
(new and existing)

development

concrete berm
1.800/2.000x600
containing tree
roots

surroundings kept
clear of trees

trench footings. See Figure 11.07b which demonstrates that pad foundations can be placed to accommodate tree roots, both existing and proposed. Trench fill (Figure 11.07a) can be used as a defensive berm, against root trespass, a point of Common Law in the

UK that has a bearing upon boundary walls.[5] Pad and beam constructions are friendly to the environment, and if hand-dug can be executed within garden spaces and with least disturbance to ground conditions. Trial digs can be made and the pads resited, provided the beam design is adjusted. Some estate walls, such as those built in the early nineteenth century around Buckingham Palace, were formed with brick piers instead of concrete pads. The piers supported massive arches to permit root spread for the forest trees planted within the palace gardens and along Constitution Hill.

11.8 Trees and Foundations on Cohesive Soils

London squares have fine forest trees growing on clay which cause no problems to the adjacent terraced houses. This is due to the cellar walls which form a berm below pavement level, as shown in Figure 11.08a. A modern version is shown in Figure 11.08b where tree-planted areas are enclosed below ground level to avoid tree-damage litigation. Cohesive soils, such as clay or loamy clays and peat or silty soils, will be at greater risk to tree root penetration and drying out than chalk, gravel or rock. Speed of root growth with fast-growing trees such as elm, poplar, sycamore and willow will threaten ground conditions for a distance equal to the height of a mature specimen, say 18 m. Plant trees in groups and the root spread may equal three times the mature height (for example, 60 m in the case of a popular plantation – see Figure 11.09c for comparison). The hair-net growth of roots extends to 900 mm depth, but will drive downwards at obstructions, hence the need for a 1200 mm minimum depth for domestic foundations in clay soil. It is certainly true that a 2 m depth will be needed for an effective berm, or where pad or trench-fill foundations abut mature trees.

A spate of insurance claims made by house owners with foundation settlement problems follows every dry summer in the UK. Insurers and speculative builders dislike trees and will insist upon tree removal up to 18 m from domestic structures. Landscape designers have different priorities and need to be aware of root containment when fast-growing trees are planted. Conifers and shallow-rooted trees like silver birch are safer. A sad comment upon

11.08c Fast growing trees in cohesive soils.
Typical growth pattern and root spread

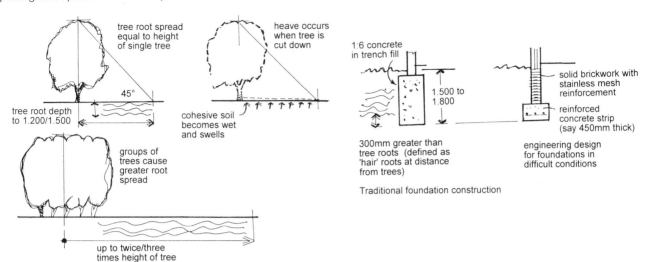

tree root spread equal to height of single tree

45°

tree root depth to 1.200/1.500

heave occurs when tree is cut down

cohesive soil becomes wet and swells

groups of trees cause greater root spread

up to twice/three times height of tree

1:6 concrete in trench fill

1.500 to 1.800

300mm greater than tree roots (defined as 'hair' roots at distance from trees)

Traditional foundation construction

solid brickwork with stainless mesh reinforcement

reinforced concrete strip (say 450mm thick)

engineering design for foundations in difficult conditions

speculative builders is not only their concern for dodging liability but their habit of stripping all the topsoil from the surroundings of their developments so that planting is hard to establish — a very different attitude from those architects and urbanists who created Hampstead Garden Suburb and Bedford Square, London, looking for a balance between town and country.

11.9 Brick Bonds and Modules

The sizes of stonemasonry are dictated by quarry production or by the need to blend in with existing stonework. 'Dimension stone' is the trade's description for the work of cutting and preparing blocks of wall masonry.
The recent repairs at Biddulph Grange Gardens, Staffordshire involved blocks measuring

a Brick types and sizes

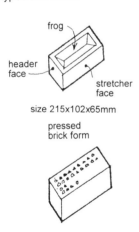

frog

header face

stretcher face

size 215x102x65mm

pressed brick form

extruded wirecut brick with perforations

module size: 290/190x90x90mm also made to normal sizes: 215x102x65mm

irregular form of handmade brick (pressed and extruded bricks also vary in size)

b Stretcher and related bonds

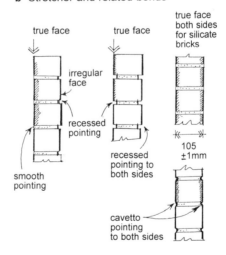

true face

true face

true face both sides for silicate bricks

irregular face

recessed pointing

smooth pointing

recessed pointing to both sides

105 ±1mm

cavetto pointing to both sides

11.09 Brick bonds and modules

c Stretcher bonds

11.09b Stretcher and related bonds   **d** English and cross bonds

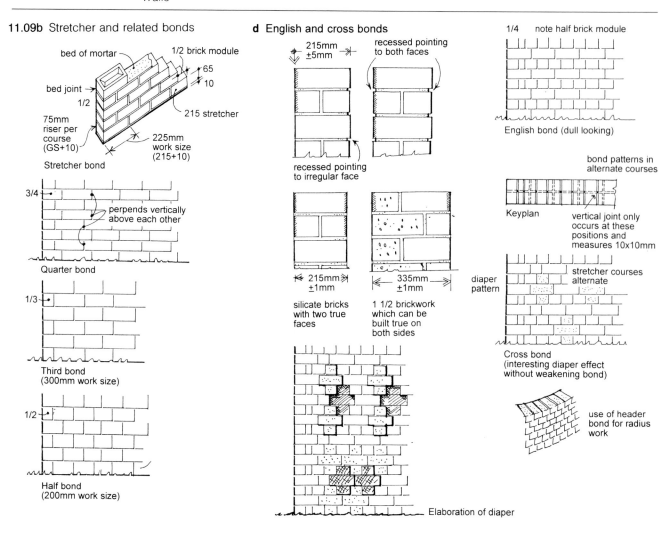

bed of mortar   1/2 brick module
65
10
bed joint
1/2   215 stretcher
75mm riser per course (GS+10)   225mm work size (215+10)
Stretcher bond

3/4   perpends vertically above each other
Quarter bond

1/3
Third bond (300mm work size)

1/2
Half bond (200mm work size)

215mm ±5mm   recessed pointing to both faces

recessed pointing to irregular face

215mm ±1mm   335mm ±1mm
silicate bricks with two true faces   1 1/2 brickwork which can be built true on both sides   diaper pattern

Elaboration of diaper

1/4   note half brick module
English bond (dull looking)

bond patterns in alternate courses
Keyplan   vertical joint only occurs at these positions and measures 10x10mm

stretcher courses alternate
Cross bond (interesting diaper effect without weakening bond)

use of header bond for radius work

900×750 mm on face and 200 mm thick. Such masonry units have to be mechanically handled into place. There is no need for standard sizes for stone cut at a quarry. The only standardized production occurs with the making of reconstructed or artificial stone wall blocks, which tends to follow a 75 mm module, though in multiples of 150, 300, 450, 600 mm, etc.

Bricks have always been made to sizes that can be hand-held, because of the laying procedure adopted by brick layers, with the brick and trowel held in each hand. Roman bricks measured roughly $300 \times 160 \times 40$ mm, but this unit has the same weight as the modern standard bricks, whether $215 \times 102 \times 65$ mm or $190 \times 90 \times 65$ mm. Figure 11.09a compares the different forms. The hollow upper mould of a brick, called the 'frog', serves to reduce the weight of bricks and to increase the mortar bond in bedded courses. Perforating bricks is another way of reducing weight and improving the kiln-firing of clay. There are also plain bricks which are extruded through a die and called 'wire cuts'. Figures 11.09b−i develop the theme of brick bonds and the way the pattern

of interleafing bricks keys the components together. Straight jointing destroys the structural unity, hence its use in movement joints.

Stretcher bond

Stretcher bond (Figures 11.09b−c), so named because of the long face exposed, is used for half-brick walls. It is cheap and fast to construct, and dull in the common form. Quarter or third bond is far more attractive and has a pleasant horizontal character which suits long walls. Refer to Figure 11.09b to compare various styles of stretcher bond. Half-brick walls are reserved for low walls up to 750 mm height, and for panel walls built between piers up to 2.1 m height. The shortcomings concern obtaining a good face (one that is uniform in texture) to both sides of half-brickwork where clay facing bricks are used. The effect of firing clay distorts the ceramic, with the result that bricks vary in girth by up to 6 mm. Bricklayers build thin walls with one true face and one rough. Recessed pointing will make a feature

f Flemish and honeycomb bonds

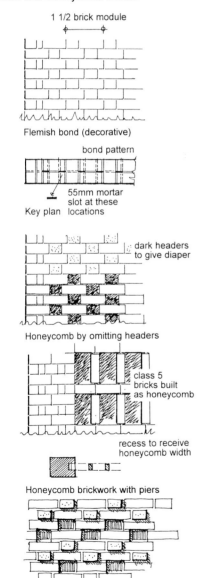

1 1/2 brick module

Flemish bond (decorative)

bond pattern

55mm mortar slot at these locations

Key plan

dark headers to give diaper

Honeycomb by omitting headers

class 5 bricks built as honeycomb

recess to receive honeycomb width

Honeycomb brickwork with piers

Multi-plane textures

of the unevenness on the rough side. To be democratic, recessed pointing could be offered on both faces. Silicate bricks hold to a constant size and can be built with a true face on both sides in half-brick and one-brick walls.

English and cross bonds

English and cross bonds (Figures 11.09d–e) are favoured for structural work, and are used where the highest strengths are needed. The thicknesses are one, one-and-a-half, two-brick, etc. The same problems exist in obtaining a true face on either side of one-brick walls in clay brick, the solution of raked pointing or switching to silicate facings being similar to that for stretcher bond. One-and-a-half brick walls and thicker present no problems since the discrepancies in brick sizes are taken up within the total wall thickness.

Bonding strength depends upon keeping the vertical matrix of brick and mortar in a tight configuration. English bond permits a 10 mm square vertical shaft of mortar to occur only at half-brick intervals in the length of walling. (Refer to bond plan in 11.09d). English bond is one of the plainest effects, but can be improved by varying the stretcher pattern (the long face of the brick) in every second course. This adjustment creates a 'diaper effect', which can be enlivened by picking out groups of facings in a darker colour, as occurred in Tudor buildings.

Bond pattern should be retained throughout the elevation, and designers ought to retain a half-brick dimension, which is the module for wall lengths, piers, openings and for spaces between openings. Figure 11.09d reveals the differences between the dull, stripy look of English and the delights of cross bond (also called Dutch cross or Scots cross bond). The repeating module in both English and cross bonds must be half-brick if the bond pattern is to be maintained.

Flemish and honeycomb bonds

Flemish bond (Figures 11.09f–g) is associated with the Flemish Netherlands. This handsome bond is selected for its appearance and the patterns that can be formed. It is also the prototype of all garden wallbonds. It is not employed where high strength is required, since the mortar slots occupy almost half of the central joints. These represent a cleavage

11.09e Cross bonds. movement joints hidden by set back in wall

g Flemish bonds
(Wren's work at
Hampton Court,
London)
i Garden wall bonds

g

i

h Garden wall bonds: typical dimensions

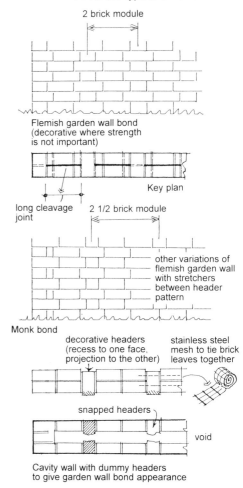

2 brick module

Flemish garden wall bond
(decorative where strength
is not important)

Key plan

long cleavage
joint

2 1/2 brick module

other variations of
flemish garden wall
with stretchers
between header
pattern

Monk bond

decorative headers
(recess to one face,
projection to the other)

stainless steel
mesh to tie brick
leaves together

snapped headers

void

Cavity wall with dummy headers
to give garden wall bond appearance

plane which weakens the homogeneity of the brickwork. The natural diaper effect is richer than cross bond, and enables the designer to explore perforated brickwork in the manner of Persian architecture. Clearly the use of open trelliswork in facing bricks demands the highest performance in terms of frost-resistance as well as strength where bonding is reduced to a minimum. The attractive, repeating cross-form motif relies upon maintaining the header pattern with the setting out. The module is one-and-a-half bricks, which entails greater care in sizing openings, piers and wall units.

Garden wall bonds

Garden wall bonds (Figures 11.09h−i) arose through the need to build one-brick walls with good faces to either side despite the irregularity of facings. The walls resemble composite brickwork, where two skins of brickwork are built back-to-back, the occasional header brick serving as a tie between both leaves. The header brick could be emphasized by using

contrasting colours or textures and appropriate larger sizes to fit the overall thickness required as in monk bond and other designs where headers are far apart.

The strength of garden walls is minimal since large cleavage planes exist down the centre of the wall, apart from the occasional headers to connect both leaves of brickwork. The lateral strength can be enhanced by building stainless steel mesh into the bedding courses to tie the wall together, say in every fourth course. Garden wall bonds are also useful for dummy bond work, where half-brick walls, normally built in stretcher bond, are constructed to resemble Flemish and the garden wall variations. The header spacing is critical in maintaining the bond module, and typical modules for the bonds are given in Figure 11.09h. Breaking the module means that the bricklayer inserts a broken bond, which is most unsightly. Refer to Figure 11.09g for an example of what happens when the setting out fails.

a Composite walls

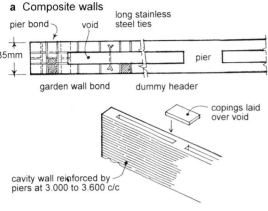

pier bond • void • long stainless steel ties

35mm

pier

garden wall bond • dummy header

copings laid over void

cavity wall reinforced by piers at 3.000 to 3.600 c/c

b

c

d Retaining structure to paved terrace

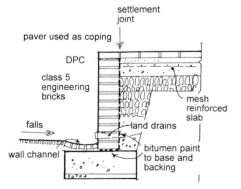

settlement joint

paver used as coping

DPC

class 5 engineering bricks

falls

wall channel

land drains

mesh reinforced slab

bitumen paint to base and backing

11.10 Composite Walls

Composite walls of reinforced concrete and brickwork have already been shown in Figure 11.06g. Variations exist where the brickwork incorporates 'secret' piers within the overall thickness (Figure 11.10a). The origins lay with forcing-houses built in the seventeenth century, where flues were incorporated within cavity brickwork to provide heated surfaces in conservatories. Cellular brickwork is still employed where appearance is important, but engineering advice is essential for calculating pier sizes and the ties to connect the two leaves of brickwork. An understanding of structural pier bonding is essential for this walling pattern, and reference must be made to bricklaying manuals. It is essential to maintain a balance of brick elements within each course to avoid wide vertical joints (called perpends) which otherwise occur to make up the dimensions. Refer to Figures 11.10b–c for an example of the problem and the resolution to achieve a uniform scale in the perpends. The free-standing pier shown was built as a composite construction with a half-brick drum filled with lean-mix concrete. The dummy bond was selected to balance the perpends and has no structural significance.

11.11 Copings and Details

It seems perverse that the bricklayer's skill with bonds and piers frequently does not extend to finishing a suburban front garden wall in a simple and effective manner. The commonplace clumsy abominations of precast slabs or tile creasing are not necessary. Coping bricks should be bedded in cement mortar (1:3). An underlay of bitumen felt or bitumen paint as a damp-proof course will prevent saturation in the wall below, and a slight overhang in the damp-proof course will also assist. A better precaution is to insert an aluminium or zinc flashing strip which sheds rain away from the wall face as Figure 11.11a. Vandalized copings can be avoided by omitting overhangs with precast concrete or quarry tile cappings. Anchored elements, such as perforated brickwork threaded with short lengths of steel bar, form the ultimate deterrent, provided that the penultimate blocks are firmly anchored. Metal tie irons can be used, but

11.10 Composite walls

b Brick core built as sluttering for concrete
c Finished free-standing pier

a Copings and details

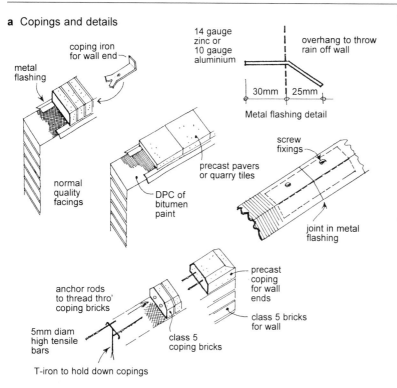

Metal flashing detail

14 gauge zinc or 10 gauge aluminium

overhang to throw rain off wall

30mm | 25mm

coping iron for wall end

metal flashing

normal quality facings

precast pavers or quarry tiles

DPC of bitumen paint

screw fixings

joint in metal flashing

anchor rods to thread thro' coping bricks

5mm diam high tensile bars

class 5 coping bricks

precast coping for wall ends

class 5 bricks for wall

T-iron to hold down copings

Vandal-proof copings

11.11 Copings and details

b Detail of garden wall with brick tile copings laid over metal flashing. Aarhus University, Denmark (1938). Architects: Fisher & Møller
c Coping slabs and aluminium sub-flashing to walls on left and right. St Catherine's College, Oxford (1964)

a cast in-situ pad of concrete will be more effective under tough usage. Continuous runs of cast in-situ concrete make a robust capping to brickwork, but weather flashing and a brushed bitumen underlay are wise precautions to avoid efflorescence.

Figure 11.11b shows the garden wall details which grace the campus at Aarhus University in Denmark. The construction dates back to the 1930s and reveals the care taken with essential elements. The wall base and coping are made from 'clinkers', a European form of frost-resisting engineering brick. The pale yellow stocks are not disfigured by run-off thanks to the neat aluminium flashing. Figure 11.11c shows a similar detail, but built more economically in silicate bricks and precast concrete copings.

11.12 Pointing

The pointing of brickwork and masonry is the finish given to the exposed mortar joint on the wall face. The soundest pointing is that struck with the trowel or tool as the work proceeds, ensuring consistency with the masonry mortar. The colour and texture need to be assessed from sample panels which are maintained as a reference for the work in progress. A typical sample is shown in Figure 11.12a, built in

Flemish garden wall bond using mortar mix iii with a 'cavetto' joint struck with a pointing tool as the panel was built. The advantage of tooling is the compaction of the mortar face and the way that the brick texture is expressed in the wall. Irregular bricks and rough stone require greater skill, and a slight recession of the joint will be needed to emphasize their character. This technique has the advantage of camouflaging the secondary faces of half- or one-brick walls (Figures 11.09b and 11.10a) and for work that adjoins older buildings. Flush pointing needs a clean style of working if the mortar is not to be smeared. Addition of crushed stone to the mortar improves the texture and masks shrinkage cracking in wide joints, and is valuable when repointing old walls (see Figure 11.05g). Flush pointing masks uneven sizing in brick and stone units and presents a uniform surface. Evenness of colour is important in all pointing, but it pays to obtain supplies of pre-mixed mortar where flush pointing is envisaged. The colour range is limited by natural sands, but present-day technology permits a guaranteed group of tinted mortars, many designed to blend with brick colours.

The pointing of walling after completion or repointing existing walling requires the joints to be raked out 20 mm deep to give space for the pointed work. Flush pointing has the advantage that chipped and damaged bricks or

a

d

b Pointing

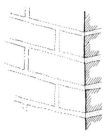

Westminster rag pointing

flush pointing usually
carried out as bricks are
laid : also useful for
repairing old work

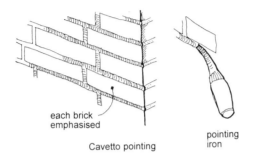

each brick
emphasised

Cavetto pointing

pointing
iron

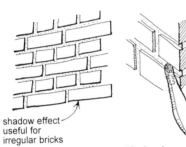

shadow effect
useful for
irregular bricks

Recessed pointing

stubby brush
used for cleaning
recessed joints

11.12 Pointing

c

e

f

stones are masked in repointed work. Rusticity
is often associated with garden architecture,
and it is worth exploring the recessed style
provided the existing bricks or stones still have
sound frost-resistant arises. Badly-executed
pointing can ruin old brickwork by bringing
into play the wrong tint of mortar, or else
emphasizing brick bonding when an overall
impression is needed. Figures 11.12e–f show
how jobbing builders ruined sound work built
under Wren that would have been better left
undisturbed.

a Rules for retaining walls

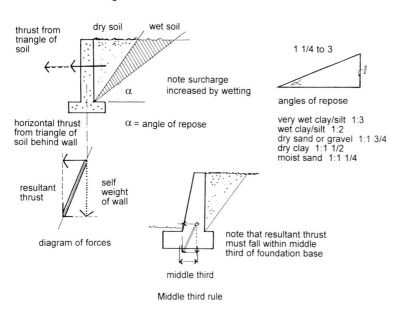

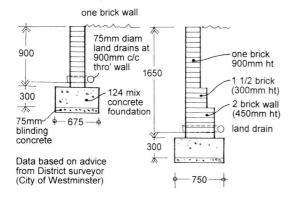

diagram of forces

note that resultant thrust
must fall within middle
third of foundation base

middle third

Middle third rule

b Area walls (rules of thumb)

Data based on advice
from District surveyor
(City of Westminster)

11.13 Rules for
retaining walls

11.13 Retaining Wall Design

Retaining walls are built to hold back earth
or subsoil exposed by excavations. Design
principles vary from 'free retaining structures'
to 'fixed' walls. The latter involve connecting
beams and are associated with deep basements
or cuttings. Most garden retaining walls are
designed as gravity retaining forms, where the
shape provides a counterbalance to the forces
exerted from the embankment behind the wall.
Engineering advice is needed, though simple
rules governing garden retaining walls in the
City of Westminster, London are given in
Figure 11.13b, where the District Surveyor
drew up details for area walls built between
rear gardens and back areas of residential
property in Paddington.

The structural geometry depends upon
resolving the overturning thrusts within the
'middle third' of the foundation girth. Thrusts
acting on the outer third of the base dimension

begin to overturn the wall. The design
principles involve calculations which convert
to a diagram of the combined forces acting
upon the centre of gravity of the retaining
structure. The weight of the wall is self-
explanatory. The horizontal effect of the soil/
sub-soil weight retained follows from the
horizontal thrust developed above the angle of
repose. Precise angles are given in Section
11.7. The proportional basis is the usual
procedure adopted by engineers when
calculating retaining work, shown in Figure
11.13a.

Trapezoid or T-shaped walls will have a
wider footprint and a larger middle third than
a slender wall, which is limited to around
900 mm height for single-brick thickness.
Small garden retaining walls in the confines of
suburban gardens could probably rely upon the
rules set out in Figure 11.13b. Large-scale
work associated with terraced construction on
steeply sloping sites or roadwork abutments
will require reinforced concrete engineering.
Stepped embankments can be made with crib
walls of timber or precast material, as described
in Section 11.18.

11.14 Simple Retaining Walls

The area walls already mentioned are typical
garden retaining walls. The configuration
of the ground in small gardens often means
cutting away soil to keep buildings dry.
Another common application is the need to
create raised planting areas, either to protect
plants from being walked over or to make
gardening easier for the elderly, disabled and
partially sighted. Individual planters made
from glass-reinforced polyester (GRP) are
limited to 3 m sizes and are illustrated in Figure
14.02c. Large-scale construction in brick
or blockwork enables garden designers to
transform a flat terrain into varied levels where
retaining walls have a significant role.

The foundation depth depends upon
subsoil conditions, as in boundary walls,
but the bearing surface should be at least
675 mm wide. A 225 mm thickness of brick or
blockwork will support a 900 mm thickness
of soil. It should ideally be built without a
horizontal damp-proof course (of bitumen
felt) since this will give a 'hinge' point under
surcharge loads from the soil. Two- or three-

course engineering bricks will make an adequate protection, or else the whole wall can be built in this manner (Figures 11.14a—c).

A triple coating of bitumen paint as a wall backing will guard against ground salts like sulphates soaking into the brickwork. These can cause discolouration and in some cases trigger a sulphate attack in brick and cement mortars. Figure 11.14d shows my neighbour's retaining wall built below a clay bank holding sulphate-bearing springwater. The bricks have above-average sulphate content and were built in a cement mortar. No back-protection or damp-proof course was provided, and breakdown of the brick face and general exfoliation occurred within ten years. The relief of groundwater is beneficial in ensuring that the angle of repose behind the retaining wall does not surcharge greater loads on the vertical face. Remember that wet subsoils have a lesser angle of repose than dry material. Land drains are laid to falls on a concrete bed but encased in loose shingle or broken stone with T-branches to discharge above the paving at the lower level.

Where doubts exist about water penetration or the quality of the structural wall it is wise to use composite construction with an open cavity and a leaf of decorative facing material. This can be facing brick, stonework or reconstructed stone, whichever fits the garden context. Earth filling in planters always settles, and it is better to heap the soil so that the final result will be flush with the copings. The coping treatment resembles that for other walls, with the selection of durable frost-proof elements and an underlaying damp-proof course to prevent saturation in the wall below. Retaining structures are often designed in conjunction with staircases, particularly those related to stepped terraces, as shown in Figures 2.08c—d. In these examples coping and the upper terrace paving continue as a single surface. Paving always settles when laid over infilled ground behind retaining structures, and it is sensible to run a movement joint at the junction of the paving and the wall slabs so that relaying can occur, rather than suffer broken-backed pavers (Figure 11.14d).

11.15 Structural Blockwork

Precast concrete featuring perforations permits steel rods to form a vertical reinforced wall and

a Brick retaining wall constructed in engineering bricks

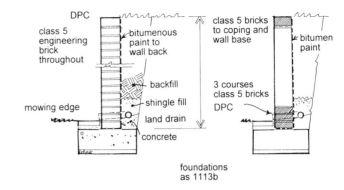

foundations
as 1113b

b Structural blockwork retaining walls

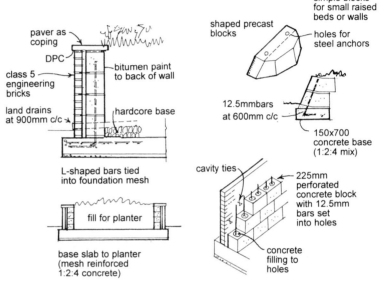

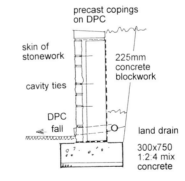

base slab to planter
(mesh reinforced
1:2:4 concrete)

c Facing and cavity construction in retaining structure

11.14 Simple retaining walls

d Sulphate attack of flettons with poor construction

11.4 Structural blockwork

Thickness	Length	Depth
75	390 or (440)	190 or (215)
100	390 or (440)	190 or (215)
140	390 or (440)	190 or (215)
190	390 or (440)	190 or (215)
215	390 or (440)	190 or (215)

Structural blockwork

Typical sizes (actual work sizes)

work size
eg: 440+10mm

thickness
440
10

vertical height
215+ 10mm joint

10mm bed joint

half units

ashlar
pattern:
solid form

brick form
100x100x
390/440

split units
to give
'riven' face

quoin blocks

perforated
form

hollow form

weathered coping
with throating

weathered coping
equal to wall
thickness

rounded face

split face

interlocking unit

stretcher bond

third bond

composite bonding

rounded face   split face

Use of rebated blocks
to form sloping
retaining wall

Random bond using different
sizes of block units within
400x200 work size

11.15 Structural blockwork

is manufactured for structural work. (Figure 11.15) The perforations in brick are too small to be effective, but blockwork is made on a $225 \times 225 \times 450$ mm module, and the working sizes are 10 mm smaller to give space for mortar beds and joints. The cellular patterns have circular or square holes which enable the blocks to be threaded over steel bars, the mortises then being grouted with fine concrete grout. Engineering input to the design and supervision is essential, but the resulting construction gives a robust wall which acts as a composite structure with the foundation slab. Appearance is poor compared to cavity work, and a decorative facing leaf will have to be built. Small-scale retaining kerbs up to 450 mm height can be built up with half-hexagonal units.

Synthetic stone products are not structural units but have to be considered as alternative facings to real stonework. Their shortcomings stem from their thin profile – usually around 100 mm – and their monotonous pattern. Genuine stone cast integrally with concrete looks superior (see Figures 11.05e–f). It can also serve a structural role. Fair-faced structural blocks are made to high standards, and are described in Section 11.19.

11.16 Reinforced Concrete Walls and Finishes

Various forms of reinforced concrete retaining walls are shown in Figure 11.13a and this application relates to structures in excess of 3 m height. At least one-third of the expenditure in casting concrete walls or kerbs will arise from the shuttering, which involves making up timber moulds stayed by framing to support the concrete matrix until cured, taking 14 days for wall elements. Civil engineering contracts may entail casting a considerable volume of concrete in road decks and allied retaining structures. Related landscape works can therefore benefit from a skilled labour force who have expertise in reinforced concrete. Concrete, though a cheap material to mix and to cast, needs skill if the surface finishes are not to be disappointing. The first priority is the selection of colour in the cement, sands and coarse aggregate. The guidance on concrete paving in Section 1.4 is just as relevant to casting walls.

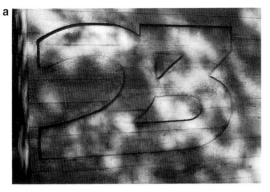

11.16 Reinforced concrete finishes

a Board-marked concrete in a river defence wall at The Strand on the Green, London. Architect: Timothy Rendle
b Exposed aggregate finish showing grading
c Granite aggregate
d Aggregate transfer on right-hand side and body of sculptured concrete. Architect: George Mitchell

The mould imprint for vertical or sloping surfaces is transferred from the shutter face, so that smooth sheets of steel plate or ply will provide a hard, flat character, while sawn boards will give wood textures. Smooth, shiny materials like plastic sheet or polished timber give a marble-like facing to concrete. The main character of cast concrete arises from the cement element, whose buff or grey aspect dominates the weathering process. The selection and exposure of stone aggregates will modify the cement colour and eventually produce an exposed character which harmonizes with natural stone. Guidance on selection is given below.

Board-marked concrete

The secure containment of wet concrete for casting in timber shuttering entails double-lined shutters of plywood lined with sawn boards. The Hayward Gallery on London's South Bank used this technique internally and externally, and the cost of the lined shutters equalled a veneer of thin Portland stone. Refer to Figure 11.16a for an example of similar concrete used for a river defence wall.

Exposed aggregate concrete

Exposing the aggregate of vertical surfaces can be performed by grit-blasting to remove the cement laitance, and varying depths of exposure can be obtained. Figures 11.16b−c shows variation in grade of exposure. Precast elements, such as copings or building blocks, can be similarly treated.

Aggregate transfer

This is the most expensive technique, and relies upon aggregate being stuck to the shuttering with short-life glues prior to encasement. The work requires a highly-skilled workforce, but it is possible to produce effects such as pebble and flint walling or a mosaic of stone resembling random rubble (Figure 11.16d).

Plastic inserts

Polystyrene inserts or rubber sheeting can be applied to shutters to give sculptural relief patterns (Figures 11.16e−f). Burning off the embedded plastic reveals the pattern, which can be enhanced with grit-blasting.

11.16e Patterns created by polystyrene insets and grit-blasting. Designer: George Mitchell

f Ribbed concrete that has been cast against synthetic rubber sheeting and bush-hammered

11.17 Reinforced Concrete Elements

The International Garden Show at Bonn in 1982 included a sample garden where reinforced concrete was the key material. Figures 11.17a–b show two views, including a free-standing wall, a fender wall, paving and steps. The related details in Figure 11.17c show the method of construction employed and the alternative finishes.

Sound production of horizontal elements such as fenders or steps is often best arranged by casting upside down and then turning the moulds over before placing them in their final location. It is relatively simple to compact concrete into a mould and to strike off the top surface with a rule, and this gives a good bedding surface when placing on site. Moulds can have hook bolts to facilitate handling, with the casing made in sections so that it can be re-used for repetitive components. Arrises

are vulnerable during mould removal and subject to frost erosion as well as accidental damage. An arris mould of 40 × 40 mm or 50 × 50 mm shape will prevent corner loss, and can be modified by grit-blasting to give softened edges to precast blocks. One problem with concrete is the way it darkens under prolonged exposure to rain, and the fact that algae or moss take years to take hold. Figure 11.17d shows precast copings at St Catherine's College, Oxford, which have a vegetation growth almost as thick as the original units after 30 years. It should always be remembered that exposed concrete eventually weathers like limestone walling due to the character of Portland cement. Erosion of the surface is a part of the ageing process. This is why concrete forms need a basic robustness in outline in order to weather in a satisfactory manner. The loss of 'face' in concrete work could be 6 mm per hundred years.

11.17 Reinforced concrete elements

a Danish Garden, Bonn International Garden Show (1982)
b Detail of concrete work in Danish Garden

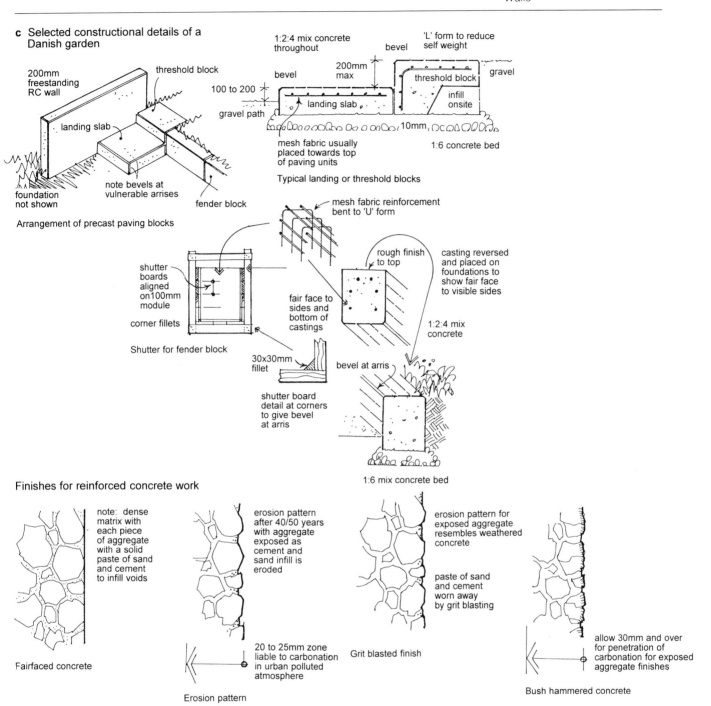

c Selected constructional details of a Danish garden

200mm freestanding RC wall

threshold block

landing slab

note bevels at vulnerable arrises

fender block

foundation not shown

Arrangement of precast paving blocks

1:2:4 mix concrete throughout

bevel

bevel

200mm max

'L' form to reduce self weight

threshold block

gravel

100 to 200

gravel path

landing slab

infill onsite

10mm

mesh fabric usually placed towards top of paving units

1:6 concrete bed

Typical landing or threshold blocks

mesh fabric reinforcement bent to 'U' form

shutter boards aligned on100mm module

corner fillets

Shutter for fender block

fair face to sides and bottom of castings

rough finish to top

casting reversed and placed on foundations to show fair face to visible sides

1:2:4 mix concrete

30x30mm fillet

shutter board detail at corners to give bevel at arris

bevel at arris

1:6 mix concrete bed

Finishes for reinforced concrete work

note: dense matrix with each piece of aggregate with a solid paste of sand and cement to infill voids

Fairfaced concrete

erosion pattern after 40/50 years with aggregate exposed as cement and sand infill is eroded

20 to 25mm zone liable to carbonation in urban polluted atmosphere

Erosion pattern

erosion pattern for exposed aggregate resembles weathered concrete

paste of sand and cement worn away by grit blasting

Grit blasted finish

allow 30mm and over for penetration of carbonation for exposed aggregate finishes

Bush hammered concrete

11.18 Other Forms of Wall

This section highlights details already alluded to in the text but not fully illustrated.

Perforated brick patterns

The inspiration comes from Persian brickwork and the skilled pattern-making developed for Islamic architecture (Figures 11.18a–b). The examples from Bhokara and Samarkand show window screens which provide ventilation or glimpsed views of gardens. This form of lightweight infilling can be incorporated between

d Moss and algae on precast coping at St Catherine's College, Oxford (1963–93). Architect: Arne Jacobson

11.18 Other forms of wall

a Perforated brick pattern in Bhokara grille

b Perforated brick pattern in Samarkand grille

c Multiple-plane brickwork in decorative wall, Louisiana, Denmark

d Multiple-plane brickwork at National Cemetery, Prague, Czechoslovakia

e Crinkle-crankle wall, University of Charlottesville, Virginia (1820s). Architect: Thomas Jefferson

f Early example of crinkle-crankle walling in Haarlem, Holland

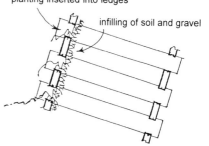

g Crib wall in timber
using joists of preserved softwood

planting inserted into ledges

infilling of soil and gravel

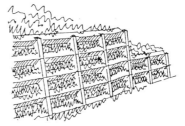

h Crib wall in reinforced concrete
using interlocking reinforced precast units (engineering design input needed for timber and precast forms: heights for retaining structures up to 9 metres)

structural piers, providing light and shade even
on the dullest day.

Multiple-plane brickwork

This variation of the Persian source is seen
in central Europe (Figures 11.18c–d). The
purpose is decorative, and it is often found in
churchyard walls. Flemish bond can provide
these designs by using three planes in the wall
face.

Crinkle-crankle (zig-zag) walls

There is considerable debate as to the origins of
these. The structural reason is obvious, just
as corrugated card is stouter than a sheet.
However, horticulturalists also maintain that a
crenellated wall gives protection to plants and
affords a concentration of warmth within the
recesses. Crinkle-crankle walls of half-brick
design at an orchard in Haarlem, Holland date
from the sixteenth century (Figure 11.18f), and
there are many examples from East Anglia
dating from the seventeenth and eighteenth
centuries. Jefferson's so-called invention of
serpentine walls at Charlottesville, date from
designs of 1823 and are half-brick thickness and
still stand intact (Figure 11.18e). They enclose
the rear gardens to the students' lodgings at the
University of Charlottesville. There are miles
of such wall which divide up the garden space
into small promenades. The extent of wall-
building required led Jefferson to seek the most
economic answer with half-brickwork, namely
serpentine layouts.

Crib walls

Crib walls (Figures 11.18g–h) resemble timber
revetments which step back along the slope.
The intent is to prevent erosion and to hold the
embankment in a stepped profile. Timber units
are supplied as kits for motorway/highway
embankments, and envisaged as a short-term
solution until the plant material growing
between the struts is sufficiently mature to
retain the subsoil.

Other structural solutions use permanent
materials such as precast concrete linked to
piles or rock anchors. The cribs form an
integral structure with the plant material to
overcome erosion and landslip on steep slopes.

Gabions

This is another form of revetment to stabilize
embankments. The masonry cores of broken
rock or large pebbles are caged by galvanized
steel mesh into large building blocks, up to
1 m square by 2 m length. Other shapes are
possible, and the sub-base can be overlaid by
boulders held in place by mesh screening.
Figures 11.18i reveals the way pebble-filled
gabions can dramatize mundane retaining
structures.

Fair-faced structural concrete block walling

Blockwork rivals brickwork for use in the
internal walls of buildings — for example, the
ubiquitous breeze block of yesteryear (Figures
11.18j–l). Today, industrialized production
facilities can produce both structural and facing
grades, and blockwork as a competitor to
brick-sized units made from silicate (cement/
sand mixtures) and concrete. The advantage of
blockwork is the large elevational scale
(225 × 450 mm or 200 × 450 mm) which blends
well with coursed stone masonry. The selection
of coloured cement and durable aggregates,

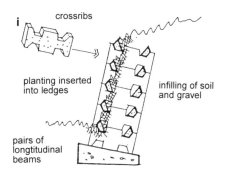

i   crossribs

planting inserted
into ledges

infilling of soil
and gravel

pairs of
longtitudinal
beams

j Gabions used
decoratively and
structurally at Zurich
Technical University,
Switzerland

11.18k Crib wall in timber
11.18l Cumberbatch

such as Portland stone, sound sandstones or granite, produces a quality which matches artificial stone. Blocks are available in 100, 150, 200 and 225 mm thicknesses, and return quoin units are made so that the spineless look of synthetic Cotswold walling is avoided. The blocks are made with perforations to reduce self-weight, or hollow to enable vertical rod reinforcement.

Structural load-bearing masonry is made from solid blocks. Standard 'special' components are available which perform similar tasks to moulded bricks, namely copings, sills and threshold units. Weathering darkens the colour of concrete blockwork, but differential weathering from top to bottom of a free-standing wall will be countered by capping the wall with a metallic trim instead of relying on the flush-fitting coping stones offered by blockwork suppliers. Damp-proof course detailing and backings with bitumen paint

resemble those described for retaining walls in Section 11.15. The material can be chosen to blend with the tints and textures of natural stonework, and provides a valid contemporary solution where budgets will not cover the cost of quarried stone. An excellent example of 'buildings in keeping' using modern blockwork can be seen in the Cumberbatch Quad extensions at Trinity College, Oxford (Figure 11.18k).

12 TRELLISES

12.1 Garden Trellises

The significance of trellises in garden architecture has been mentioned in Chapter 6,[1] with reference to Raymond Unwin. The trellis arrangements at Letchworth, Hertfordshire, or Hampstead Garden Suburb have long since been overwhelmed by the hedges that were designed to overrun their temporary support. The use of trellis screens is just as relevant today when seeking to soften the appearance of newly-built habitations. Square mesh appears less distracting than diamond forms and is easier to adapt to a regular framework of posts and rails, 20 mm square profile battens cut from larch provide reasonable impact strength

a Square trellis construction.

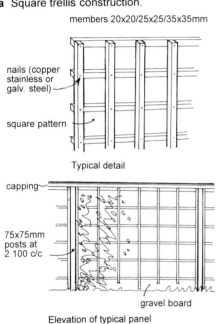

members 20x20/25x25/35x35mm

nails (copper stainless or galv. steel)

square pattern

Typical detail

capping

75x75mm posts at 2.100 c/c

gravel board

Elevation of typical panel

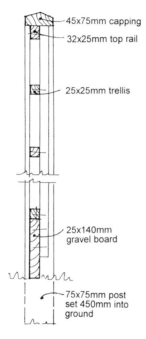

45x75mm capping

32x25mm top rail

25x25mm trellis

25x140mm gravel board

75x75mm post set 450mm into ground

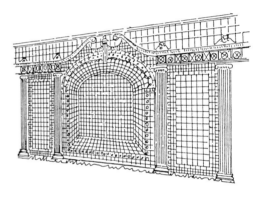

c Perspective trellis. Gable end in the Marais, Paris.

12.01 Garden trellises

b Oak trellis to support roses, Lakeside terrace, Hever Castle, Kent, (original installation 1908). Architect: Frank L. Pearson
d Lift-off trellis framing. Arnhem Farm Museum, Holland.

12.02 Architectural trellises

a Trellis pattern used in glazing forcing-houses at Chatsworth Derbyshire (1848). Designer: Joseph Paxton

b Wall trellis and glazed screen to the terraces below the Palace of Sans Souci at Potsdam, Germany (1745–7, restored 1982). Designer: C. W. von Knobelsdorff

c Glazed screen to define extremity of terrace in relation to glazed fenestration, Bentley Wood, Holland Sussex (1938). Architect: Serge Chermayeff, landscape architect: Christopher Tunnard

d Sculpture Pavilion, National Park de Hoge Veluwe, Otterloo, Holland (1954, rebuilt 1965), general view. Architect: Gerritt Rietveld

e Detail of trellis screen at Sculpture Pavilion

f Clear perspex screens, held secure by tubular steel frames. Toronto Zoo, Ontario, (1978)

g Opalescent toughened glass screens at exit path, Rhine Park, Cologne. Designed for the International Garden Exhibition (1956)

h Armoured glass screen, house on the Falmouth estuary, Cornwall. Architect: John Crowther.
i A trellised bamboo 'window' in a wall
j A sliding trellis screen to the right of tea house
k Patterned fretwork to symbolize landscape in wall trellises

and sufficient weight in the visual sense.[2] Overall framing will be required at four edges — the usual pattern comprises 75 × 75 mm square posts with a gravel board or bottom rail and capping timber. Heavier sections of 25 × 25 mm or 35 × 35 mm will allow the height to be increased from 1.2 to 2 m, and have sufficient stability to support pleached trees or vines. Refer to Figures 12.01a—d for typical applications.

12.2 Architectural Trellises

The architectural character will be enhanced by constructing a framework of fully-prepared timber (planed and sanded) or timber combined with rectangular steel tube. The woodwork can be tenoned together instead of 'trellis lapped' and provide a painted background framing to the planting. The scale can be extended beyond the 150 mm grid to a 300 mm module of garden trellising to embrace the window proportions of adjacent buildings — for example, conservatory glazing or the rhythm of a fenestrated façade. The most evocative ideas can be seen in the forcing-houses at Chatsworth, Derbyshire designed by Paxton (see Figure 12.02a). The counterpoint between wall, trellis and glazing is exploited to the full in the pleached tree frames and glazing created alongside the stair cascade at Potsdam, Germany. Figure 12.02b shows the restoration in process. Another application of glass is the glazed trellis screen designed by Serge Chermayeff for the terrace at his house near Halland, Sussex which acts in counterpoint to the main elevation of the house (Figure 12.02c). The advantage of trelliswork in architectural design is the more generous proportions which can be used as a reference point to scale within the total landscape. The Sculpture Pavilion at the National Park de Hoge Veluwe, Otterloo, Holland, stands within parkland. The Hepworth exhibits are small-scale and would be lost in the open landscape, so trellis screens — sometimes glazed, otherwise left open — act as picture

a Detail of straining wires

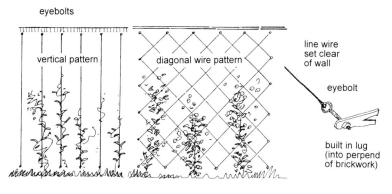

eyebolts

vertical pattern

diagonal wire pattern

line wire set clear of wall

eyebolt

built in lug (into perpend of brickwork)

b Detail of lift-off timber trellis.

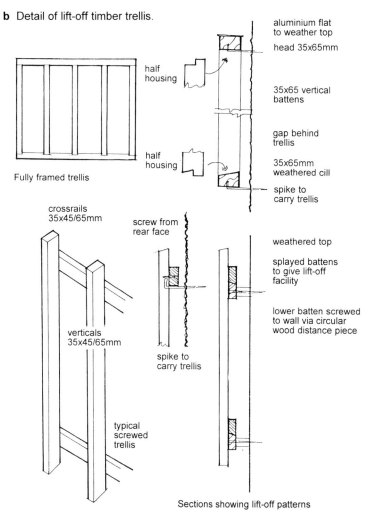

Fully framed trellis

half housing

half housing

aluminium flat to weather top

head 35x65mm

35x65 vertical battens

gap behind trellis

35x65mm weathered cill

spike to carry trellis

crossrails 35x45/65mm

screw from rear face

verticals 35x45/65mm

typical screwed trellis

spike to carry trellis

weathered top

splayed battens to give lift-off facility

lower batten screwed to wall via circular wood distance piece

Sections showing lift-off patterns

12.03 Wall trellises and plant trainers

c Virginia creeper (planted circa 1780) kept in place and retrained for the modern building. St Ann's, Chertsey, Surrey (1937) (view taken in 1989). Architect: Raymond McGrath, landscape architect: Christopher Tunnard

frames for the works exhibited. Figures 12.02d—e show relevant details of the elegant steel framing, and exemplify space division within landscape without recourse to walls or the fussiness of palisading.

Boundary situations between private and public space often need special treatment — total enclosure may be required for security, but transparency may be necessary for the sake of plant material. Unbreakable glazing such as perspex or polycarbonate can be used to make vandalproof screens. All plastic sheeting materials can be scratched, but the embossed or opalescent forms are difficult to deface badly. Flexing under impact has to be guarded against, either by subframing in sizes around 1.2 m square or by using stout steel frames, such as 25 mm tubular steel. Transparent versions are often used for animal enclosures at zoological gardens, as shown in Figure 12.02f. Figures 12.02g—h show other designs using toughened opalescent glass, which has the advantage that plant material can be seen in silhouette — a detail which resembles Oriental rice paper screens. Coastal situations often need windscreening, and here toughened glass balustrading is superior to any other form of sheet material. Figure 12.02h shows a terrace garden screen on the Falmouth estuary, Cornwall, where the glass, if kept clean, provides a perfect 'window' to the view.

The notion of the 'window' in landscape — either clear or divided into a patterned jalousie — is a feature of Oriental landscape. The trellis is made from bamboo or fretted woodwork and can take the symbolic pattern of plant or landscape as the infilling. Figures 12.02i—k are taken from a series of Chinese and Japanese gardens where trellising is featured either as a total enclosure or as a 'window' in the wall.

12.3   Wall Trellises and Plant Trainers

Trelliswork or straining wires can be used to train plants over walls and buildings. The need for access to maintain paintwork or façades should not be forgotten. Lift-off designs have advantages over fixed frameworks of timber or wire. Figures 12.03a—b show metal strainers and timber trellises designed to be removable for building repairs. Clearly, winter working will cause less damage to climbers, and one of

12.03d Lift-off trellis on eighteenth-century cottage, Arnhem, Holland
e Grid trellis to cover whole elevation. Louisiana Museum, Denmark (1958). Architects: Jorgan Bo & Vilkelm Wohlest
f Trellis held off wall by screwed distance pieces. Author's house, Coombe Hill Kingston upon Thames (1957). Architects: Alan & Sylvia Blanc

12.04 Trellises versus fences

a and b The advantage of sturdy trellis framing. Architect's garden, Walmer, Kent. Architect: John Bruckland. (Note that the two views were taken at six-year intervals)
c Adapting standard palisading with trellis topping, Energy Village Milton Keynes, Buckinghamshire

12.04d As illustration
12.04c but with trellis
inserts
e As illustration 12.04c
with further variations

the most remarkable examples of 'refixing'
Virginia creeper is the eighteenth-century
climber at St Ann's, Chertsey, Surrey, which
survived the demolition of the older house
and retraining on the modern façade in 1937
(see Figure 12.03c).

Wood-framed buildings need to be separated
from the clinging wall roots of climbers which
will grow into the timber grain, and a simple
solution is found in Holland, where 'hook
nails' secure trellis frames. Figures 12.03d–f
show various examples.

12.4   Conclusion

Most trelliswork is intended as a temporary
framework, as discussed in Section 12.1.
A telling example is given in Figures 12.04a–b
which show views taken six years apart. The
context is an urban garden in the fisherman's
quarter of Walmer, Kent. The rear yards are

tight spaces between the backs of terraced
houses. The framework of 50 × 35 mm treated
Douglas fir studs gave a visual reference in
the early days, but was speedily greened by
climbers planted adjacent.

Many designers seek to modify the firm
enclosure of palisade fencing adding trelliswork,
and Figures 12.04c–e show the way this was
achieved at the Energy Village, Milton Keynes,
Buckinghamshire. Here standard fencing
packages were modified to provide trellising,
either in the form of over-framing or by
interleaving with larch slats within the framing
pattern. The contrast was reinforced by the use
of differing timber stains, with darker colours
used for the structural elements while bright
shades were used on the decorative infill.
This is an infinite improvement on the dullness
of close-boarded fences or the clumsiness
of interwoven panels, which feel and look
temporary without the virtue of giving
support to climbing plants.

13 PERGOLAS

13.1 Historic References

Pergolas originated in vineyards as rafter-like frameworks to carry grape vines overhead, partly to give a variety of growing conditions — light versus shade — and partly to allow easier access to the fruit. Stone or brickwork supports are often selected for the vertical structures due to their durability and strength.

Figure 13.01a shows a traditional vineyard in the Ticino region of Switzerland, with granite shafts placed as columnar props to the purlins and rafter frames. The classical version of this design features Doric columns carrying beams and shaped roofing members, as if the construction represented a primitive temple from antiquity.

The sturdy rustic design portrayed in Figure 13.01b stems from 1905 and is part of the embellishments designed by T. H. Mawson for 'The Hill', Hampstead, London. The heaviness of construction and the constricted proportions between the open sky and the shaded areas appear sombre under northern skies.

A more successful design with balancing light and shade effects is the pergola at Hever, Kent, where the timberwork is widely spaced, or in places absent, to lighten the canopy of

larch poles (Figures 13.01c−e). These are arranged as in a vineyard pergola with *traversi* and *cordoni* — large beams and smaller poles. The construction dates back to Frank Pearson's designs for the Italianate Garden between 1904 and 1908. The quality of the work results from the following details. Firstly, the larch pole framework is designed to be self-weathering, without flat, sawn areas which collect rainwater. Secondly, the bearing holes within the masonry are left open to prevent rot pockets. Finally, the stonework is built as free-standing piers of substantial girth but of hollow form to give box-like strength, while the smaller shafts are constructed of solid blocks. The stonework has raked-out joints to avoid a cementacious look. The other architectural quality of note at Hever

b

c

d

13.01 Historical references

a Traditional vineyard pergola resting on granite shafts. Ronco, Ticino, Switzerland
b Heavy classical pergola with stone Doric columns. The Hill, Hampstead, London (1905). Architect: T. H. Mawson
c Light and shade pergola. Italianate Gardens, Hever, Kent (1904−8). Architect: Frank Pearson
d Detail of Hever pergola. Note the use of large and small poles with ample pockets in masonry

a

13.01e Details of large piers at Hever, with hollow box masonry and solid blocks for smaller shafts
f Pleached limes on parabolic metal frame. Boboli Gardens, Florence
g Pleached plane trees with metal supports, Jardin de Plantes, Paris (1870s)
h Arbour as outside room. Timber trellises and vaults to the pavilions, Sans Souci, Potsdam, Germany (1747, reconstructed in the 1970s)
i Princess's Garden, Het Loo, Holland (original work started in 1687, restored 1982). Designer: Jacob Roman

is the way the pergola forms not only give an airy canopy to the covered way but provides sufficient robustness to support crab apple and other sturdy climbers 80 years later.

The other relevant historical reference is the arbour, a curved network of branches which initially requires support from metal or timber arches. Pompeiian designs reveal such features (see Figure 14.01a), which appear again in early Renaissance gardens as shaded walks. The arrangement is often sequential, with enclosed vistas broken by open spaces giving the variety of visual delights experienced in the gardens of the Villa Garzoni (see Figure 2.06f).

Other layouts utilize arbours and pergolas as frameworks to surround open gardens. The Italianate theme at Hever follows this example, as shown in Figure 13.03c. The views in Figures 13.01f–i highlight seminal historic designs, and the significant features are as follows.

The arbours constructed for the shaded

a Pergola between walls

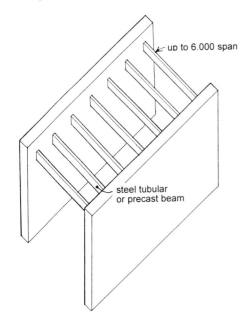

↙ up to 6.000 span

steel tubular
or precast beam

b Pergola built with joist ends running through

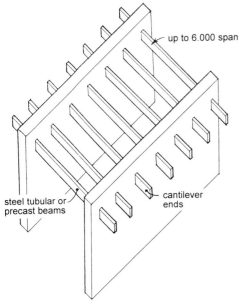

↙ up to 6.000 span

steel tubular or
precast beams

cantilever
ends

c Steel beams

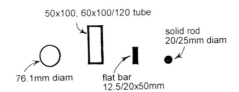

50x100, 60x100/120 tube

solid rod
20/25mm diam

76.1mm diam

flat bar
12.5/20x50mm

d Precast concrete beams

standard
aluminium
channel

200/225/250/300
depths

3.000 to
6.000 span

standard precast
prestressed concrete joists
natural grey concrete finish
usually painted to
protect reinforcement

50mm thickness

e Well-made concrete
pergola at Cement
and Concrete
Headquarters, Wexham
Springs
Buckinghamshire

e

vistas at the Boboli Gardens, Florence resemble the idealized arch made below an avenue of trees – a parabolic curve, not semi-circular. Trees as diverse as lime, plane or poplar can be pleached over a metal framework in a variety of forms, curved or rectangular. The view shown in Figure 13.01f is one of the twin vistas rising from the Pitti Palace to the hills opposite. The notion of art imitating nature is epitomized at the Jardin de Plantes, Paris (Figure 13.01g). Here, the plane trees planted after the siege of Paris have iron supports, and this profile coupled with adroit pruning has formed a natural arch. Architectural ideas for arbours more often assume built forms, with trellises and curving rafters simulating outdoor rooms and following French seventeenth-century taste. The garden constructions at Versailles and Potsdam (Figure 13.01h) share common features, particularly the pair of pavilions to the east and west of Sans Souci. Their excellent condition results from careful reconstruction carried out in the 1970s. The eventual 'green' appearance will resemble the arboreal palaces placed alongside Het Loo in the early 1980s (Figure 13.01). There, historic renewal is based upon surviving drawings of the works undertaken by Jacob Roman (former sculptor appointed to William III for the gardens at Het Loo and Dieven) from 1687 onwards.

13.03 Pergolas propped against or over walls

a Pergola propped against a façade. Maison Columbier L'Hameau, Versailles (1770)

a

13.2 Pergola Construction

The generic forms of construction are given below in order of complexity:

- Spanning between walls (Figures 13.02a—e)
- Propped against or over walls (Figures 13.03a—g)
- Free-standing structures carried on piers and/or columns (Figures 13.04a—e)
- Free-standing timber post and beam frames (Figures 13.05a—e)
- Free-standing metal frames, usually made for arbours (Figures 13.06a—g)

The simplest concept consists of existing walls or buildings bridged by pergola beams, resembling an outdoor room or passage that is largely open to the sky. Timbers solidly embedded into external masonry are subject to the ravages of wet rot. This also occurs where timber is in face contact with wet construction.

b Pergola propped against a wall

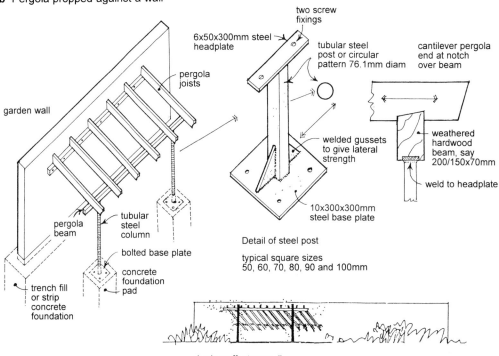

two screw fixings

6x50x300mm steel headplate

pergola joists

garden wall

tubular steel post or circular pattern 76.1mm diam

cantilever pergola end at notch over beam

welded gussets to give lateral strength

weathered hardwood beam, say 200/150x70mm

weld to headplate

pergola beam

tubular steel column

bolted base plate

concrete foundation pad

10x300x300mm steel base plate

trench fill or strip concrete foundation

Detail of steel post

typical square sizes
50, 60, 70, 80, 90 and 100mm

shadow effect on wall

c Bolted wall plate with gap to wall

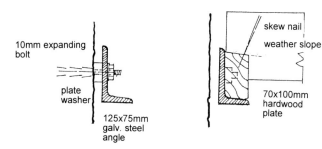

10mm expanding bolt

plate washer

125x75mm galv. steel angle

skew nail

weather slope

70x100mm hardwood plate

d Use of galvanized steel joist hanger

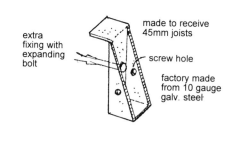

extra fixing with expanding bolt

made to receive 45mm joists

screw hole

factory made from 10 gauge galv. steel

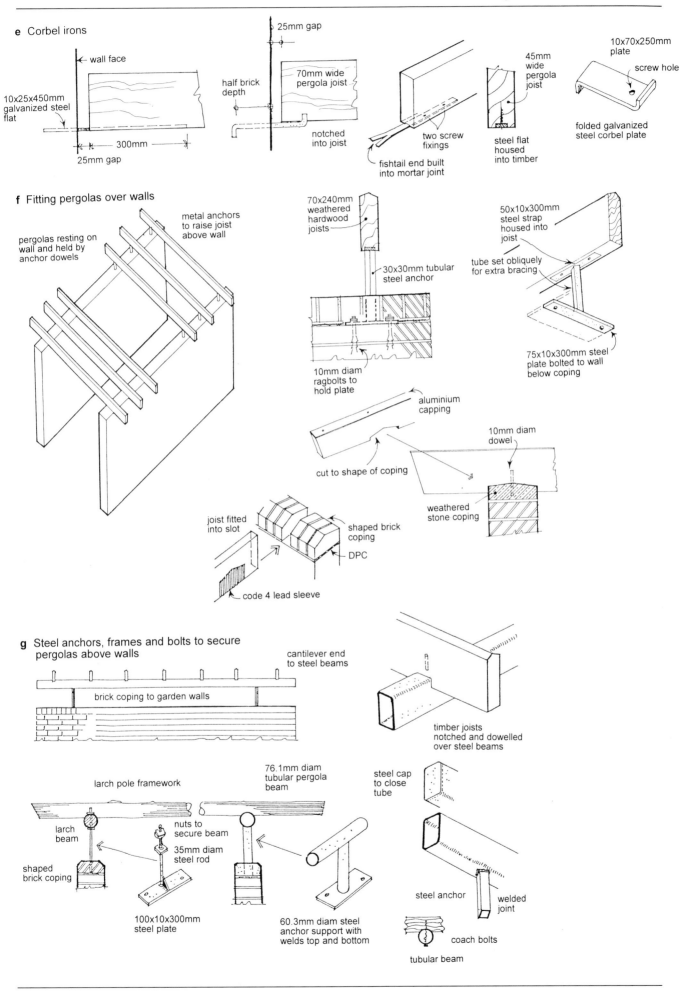

e Corbel irons

wall face

10x25x450mm galvanized steel flat

300mm

25mm gap

25mm gap

half brick depth

70mm wide pergola joist

notched into joist

two screw fixings

fishtail end built into mortar joint

45mm wide pergola joist

steel flat housed into timber

10x70x250mm plate

screw hole

folded galvanized steel corbel plate

f Fitting pergolas over walls

pergolas resting on wall and held by anchor dowels

metal anchors to raise joist above wall

70x240mm weathered hardwood joists

30x30mm tubular steel anchor

10mm diam ragbolts to hold plate

50x10x300mm steel strap housed into joist

tube set obliquely for extra bracing

75x10x300mm steel plate bolted to wall below coping

aluminium capping

cut to shape of coping

10mm diam dowel

weathered stone coping

joist fitted into slot

shaped brick coping

DPC

code 4 lead sleeve

g Steel anchors, frames and bolts to secure pergolas above walls

cantilever end to steel beams

brick coping to garden walls

timber joists notched and dowelled over steel beams

larch pole framework

76.1mm diam tubular pergola beam

steel cap to close tube

larch beam

nuts to secure beam

35mm diam steel rod

shaped brick coping

100x10x300mm steel plate

60.3mm diam steel anchor support with welds top and bottom

steel anchor

welded joint

coach bolts

tubular beam

165

Designers therefore look to more permanent materials such as precast concrete or galvanized tubular steel for pergola beams. Figures 13.02a—c show locations and materials for built-in details. Precast joists are made for domestic floor construction and have inadequate cover to the embedded steel reinforcement for pergola applications, therefore it is necessary either to paint the concrete for protection or to specify galvanized steel or stainless reinforcement bars. Standard tubular steel can be factory-finished with a phosphate primer, but this does not apply to the interior faces nor to cut ends, so better rust protection will be necessary. It is customary for tubular sections to be capped with welded plugs or plastic caps and for the external faces to be hot zinc-dipped. The same precautions should be used for solid rods or flat bars assembled as pergolas.

Precast concrete beams can simulate natural stone but tend to darken with exposure. Figure 13.02e shows a well-made concrete pergola after 15 years' weathering, giving a result close in tonal value to stonemasonry. Another advantage of precast work is that it is resistant to vandalism.

13.3   Pergolas Propped Against or Over Walls

The propped pergola is often utilized to relieve a dull run of walling or to give a feature which defines entries or particular windows on a façade, as at Versailles (Figure 13.03a). The rotting problem with embedded timbers is similar to that already described in Section 13.2. The construction tends to occur as an embellishment after buildings have been completed. The designer therefore relies on fixings that are bolted in place for the pergola (Figures 13.03b—d) rather than built-in construction, which may disturb existing walls. The free-standing framework erected away from the wall supports needs to have firm base fixings to give longitudinal strength. A clear gap of at least 25 mm is sufficient to prevent wet rot occurring in timber that is placed in proximity to external masonry or paving. The wall to beam interface can be achieved by inserting expanding bolts with distance washers or nuts, as shown in Figure 13.03c.[1] These will securely fix a wall plate – a bearing timber run parallel to the wall – but will separate the wood face from the masonry.

Galvanized steel joist hangers, as shown in Figure 13.03d, can be used for each pergola timber bearing. Iron corbels or bars (Figure 13.03e) can be used instead but are expensive to fabricate, and their installation involves accurate and skilled work.

Construction which overlaps masonry is easier to install and has the advantage of providing a decorative and planted canopy when seen from the opposite side. Anchoring the pergola beams can depend upon a rebated fit between the timbers and the coping bricks. A lead undersleeve is inserted as a damp-proof layer to separate the woodwork from damp masonry, as shown in Figure 13.03f. Lifting the beams to give a clear gap above the wall, as in Figure 13.03g, is another method. Stability will, however, have to depend upon a steel subframe or upon steel anchors firmly fixed to each timber and to the wall below, using welded base plates and a pair of inset expanding bolts set into the walling.

13.4   Free-standing Structures Carried on Piers, etc

The Italianate tradition has already been described in Section 13.1. The significant advantage of the hollow masonry piers developed at Hever (see Figure 13.01e) is the fact that the self-weight is reduced, thus reducing the risk of overturning. The hollow box form is buttressed within its own geometry at the corners and is superior to solid piers, which usually have rubble cores which add nothing to the overall stability. Minimal dimensions could be 675 mm for half-brick skins or 900 mm for single-brickwork drums. Infilling with reinforced concrete will produce a stronger structure, and the brickwork could form an armature for the reinforced element. The combination of vertical steel bars and the concrete core provides a composite structure where the steel members take care of tensile or bending stresses and the concrete and brick casing takes the compression loading. Figures 13.04a—c show hollow and reinforced masonry piers, while Figures 13.04d—e show details of large-scale pergola frames acting as a tartan grid which expands the design concept in any direction. Ladder frames are often used with the main beams, and these are installed in duplicate, with the cross-rafters (called ladders) arranged to support climbing plants.

a Half brick skins to hollow piers

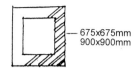

675x675mm
900x900mm

b Full brick drums

750/900mm diam.

c Half brick armatures to reinforced concrete cores.

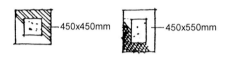

450x450mm   450x550mm

d Tartan grid with main beams connecting to piers and cross members to form a ladder frame.

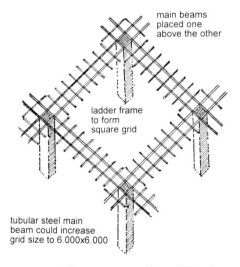

main beams placed one above the other

ladder frame to form square grid

tubular steel main beam could increase grid size to 6.000x6.000

e Variation on tartan grid

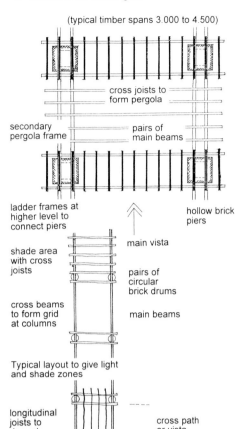

(typical timber spans 3.000 to 4.500)

cross joists to form pergola

secondary pergola frame

pairs of main beams

ladder frames at higher level to connect piers

hollow brick piers

shade area with cross joists

main vista

pairs of circular brick drums

cross beams to form grid at columns

main beams

Typical layout to give light and shade zones

longitudinal joists to demark cross vista

cross path or vista

13.04 Free-standing structures carried on piers/columns

13.5 Free-standing Timber Post and Beam Frames

Standard kits

These are favoured for small gardens or where space is at a premium. The DIY market offers pergola kits which embrace differing styles and are much in evidence in the speculative housing that is a feature of international garden exhibitions in the UK. Figure 13.05a shows a typical example.

Base fixings

Rigidity depends upon the timber framing, but the critical element is the post–to–ground

13.05 Free-standing timber post and beam frames

a Standardized pergola kit at Liverpool International Garden Exhibition (1983)

13.05b Rigid base supports to pergola posts

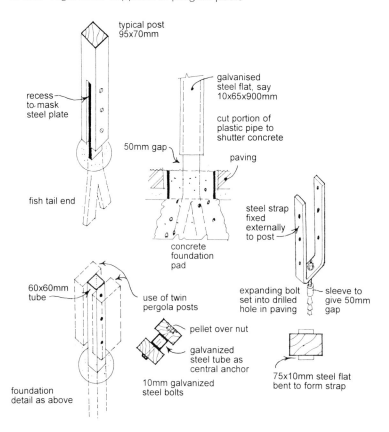

typical post
95x70mm

recess
to mask
steel plate

fish tail end

galvanised
steel flat, say
10x65x900mm

cut portion of
plastic pipe to
shutter concrete

50mm gap

paving

concrete
foundation
pad

steel strap
fixed
externally
to post

expanding bolt
set into drilled
hole in paving

sleeve to
give 50mm
gap

60x60mm
tube

use of twin
pergola posts

pellet over nut

galvanized
steel tube as
central anchor

10mm galvanized
steel bolts

foundation
detail as above

75x10mm steel flat
bent to form strap

c Head frame fixings

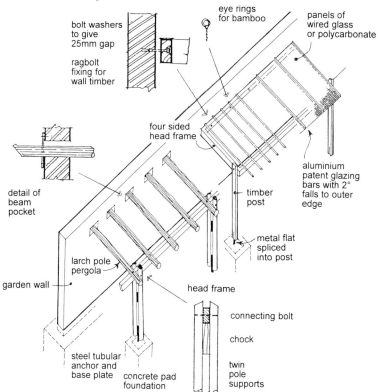

bolt washers
to give
25mm gap

ragbolt
fixing for
wall timber

eye rings
for bamboo

panels of
wired glass
or polycarbonate

four sided
head frame

detail of
beam
pocket

timber
post

aluminium
patent glazing
bars with 2°
falls to outer
edge

metal flat
spliced
into post

larch pole
pergola

garden wall

head frame

connecting bolt

chock

steel tubular
anchor and
base plate

concrete pad
foundation

twin
pole
supports

connection, which has to be firmly made to keep the frame upright and prevent it distorting.

A steel fishplate or shoe is the sturdier solution and avoids the problem of contact between wooden posts and wet ground. Figure 13.05b shows the principles which are explained below:

- Fishplates are often the simplest answer, and can be fitted on site, provided that the maximum post dimension is 100 mm. The post will need to be propped and stayed. It is possible to contain the concrete foundation neatly by casting the upper section within a plastic/clayware pipe.
- U-Shaped straps/shoes are preferred on engineering grounds since there is less likelihood of splitting the post when under strain. These require greater accuracy if the fixing bolt is pre-fixed into paving or base slabs. However, the pre-assembly of strap, post and anchor bolt permits the concrete base to be cast as the last operation, with the final paving unit cut around the bolt shank.
- Tubular bases are used ideally as a space-filler between twin pergola posts. They are not recommended as a sleeve fitted to the base of posts due to the risk of rot in the hidden timber work. Welded shoe boxes, although neat in appearance, also cause problems with rotting of post ends where open drainage and ventilation cannot occur.

Head fixings

Head frames require secure bolting and reinforcement using sawtooth washers or triangulation. Figure 13.05c shows various solutions for these fixings. Angled struts between posts and the horizontal frames may look clumsy but are effective in giving rigid framing.

Weathering details

The exposed surfaces of wooden pergola beams need to be shaped or clad to protect them from weathering, unless oak or chestnut is used.

Rounded poles or beams will throw off rain, and work well where larch poles are made up as pergola frames. An outstanding example is the work at Hever (see Figures 13.01c–e).

Cappings can be either timber or metal – the former resemble fence cappings for close-boarded fencing and are usually run with oak or chestnut moulded timbers.

Metal trim is used for flashing details for roof edges and are fabricated by metalsmiths or plumbers from folded sections of 14-gauge aluminium or zinc sheet, which can be machine-folded on a workbench into complex shapes. They can be secretly fixed using undersleeves, as shown in Figure 13.05d. The simplest answer is to obtain cut lengths of aluminium (in either 10 or 8 gauge) which has been guillotined into flat strips of the width required. A slight overhang of 4–5 mm will improve the appearance and prevent streaking. Most sheet matals can be worked in lengths up to 3 m. Joints can be butted, but undersleeves are preferred where full weather protection is needed. Figure 13.05d shows different materials and fixing methods.

The aesthetics of trimming the ends of pergola beams and rafters are governed by practical considerations. Overhanging timbers permit bolt holes to be made at a distance from the ends of members, thereby reducing the risk of splitting at bolt positions. End rot may occur, but a generous overhang allows trimming without sacrificing strength. The cantilever effect of extended timbers permits an overhang equal to one-third of the span without causing undue stressing. Finally, the splay-cutting of overhung ends will give some protection to the exposed end grain, which has greater susceptibility to rot than the vertical exposure of timber. The interface between post, main beam and rafter can be bolted through from more than one direction. This procedure, coupled with toothed washers, provides a non-slip connection between the timbers and is equal in strength to conventional triangulation (Figure 13.05e).

Timbers need to be specified according to the anticipated life span of the components and the finish required. The following data is given for general guidance, but it must be noted that a mixture of timbers is often selected according to the structural role adopted.

Posts Oak, teak or jarrah will provide the maximum life span (100 years or more) and will need minimal treatment if kept clear of the ground.

Main beams The hardwoods listed for use as posts will perform well, though oak in small profiles tends to twist when not restrained.

13.05d Pergola shapes and cappings

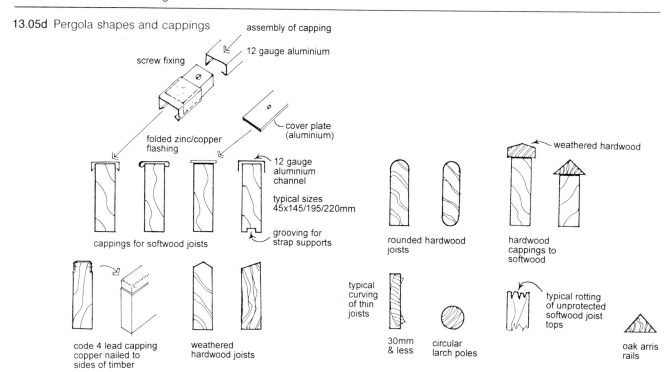

assembly of capping

screw fixing

12 gauge aluminium

cover plate (aluminium)

folded zinc/copper flashing

12 gauge aluminium channel

typical sizes
45x145/195/220mm

grooving for strap supports

cappings for softwood joists

rounded hardwood joists

weathered hardwood

hardwood cappings to softwood

code 4 lead capping copper nailed to sides of timber

weathered hardwood joists

typical curving of thin joists

30mm & less

circular larch poles

typical rotting of unprotected softwood joist tops

oak arris rails

e Assembly of post, beam and rafter components.

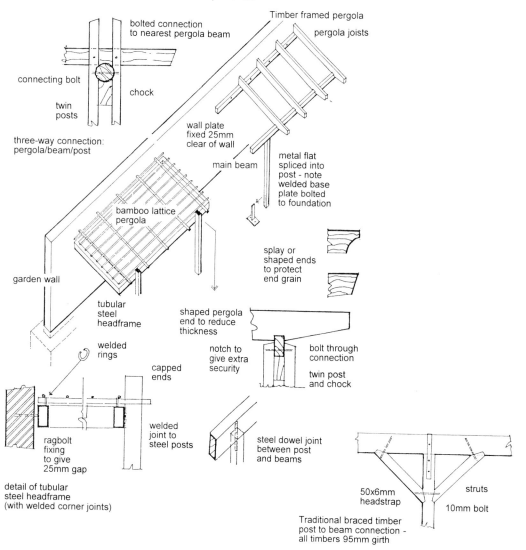

bolted connection to nearest pergola beam

Timber framed pergola

pergola joists

connecting bolt

chock

twin posts

three-way connection: pergola/beam/post

wall plate fixed 25mm clear of wall

main beam

metal flat spliced into post - note welded base plate bolted to foundation

bamboo lattice pergola

garden wall

tubular steel headframe

welded rings

capped ends

splay or shaped ends to protect end grain

shaped pergola end to reduce thickness

notch to give extra security

bolt through connection

twin post and chock

ragbolt fixing to give 25mm gap

welded joint to steel posts

steel dowel joint between post and beams

detail of tubular steel headframe (with welded corner joints)

50x6mm headstrap

struts

10mm bolt

Traditional braced timber post to beam connection - all timbers 95mm girth

Softwoods such as impregnated larch or Douglas fir will last 60–70 years provided the details avoid water pockets. Top protection by metal or oak cappings will prolong life. Impregnated European redwood is liable to rot at joints and where lapped over other timbers.

Rafters These are usually constructed from softwoods such as impregnated larch or Douglas fir. Bamboo provides a slender and strong rafter timber with a life span of 20–30 years. Keruing, often used for decking, makes an excellent roof batten frame where shade screens are required.

13.6 Free-standing Metal Frames and Arbours

Metal framing in steel tubular sections imparts higher strength than timber, and the connections can be made by welding the components together. Such construction is fire-resistant and vandalproof and should be considered for public areas in urban landscape.

Standard kits

Railing manufacturers such as Orsogril (see Chapter 8.2 and Figures 8.02g) fabricate curved and rectangular pergola frames as standard assemblies for urban landscape intended as free-standing items such as those featured in Figure 13.06a. The steel grilles are galvanized and enamelled or plastic-coated, with stainless fastenings where units are connected together.

Purpose-made frames

Purpose-made frames are supported by steel tubular verticals connected by head frames which make up rectangular platorms. Steel bars, straining wires, precast beams or larch poles overlay the head frame to carry climbing plants. The use of tubular steel posts is often combined with timber head frames where additional security is needed in public areas. The details given in Figure 13.06b–c cover a range of constructional forms and include arched arbours that are traditionally made from steel flats and rods. External steelwork in landscape constructions such as pergolas needs to be galvanized after manufacture and should

13.06 Free-standing metal frames and arbours

a Standard kits for pergola construction

a Standard kits for pergola construction

b Purpose made pergola supports and head frames.

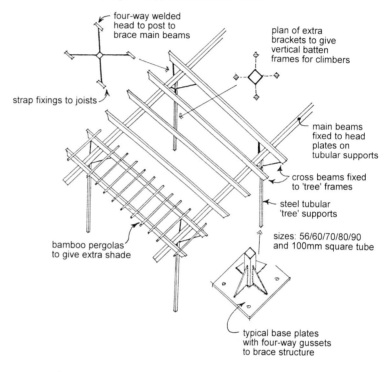

four-way welded head to post to brace main beams

plan of extra brackets to give vertical batten frames for climbers

strap fixings to joists

main beams fixed to head plates on tubular supports

cross beams fixed to 'tree' frames

steel tubular 'tree' supports

sizes: 56/60/70/80/90 and 100mm square tube

bamboo pergolas to give extra shade

typical base plates with four-way gussets to brace structure

c Traditional arbour frames formed with steel rods and flat bars.

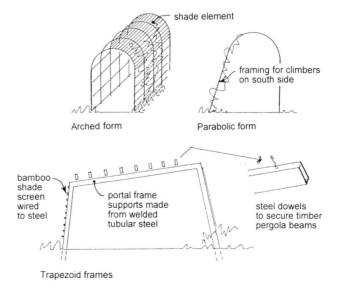

shade element

framing for climbers on south side

Arched form

Parabolic form

bamboo shade screen wired to steel

portal frame supports made from welded tubular steel

steel dowels to secure timber pergola beams

Trapezoid frames

be plastic-coated (in a similar manner to chain link material). Alternatively the zinc coating should be factory-treated with a 'mordant' solution to improve paint bonding. The decoration could be conventional brush-applied paints but, increasingly, steel products are factory-finished with powder coatings, fired to give an enamel surface (see Section 9.11 for further details).

13.7   Other Examples of Pergola Design

Shade screen

The ferns and shade-loving plants are protected by slatted screens mounted above pergola beams in this example, (Figure 13.07a), and

the same screening is extended to part of the open-air restaurant to give summer shading. The main beams are laminated timber with metallic cappings, while the slats are made from a durable hardwood, like keruing.

Light and shade pergola

The Huntington Gardens at Pasadena, LA, simulate examples of landscape worldwide (Figure 13.07b). The English rose garden has extensive pergolas to suggest a Lutyens setting, but also to provide shelter from the glare of the summer sun. The framework is of generous proportion, using a tartan grid of beams so that the 'window' to the open sky is limited in extent. The timber is untreated redwood (native to the West Coast), a superb, durable timber which weathers to a silver grey colour.

13.07 Other examples of pergola designs

a Shade screen for outdoor terrace, Louisiana Museum, Denmark (1958). Architects: Jorgan Bo & Wilkelm Wohlest
b Light and shade pergola, Huntington Gardens, Pasedena, Los Angeles, California (1980)
c Lattice construction of posts and beams. Lower terrace garden, Bodnant, North Wales (1908)
d Serpentine spine pergola frame separating car park from shopping arcade, Heritage Close, Stony Stratford Buckinghamshire (1978)
e Steel tubular frames. Freely-planned trapezoid pergola frames, Rhine Park, International Garden Show, Cologne (1956)
f Glazed pergolas. Glass-covered walkways, St Catherine's College, Oxford (1964). Architect: Arne Jacobsen

Lattice construction of posts and beams

A remarkable piece of construction (Figure 13.07c) where lattice structures are applied to both vertical and horizontal members for the terrace pergolas at Bodnant Gardens, North Wales. The larch was grown locally and pressure-impregnated with copper-based preservatives. It is still in fine condition due to the open quality of the construction and the way built-in timber has been avoided. Small pieces of code 4 lead (4 lb) were placed as damp-proof courses wherever post members rested on stone bases or copings.

Serpentine spine

A similar concept to Bodnant, with a serpentine spine serving as a dividing screen within an open area (Figure 13.07d), this time in a car park separated by a raised planted screen from the shopping mall arcade called Heritage Close, Stony Stratford, Buckinghamshire. The materials are stained and impregnated Douglas fir throughout, with metal dowels used as anchors to concrete pad foundations.

Steel tubular frames

Steel tube has significant advantages over timberwork in pergola construction (Figure 13.07e). Firstly, the size of members can be minimal, and similar-sized spars can be framed together as trussed components. This gives a lightness of construction that is a far cry from the classical approach using piers and beams which suggest a colonnade (for comparison see Figure 13.01b). The sense of light and openness is captured by the freely-sited pergola frames at the Rhine Park in central Cologne. The designs form a stepped central feature to embrace a water cascade. The white paint is retained as an accent for all artefacts within the park other than boundary walls or permanent buildings.

Glazed pergolas

Water drip and lack of protection are the usual complaints concerning open pergolas adjoining buildings. It is, however, possible to combine the lightness of construction seen at Cologne with glazed covering (Figure 13.07f). The glazing forms are rectangular, similar to greenhouse roofing, and can be laid almost horizontal if the panes are mastic-sealed and limited to single lengths of glass. St Catherine's College, Oxford is distinguished by open-sided pergolas formed with slender brick piers surmounted by tubular steelwork frames and long runs of patent glazing, namely aluminium T-bars with wired glazing panels. Clipped yew hedges create 'green' breaks in the covered way in lieu of creepers which are left to climb the 'blind' end walls of nearby façades.

14 PLANTERS

The use of containers or pots for plants is illustrated in the wall paintings at Pompeii, which suggests a Mediterranean tradition that may be as old as garden history itself. The continuity in this theme can be seen by comparing Pompeiian views (Figure 14.01a) with those of the reconstructed gardens of Alcazar in Seville (Figure 14.01b). The lineage between Spanish and Italian gardens helps to explain the prevalence of planted pots in the Italianate manner used on buildings or in landscape (Figure 14.01c−d). For further examples see Figures 2.06a−c and 2.06f and the descriptions in Section 2.3. Large clayware pots have the advantage of greater depth for root development than the bowl or saucer pattern favoured for concrete or glass-reinforced cement (GRC) planters. The other disadvantage of cement-based materials is their lack of absorbency and their tendency to dry out and overheat.

14.01 Pots and containers

a House of Vettî Pompei
b Pots in reconstructed garden of the Alcazar, Seville. (Foundations to garden date back to twelfth century)
c Italianate pots from Chatsworth Derbyshire

d Use of clayware pots fixed to balcony railing, in Seville

e Sorensen's method of making timber pots for Tivoli Gardens, Copenhagen. (early1940's)

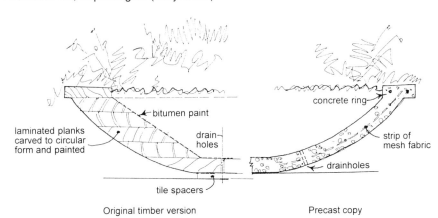

laminated planks carved to circular form and painted — bitumen paint — drain-holes — tile spacers

Original timber version

concrete ring — strip of mesh fabric — drainholes

Precast copy

14.1   Precast Planters

The development of reinforced concrete is said to date back to 1868 with Monnier's efforts at Versailles to make concrete pots for the palace gardens, which it was hoped would be more frostproof than clayware. The advantages of cement-based products (made as precast reinforced units or from cement fibre castings) are high strength coupled with frost-resistance. The problem of drying out can be overcome using automatic time/temperature controlled irrigation systems which trickle water to containers connected to a ring of plastic piping. Replacing plants can be eased by the use of sub-containers (metal mesh or corrugated plastic) which can be changed over by the gardening staff. The shell-shaped saucers associated with the 1950s were first envisaged as carved timber forms by the designer C. T. Sorensen to enliven Tivoli Gardens in wartime Copenhagen. They were cast made from laminated timber moulds as shown in Figure 14.01e, and the form was adopted by precasters and makers of GRC products in the 1950s (Figure 14.01f). Present-day products use interchangeable trays to allow for irrigation and maintenance. The modules also allow composite collections of units to form a complete group of garden furniture, including seats, tables, pools and stepped planters. One of the best designs is the range of units developed for the city of Munich in 1972. Figures 14.02a–b show individual planters and their integration into street

14.01f Standard precast dished planters

furniture. Glass-reinforced polyester (GRP) is also moulded for planters, but is usually reserved for indoor use due to the glossy finish which wears badly outdoors. GRP items can be formed with internal reservoirs and automatic watering controls. In the Netherlands, large-scale GRP planters up to 3 m in diameter are fabricated with a matt finish, and have the advantage of urban scale, as shown in Figure 14.02c. These large pots

are made with wire reinforcement and can be shifted by fork-lift truck.

Designers will probably wish to create plant containers in materials which are appropriate to the context of the garden and masonry and timber frames are often employed. The GRC and GRP planters already mentioned are useful as liners, particularly where irrigation systems have to be considered. Figure 14.02d shows an installation relying on this approach. The history of moveable containers dates to the wooden boxes said to be developed for the Orangery at Versailles in the seventeenth century (Figure 1.07b), where sturdy timber boxes were made, complete with lead liners. Wrought iron sockets were fitted to either side to accept liftingshafts, and today fork-lifts are used instead of manual labour. The timber framing was also arranged with hinged or sliding loose panels so that potbound roots could be pruned.

14.02 GRC and GRP forms

a Modules of GRC units
b Integration of planters and seating as a complete system of street furniture, Munich (1972)
c Large-scale GRP planters in a pedestrianized street in Holland
d Use of precast concrete enclosures for GRP containers

a

c

b

d

15 GARDEN LIGHTING

15.1 Functional and Aesthetic Factors

The best effects of exterior lighting should equal the success of stage lighting. Darkness can be the starting point for both processes, the illumination brought to bear on dramatizing scenes and emphasizing the character of a setting. An obvious device is the juxtaposition of varying degrees of light and shade, as shown in Figure 15.02g, rather than the glare of floodlighting or the bland overall illumination developed by security firms. Exterior lighting seldom replaces daylight except in sports stadiums. Artificial lighting in the garden is a matter of setting priorities, since running costs will usually dictate that paths and steps take precedence over landscape features. The following guidance covers functional and visual delights in external lighting design. Detailed advice will be needed from lighting engineers – in fact, most fitting suppliers offer a design service which embraces all forms of artificial illumination.

Functional requirements

Definition of paths and steps This includes the provision of emergency lighting where required by local licencing regulations, for example, exit signs in public areas and illumination of steps and ramps where premises and their surroundings are licensed for public entertainment in the UK.

Security lighting This needs to meet insurance requirements, where aesthetic considerations will not figure. It is worth remembering, however, that a well-designed scheme of garden lighting is a good defence against intruders, particularly if sensor-controlled spotlights are included within the layout.

Task lighting This is necessary to allow sufficient local light, for example, to find the keyhole at significant entries or control points for water valves.

Photoperiodic lighting This can be effective in triggering the timing of flowering. Such installations require short periods of illumination, sometimes as little as one or two hours per night. The wave lengths in the red (600–700 nm) and far-red (700–800 nm) regions of the spectrum are important. Advice on lamps used in horticulture can be obtained from leading manufacturers such as Philips Lighting Ltd.

Aesthetic considerations

These include emphasis on principal features, for example, sculpture, specimen trees and waterscapes; the lighting of detail, specific planting areas or foliage effects, and architectural flood- or spotlighting of buildings within the landscape.

Revelation of garden geometry

This is the most inviting endeavour, and one where illusion is easier to achieve than honesty. Blacking out zones of the garden can change the composition and bring a different order to the key elements. Vertical surfaces can be defined, as can texture and the silhouette of planting. Foreground and distant effects can be enhanced with coloured lighting – warm for foreground and cool for distance – while intensity can be adjusted using time-controlled dimmers.

15.2 Equipment

The type of equipment falls into two categories. Functional or task lighting systems are employed for highways, security or for sports grounds. The other ranges of exterior lights seek to combine practical considerations with a better quality of illumination, particularly with indirect lighting which achieves brightness by reflection rather than by aiming direct incident light onto landscape features.

The first consideration is the choice of luminaires, and initial costs need to be set against running expenditure. The great majority of amenity applications use high-pressure discharge lamps, such as SON-E, SON-T, MBF and MBI. GLS lamps were

15.1 Lamp properties and applications

Lamp type	Rating (watts)	Efficacy Range (Lm/W)	Lumen output Range (Lm)	Average rated life (hours)	Control gear	Colour appearance	Colour rendering	Initial costs	Running costs	Exterior lighting applications
G.L.S.	25 to 2,000	10 to 20	250 to 40,000	1,000	No	Warm white	Excellent	Low	High	Decorative lighting Amenity lighting
T.H.D.	300 to 2,000	17 to 22	5,250 to 45,000	2,000	No	Warm white	Excellent	Low	High	General floodlighting Security lighting
PL	5 to 26	50 to 82	230 to 1,650	6,000	Choke or built-in	Warm white	Good	Medium	Low	SL Replacing GLS lamps SL & PL Amenity and Decorative lighting Security lighting
SL	9 to 25	50	450 to 1,200	6,000	Built-in	Warm white	Good	Medium	Low	
MBF/U	50 to 2,000	36 to 58	1,700 to 110,000	9,000	Yes	Intermediate white	Moderate to good	Medium	Medium	Amenity lighting Public lighting General floodlighting
MBF-Delux	50 to 400	40 to 60	1,900 to 22,800	9,000	Yes	Intermediate white	Moderate to good	Medium	Medium	
MBI	250 to 2,000	60 to 85	13,600 to 166,000	4,000	Yes	Cool white	Good to excellent	High	Low	Sports grounds Sports stadia Colour TV transmission Building floodlighting Area floodlighting
SOX	18 to 180	100 to 183	1,750 to 32,300	10,000	Yes	Yellow	Non-existent	High	Low	Road lighting Security lighting
SON-E	50 to 1,000	90 to 130	3,100 to 129,000	9,000+	Yes	Golden white	Moderate	High	Low	Area floodlighting Security lighting General sports lighting High mast lighting Building floodlighting Amenity lighting
SON-T	50 to 1,000	90 to 130	3,100 to 129,000	9,000+	Yes	Golden white	Moderate	High	Low	

commonly installed, but these have been superseded by compact fluorescent sources, owing to their low wattages and longer life. Table 15.1 lays out the various lamp patterns and their applications and characteristics. Lighting columns employing direct incident light vary in size according to lamp power. Table 15.2 provides recommendations for MBH fittings.

The illumination level for amenity and garden lighting is generally low, and uniformity is not important. In general terms, the levels can be between 10−20 lux for average horizontal illuminance to paved entrances and forecourts. Steps need higher values of 20−50 lux with localized fittings, while footpath illuminance can be as low as 5 lux, a recommended minimum where public safety is a factor. In private gardens the level could be 1 lux for terraces, which should just make it possible to detect dangerous obstacles such as kerbs or raised paving slabs. Another consideration is the grading of illumination between the interior and exterior of buildings, and here canopy and porch lights can assist the transition to the external night-time environment.

The type of fittings fall into the following categories:

- Pole-mounted;
- Wall-mounted;
- Bollards, mushroom and inset lights;
- Floodlights (see Section 15.3).

The various fittings and the effects achieved are described below.

Pole-mounted fittings

These are derived from highway and pavement lighting. They are valuable in providing a spread of horizontal illumination. Baffles or shields within the fitting can focus the beam in a particular direction (Figure 15.01c). Double-headed or twin-lamp fittings are useful where dual-purpose illumination is needed − for example, full lighting when large numbers of

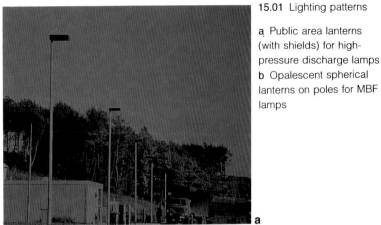

15.01 Lighting patterns

a Public area lanterns (with shields) for high-pressure discharge lamps
b Opalescent spherical lanterns on poles for MBF lamps

people are present in public spaces, or a background effect on less busy occasions. Opalescent and clear spheres have a decorative quality in day and night-time conditions, and multiple heads give a chandelier effect (Figures 15.01a−e). These are useful to signify routes through landscape areas, with dual or multiple fittings placed at significant points. Polycarbonate is the normal specification for lanterns, to counter vandalism.

Wall-mounted fittings

These fittings are similar to pole-mounted equipment, but are provided with adjustable brackets for wall mounting, either face- or corner-fixed. Reflection from walls is a useful asset and can often enhance planting schemes. The use of clear glass spheres also provides upward lighting effects and looks attractive

15.2 Recommended lamp oupput/mounting heights

Lamp	Luminous power (lm)	Mounting Height (m)
50w SON: 80w MBF	3,000 to 4,000	3m to 4m
70w: 100w SON: 125w MBF	5000 to 10,000	5m to 6m
150w SON: 250w MBF	12,000 +	8m and above

Tables 15.1 and 15.2 reprinted by kind permission of Abacus Municipal Ltd

c Clustered glass fittings for clear MBF lamps
d Wall bracket light with polycarbonate lantern
e Similar fitting to 1501 d, shown at night
f Decorative glass fitting
g Small-scale bollard light at path edge. Compare with illustrations 502 d and 602 g where shielded lenses are used
h Mushroom light used to provide low-level floodlighting
i Mushroom light used at 'change point' in path

c

g

d

h

e

f

i

under tree canopies. Shields and baffles are made to fit the luminaire so that lighting can be focused downwards, upwards or obliquely. Figures 15.01d—e show clear glass spherical fittings in day and night-time conditions. Note the brightness, which is valuable at entries to buildings. A decorative lantern is shown in Figure 15.01f which illustrates the advantage of using a white wall for reflection.

Bollard, mushroom and inset lights

Low-level fixtures are the most commonly-used garden lights, and have the advantage that horizontal surfaces and steps can be accented without competing with floodlighting or the utilitarian tasks performed by pole-mounted fittings. Bollard lanterns (see Section 5.4) are particularly useful as they are constructed in a robust manner with protected light sources.

j

k

The inset lenses permit a high standard of horizontal illumination which is valuable in traffic and pedestrian areas (see Figure 15.01h). They also make useful markers in the illumination of gardens, where lighting can serve for paths and steps and enhance the adjacent planting. A typical car park bollard is shown in Figure 5.02c, while Figure 15.01g shows a pathside bollard light. Smaller versions resemble mushrooms in form and provide accent lighting for plant displays or at 'change points' in the garden path network. Figures 15.01h—i show typical applications. The 'Span' housing estates designed by Lyons and Cunningham in the UK were developed on the Radburn layout with vehicular traffic separated from pedestrian.[1] The lighting arrangements adopted a similar division — column lights for roads and low-level illumination for paths. Figure 15.01j shows a mushroom light signalling the pedestrian route. Low-level inset lights can be used where walking routes follow walls, as at St Catherine's College, Oxford (see Figure 15.01k). 'Lighting bricks' and louvred lights are widely available and ideal for tasks such as illuminating steps and changes of level. Handrails made from channel-shaped aluminium or steel sections can accommodate continuous tube lights and provide brighter levels of illumination for escape stairs in public areas. A twin system of lights can be readily installed in handrail lights where a separate emergency system is specified by licensing authorities.[2]

a Garden floodlighting

fully adjustable mounting

screw fixings to base

long range floodlight

b

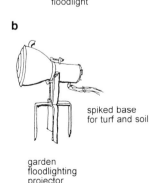

spiked base for turf and soil

garden floodlighting projector

15.01j Mushroom lights etc.
k Lights built into wall at low level is light path. St Catherine's College. A. Jacobson.

15.02 Floodlights

15.02d Recessed lighting

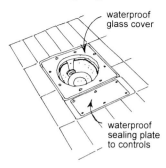

waterproof glass cover

waterproof sealing plate to controls

c Trough floodlights

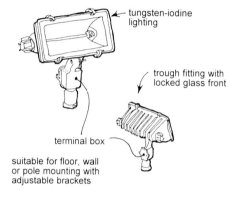

tungsten-iodine lighting

trough fitting with locked glass front

terminal box

suitable for floor, wall or pole mounting with adjustable brackets

e 12V luminaire box

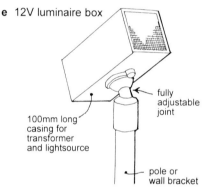

fully adjustable joint

100mm long casing for transformer and lightsource

pole or wall bracket

f Uplighting with a single floodlight

15.3 Floodlights

The equipment needs to be robust and guaranteed to be weatherproof, or waterproof where used for fountain and pool lighting. Figures 15.02a–e show the principal forms, but specialist suppliers need to be consulted for the appropriate specification for each context.

Garden floodlights

The basic tool is a mobile fitting with a spiked base. The wiring can be run over the ground surface to a waterproof insulated socket so that the fitting and cables can be stored when not required (see Figure 15.02a).

Long-range floodlights

These are usually heavier, permanent installations with lenses chosen for specific tasks, permanently wired to underground cabling. The fittings are made for ground, roof or wall mounting (see Figure 15.02b).

Floodlighting troughs

These are general-purpose fixtures designed to spread lighting over vertical surfaces or to feature shrubs and trees. They are wired permanently and made for ground or pole mounting (see Figure 15.02c). The cosmetic appearance of such equipment is seldom considered by makers and will need to be masked by planting or screens.

Recessed lighting

Many imported fittings are far superior to British-made items in terms of housing and neat appearance (see Figure 15.02d). Hydrel of California fabricate a wide range of special fittings for burial in paving or for underwater lighting, and give long-term guarantees of performance.

12–2 volt luminaire boxes

Another product from the USA is a fitting (which is here adapted to the UK market) and that includes a weather-protected transformer to power 6- or 12-volt light sources (Figure 15.02e). The 100 mm long unit is designed to be concealed amongst planting. British manufacturers are looking at similar

g

h

i

g Multiple floodlighting
h Horizontal lighting
i Silhouette lighting
j Floating restaurants
at the Swiss National
Exhibition, Lausanne
(1964)

j

applications for small-scale garden fittings. Figures 15.02f–j demonstrate the effects obtained with various garden floodlights.

Uplighting The basic application uses a mobile spotlight, as shown in Figure 15.02a, but directed vertically to uplight foliage. This method can be applied at key locations in a garden and changed according to the season (Figure 15.02f).

Multiple floodlights Multiple flood-lights enable the designer to create a sequence of spatial effects. Foreground lighting of pools or planters can be accomplished using fittings mounted high on a nearby building, with middle-ground features, such as trees, lit by spotlights hidden in the foliage. Distant items can be lit locally or by long-focus spotlights mounted on the rear of the tree. The boundary fence on the right is separately lit to define the edge of the night view (Figure 15.02g).

Horizontal lighting The lighting of horizontal surfaces from a hidden source is of great assistance in the surroundings to buildings. The shielded fittings can be tree or wall-mounted, and help to bridge the difference between interior and exterior. They can also serve as reflectors if water features are present (Figure 15.02h).

Silhouette lighting This is one of the most attractive forms of garden lighting, where a group of shrubs or a sculpture are lit in contrast to a dark background and where the 'frame' of the picture is completed by highlighting the overhang of foliage (Figure 15.02i).

Floodlighting of water features using uplighters, illuminated forms and mirror images is the most dramatic type of garden lighting, Figure 15.02h shows the Swiss National Exhibition at Lausanne, where the floating restaurants were the main night-time attraction of the lakeside setting.

15.4 Wiring

It is customary for the fuse boxes for outdoor lighting circuits to be separate from internal systems, and cables are usually terminated in weatherproof outlet boxes. Weatherproofing is essential for all exterior light fittings, as is efficient earthing. Permanent external lighting installations for public areas should be connected to cable runs buried in the ground to a depth of 450 mm and identified by cable covers and marker stones.

There is a choice of three wiring arrangements for private gardens:

- **Pyrotenax cable** – This is the usual choice since it can be laid directly in the ground. Protection is given by PVC sheathing, which should be shielded by tile cable covers. Threading through dry land-drain pipes is another precaution.
- **PVC cable** – This is no longer a popular choice since it needs to be sealed in a continuous metal conduit with an earth continuity conductor. The exterior of galvanized conduit must be painted or bound with bitumen tape if buried underground. Corrosion at cut ends and at junction box connections is a common failing.
- **PVC-sheathed armour cable** – This is the customary specification for connections run on the ground or on the surface of fences and walls. It is also used for temporary installations and for those to be dismantled for storage in winter.

16 WATER DRAINAGE

Surface water and groundwater drainage is one of the first considerations in laying out paving and landscaping. Exposure ratings for sites include rainfall and prevailing wind patterns, and survey details must take into account water tables, substrata, spring lines and watercourses. Information on surface water sewers or other means of disposal can be obtained from the local water authorities. Local water sources such as springs or streams need to be analysed, and sulphate levels checked as this aspect governs the type of cement specified for ground slabs and foundation structures. It is best to seek independent advice for large water engineering projects rather than trusting to data gleaned from trade catalogues. It is essential to calculate the run-off from roofs and paved areas, and general guidance can be found in both BS 8301 (1985) and BS 6367 (1983). Special consideration should be given to acute stormwater run-off from glass- or smooth-faced buildings and from sloping land. Conversion of landscape from a soft environment to hard surfaces provokes the worst problems when existing drains are not renewed to cope with extra discharges from buildings and paving.[1]

16.1 Surface Water Drainage

The initial draining of paved surfaces is achieved by laying to falls to gutters (open-channel or enclosed) and thence to gully outlets. Surface falls reflect the flow characteristics of paving, with the steepest slopes for textured materials and shallow inclines for smooth, and Table 16.1 can be used in conjunction with the fuller appraisal of paving in Chapter 1 to calculate the required falls.

Surface geometry, whether one-way or two-way reverse pyramids, depends upon plan areas. Refer to Figure 16.01 for guidance on applications with surface gutters and gullies. Narrow roads or terraces up to 6 m girth are best drained one-way, but the gutter element will need two-way falls to outlets. This

produces a straightforward construction using a single slope, which suits slab and tilework finishes for terraces. In the examples shown, gutter construction has to allow for level edges at road or terrace sides with sufficient breadth to be shaped as a trough towards the outlet. Detailing with asphalt or with granite setts can achieve these complex forms (see Chapter 1 and Figures 1.06c, 1.11b and 1.12b)

Asphalt, macadam/tar surfacing and cast in-situ concrete paving can be moulded to multiple falls, which enables a standard profile gutter block to be placed alongside round kerbs. The disposal of gullies on a staggered basis spreads the ponding pattern instead of bunching it in the length of the road as in the last illustration for Figure 16.01.

Surface geometry and drainage

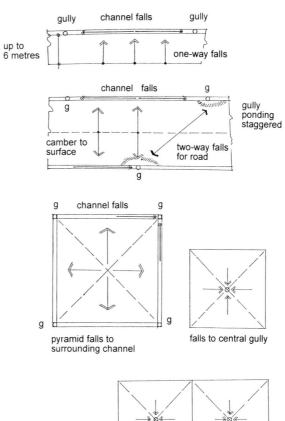

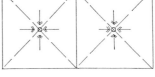

16.01 Surface geometry and drainage

16.1 Surface water drainage

Falls in varying conditions

Concrete	1 and 60 straight cross-fall (50 mm in 3.000) 1 in 100 or 150 for long fall
Bituminous surfaces	1 in 48 camber, 1 in 200 for long fall 1 in 40 straight cross fall 1 in 60 on playgrounds
Gravel	1 in 30, important to prevent puddling and therefore moss
Brick	1 in 60 minimum
Paving slabs	1 in 72 (25 mm in 1.800) minimum is commonly specified. Successful traditional practice suggests more generous falls could often be used without danger of slip.
Public pavements	1 in 48 and 1 in 32 are both common and other cross-falls may be common locally. Check with Local Authority.

a Layout for monsoon and channel drains

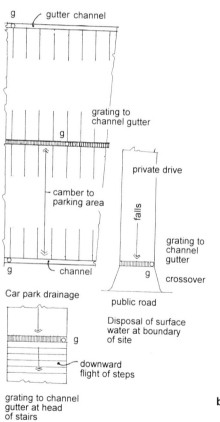

Car park drainage

grating to channel gutter at head of stairs

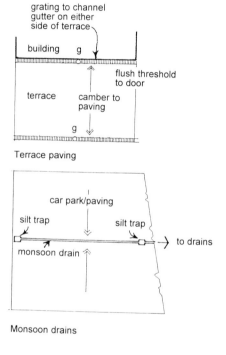

Terrace paving

Monsoon drains

Disposal of surface water at boundary of site

16.02 Monsoon and channel-grid drains

b Technical details for monsoon drains.

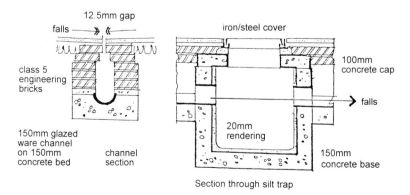

c Channel grid drains

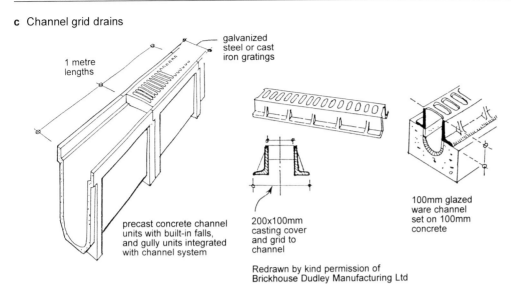

1 metre lengths

galvanized steel or cast iron gratings

precast concrete channel units with built-in falls, and gully units integrated with channel system

200x100mm casting cover and grid to channel

100mm glazed ware channel set on 100mm concrete

Redrawn by kind permission of Brickhouse Dudley Manufacturing Ltd

d Channel-grid drains. (Details extracted from data kindly supplied by Kaskade Drains Ltd)
e Failed channel-grid drain

16.2 Monsoon and Channel-grid Drains

Monsoon and channel-grid drains (Figures 16.02a–c) avoid ponding, the sunk drain drawing the surface water off the road to an underground drainage system. The arrangement of levels is simplified, as monsoon and channel-grid drains have sophisticated inner falls. Gutter grids are set level and the road surfaces formed in straightforward planes. There is less risk of ice patches, in contrast to open-channel gutters.

Monsoon drains are used for storm drainage in the tropics, and for where surface gutters may be misused for rubbish disposal. The construction is robust but labour-intensive, and amounts to a brick-built drain with a foundation slab and glazed-ware channel. Catchpits are placed at 30 m intervals or at junctions, and serve as silt traps as well as providing access points for rodding the channels. Maintenance is a regular problem, and it is significant that the system installed for the pedestrian area of Stevenage, Hertfordshire, has been largely replaced.

Channel-grid drains can be easily maintained as they are equipped with removable grids. The traditional pattern dating from the nineteenth century has a glazed-ware or cast iron channel set in concrete and surmounted by a cast iron frame and loose grid. The sizes are limited to 100, 150 and 225 mm widths of channel. The drainage runs are linked to gully pots equipped with silt buckets. Cast iron drain channels and gullies have a neat architectural style and fit in with the scale of building entries (refer to the details in Figure 2.04c).

Precast units are to be preferred for roads and car parks as grids, channels and gullies are combined in one system of assembly. This design permits the heaviest loads, and a variation on the system shown in Figure 16.02c is used for the aprons at London Heathrow Airport. Cheap alternatives exist which resemble monsoon drains: the units are precast hollow blocks about 250 × 250 × 900 mm long with a small vertical drainage slot within the paving surface. The disadvantages are difficulty in rodding and in keeping the narrow inlet slot free from obstructions.

A great deal of wrack and dirt is washed into surface water drains in gardens and soft landscape. Undersizing quickly leads to blockage, and Figure 16.02d demonstrates the difficulties caused by channels made too small for paving surrounded by planting.

16.3   Surface Water Disposal

There are three methods of disposal:

- **By river or stream** − In the UK permission must be gained from the local water authority, who can insist on petrol gasoline interceptors for car park drainage, and silt traps on exit drains.
- **By surface water sewers** − Permission must be obtained from the local authority or the water authority in the UK. Access chambers will have to be provided at bends and intersections and at the point where the owner's sewer leaves the site. Again petrol/ gasoline interceptors and silt traps may be necessary.
- **By soakaways** − Again permission must be sought from the Local Authority/ Water Authority in the UK. Soakaways are only constructed in permeable sub-soils, and are sited and sized according to legal requirements (see Section 16.7 for details).

The technical details involved in the construction of surface water drains, gullies and access chambers are explained below.

Surface water drains

The domestic layout shown in Figure 16.03a reflects the principles adopted for a drainage layout connected to a public surface water sewer. The final connection from the site boundary to the sewer is made by the responsible authority and taken by a pipe set in a saddle as shown. An access chamber (commonly called a manhole in the UK) must be constructed at the site boundary, and may have to be fitted with an anti-flood valve where back-surge is a problem in river valleys or tidal areas. Access chambers or rodding eyes must be provided at changes of direction and at 45 m intervals in straight runs so that drain rods can be used to clear blockages. Junctions with other drains also need access points. Gully terminations must have water traps to contain drain smells. Specific measures for through ventilation are not considered important unless the sewer system is combined with foul sewerage.[2] Gravity flow dictates the hydraulic engineering of pipes. Pipes laid to slack falls such as 1:80 will be liable to debris precipitation, and ponding due to uneven bedding. Pipes laid to steep falls will entail expensive excavation. The ideal design follows the fall of the land so that near-constant depths are maintained for the trench excavation. Rules of thumb for pipe sizes and falls are:

- 100 mm − 1:40
- 150 mm − 1:60.

Economy can be achieved by using the shortest possible runs of pipe, the minimum excavation and the least number of access points. To avoid claims from drainage sub-contractors it is important that tender plans include existing and proposed levels for the ground works in relation to all drain runs and fittings, and that finished inverts are carefully checked.

The types of piping for surface water drains are discussed below and are shown in Figure 16.03b. Components such as gully and access chambers are highlighted in Figure 16.03c.

Pitch fibre pipes   These are covered in BS 2760, and are used more often for land drainage, due to their friability and to the risk of damage from rats and tree roots. Their construction relies upon 'slip joints', with tapered plastic sleeves pushed over the ends of the pipes.

Plastic pipes   The choice includes unplasticised polyvinyl chloride (uPVC to BS 4660 (1973) with couplings of polypropylene copolymer; the process is covered by BS 5911:

a Surface water disposal: typical layout of drains.

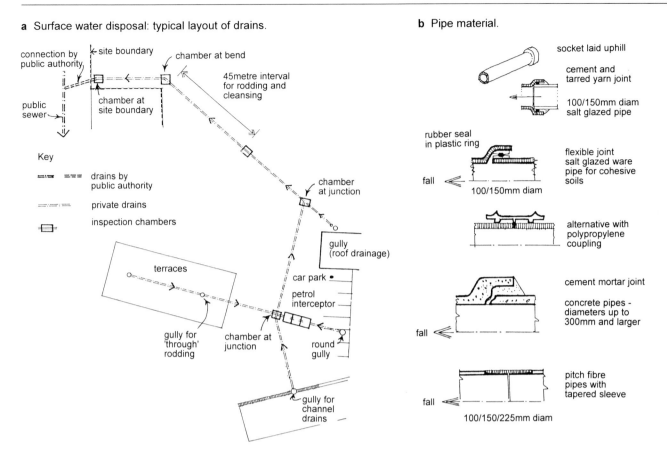

Key

drains by public authority

private drains

inspection chambers

b Pipe material.

socket laid uphill

cement and tarred yarn joint

100/150mm diam salt glazed pipe

rubber seal in plastic ring

flexible joint salt glazed ware pipe for cohesive soils

fall 100/150mm diam

alternative with polypropylene coupling

cement mortar joint

concrete pipes - diameters up to 300mm and larger

fall

pitch fibre pipes with tapered sleeve

fall 100/150/225mm diam

c Polypropylene units for access chamber and gully.

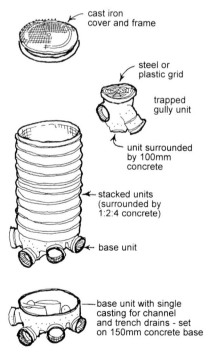

cast iron cover and frame

steel or plastic grid

trapped gully unit

unit surrounded by 100mm concrete

stacked units (surrounded by 1:2:4 concrete)

base unit

base unit with single casting for channel and trench drains - set on 150mm concrete base

Reprinted by kind permission of Wavin Plastics Ltd.

d Traditional brick-built chamber.

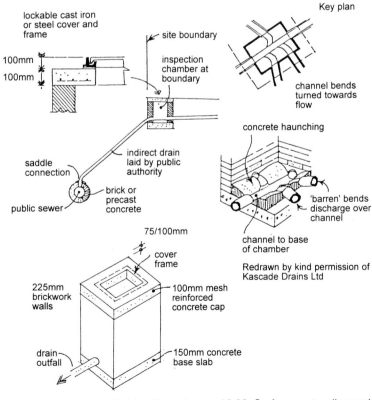

lockable cast iron or steel cover and frame

site boundary

100mm
100mm

inspection chamber at boundary

indirect drain laid by public authority

saddle connection

public sewer

brick or precast concrete

Key plan

channel bends turned towards flow

concrete haunching

'barren' bends discharge over channel

channel to base of chamber

Redrawn by kind permission of Kascade Drains Ltd

75/100mm

cover frame

225mm brickwork walls

100mm mesh reinforced concrete cap

drain outfall

150mm concrete base slab

Isometric of brick-built chamber

16.03 Surface water disposal

16.03e Well-placed circular covers. Compare with square versions
f Access chambers poorly related to levels
g The typical mess made by drainage sub-contractors
h position of manholes un-coordinated

Part 6. Plastic has superseded all other materials and is available with a composite range of fittings such as gullies and access chambers. Jointing utilizes push-fit couplings. Pipes and fittings are placed upon and surrounded by granular fill, but concrete casing will be needed for fittings set in traffic areas. The technology includes couplings to vitreous clayware, and to cast iron where required for extra strength.

Vitreous clayware Vitreous clayware is covered by BS 65 (1988), BS 2494 (1988) and BS 8301 (1985).[3] Joints can be flexible (using plastic connections) or rigid (using conventional cement and pointing around a gasket ring). Vitreous clayware is preferred in polluted subsoils and where high traffic loading is involved. Rigid pipe jointing requires concrete foundations and a construction which will withstand differential settlement in clay soils to avoid pipes breaking under ground stresses.

Steel and cast iron pipes These specialist fittings are reserved for pipes passing below buildings, and can be supplied with flexible bolted sockets to cope with severe settlement. They are covered by BS 437 (1978), BS 4772 (1988) and BS 6087 (1981).[4] They are also installed in heavily polluted sites and

where drains are laid in peaty and silt-based soils. Cast iron fittings are often installed where tough wear is expected — for example, access covers and gullies in car parks and roads — but connected to plastic drains. Useful references are makers catalogues and BS 497: *Specification for manhole covers, roadgully gratings and frames for drainage purposes*. The useful subsection is Part 1 (1976) *Cast iron and steel*. Cellular covers are manufactured which can be infilled on site with materials to match hard surfacing (concrete, macadam/tar coating, brick paving or setts).

Precast concrete These pipes and fittings are used in road works and large sewers. Precast gullies are made in large sizes, useful for road drainage, and are covered by BS 5911 (1981): *Precast pipes, fittings and ancillary products*. Precast concrete is also extensively specified for channel drainage (see Section 16.2 and Figure 16.02c).

Traditional access chambers Brick-built chambers are still constructed for deep drainage runs, say over 2 m, and are preferred for silt traps due to the range of dimensions and solidity possible. The basic details given in Figure 16.03d refer to access chamber construction where a surface water drain is connected to a road sewer. The 2.4 m deep excavation shown would need to be planked and restrained, leaving enough space for the brick layers to finish the exterior face of the brick shaft properly. The base slab is cast with structural-mix concrete and the brickwork formed with engineering-class bricks of 225 mm thickness. The interior face is flush-pointed to keep the surface clean. Some authorities may ask for 20 mm cement and sand rendering as an extra precaution. The top has a reinforced concrete slab (either cast in-situ or precast) with a hole to match the access cover. Dimensions will depend upon the purpose, but the basic operations of rodding and cleaning entail an internal size of at least 900 × 900 mm for deep drains. Step irons are provided which also serve as handholds. The pipe at the base of the chamber becomes a channel, and could be fitted with a silt sump over a flood valve if needed. The channel is haunched in concrete for security and to provide a footspace for the rodder. Access covers are selected according to the loading: heavy-duty for large vehicle traffic, medium-duty for cars and light-duty for pedestrians. The materials are cast iron, cast steel or steel plate, and can be specified by reference to BS 497: Part 7 (1976). Security can be provided by key lifting, locking or locking and hingeing. Circular patterns are more appropriate to landscape than square designs and resolve the difficulty in persuading drain-layers to align square covers or rectangular brick-built shafts to specific features which may not have been built when the drainage works are constructed.

Refer to Figures 16.03e–f for examples of good and bad designs of access covers.

Drainage details will be affected by site conditions, and the final layout will often vary from the original design. Levels are critical, and shallow drain runs near buildings have to be protected by granular infill or 100 mm of lean-mix concrete. The latter material is suitable below paved surfaces but presents insuperable problems in soft landscape such as that originally intended in Figure 16.03g.

16.4 Land Drainage Systems

Land drains perform three significant roles: firstly, to relieve groundwater pressure adjoining buildings or retaining walls; secondly, to assist with the shedding of stormwater from sloping land, and finally, to lower the water table in low-lying ground.

Relief drains

Land drains are placed as a network around or near buildings to disperse groundwater descending from higher ground. The most direct solution is to install a pipe in the foundation trench on the uphill side of a retaining wall (see Figures 11.14a–d). Buildings placed at angles to the contours call for a more comprehensive layout, and a 'moat' arrangement can be made, either L- or square-shaped, to convey the drains away from the site (Figure 16.04a).

a Moat layouts

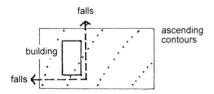

b Fanshaped layouts

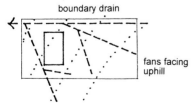

c Grid layouts

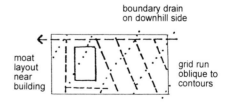

d Herringbone layouts

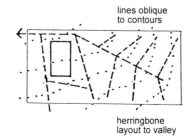

16.04 Land drainage systems

Fan-shaped layouts

Fan-shaped layouts (Figure 16.04b) are helpful in establishing the character of ground conditions and to check for ground water movement. With a rectangular plot, the drains could encompass adjacent boundaries and spread out radially but oblique to the contours. These are often used as the initial drainage scheme and could be linked to as soakaway or silt trap and surface water drain.

Grid layouts

Grid layouts (Figure 16.04b) are associated with horticultural engineering. A regular layout of machine-made land drain trenches is formed, complete with main drains or watercourses to the down hill side of the site.

Herringbone layouts

Herringbone layouts (Figure 16.04d) are used for extensive areas of undulating ground and comprise lateral drains and main drains. The laterals are run parallel to each other but at an angle to contours, and discharge via main drains run in the valley bottoms.

Existing land drainage is often found to contain a mixture of systems which will need sympathetic modification if disturbed. Cutting drains off will produce local flooding. Forming links with inadequate falls will silt up the pipes. A helpful solution is often to reconnect a broken network to a new main drain and silt trap so that existing problems can be contained until additional work or relaying can be undertaken.

16.5   Land Drains Installation

The conventional work of hand-trenching and laying butt-jointed clayware pipes within a bed of shingle or broken stone has been replaced by mechanical devices which excavate and lay drains in one operation; uPVC has revolutionized the technology and permits continuous pipe runs to be installed.

Flat sites often require immediate work to remove water, and 'mole drains' may form a short-term answer (Figure 16.05a–b). This technique consists of drawing a cutting blade through the subsoil, which leaves a soil-bound opening running to falls of 1:100. A cross-grid can be made at a shallower depth, and the outflow collected by ditches on the periphery. Pumps can be employed to keep the water at specific levels in the ditches, which in turn lowers the water table for the intervening mole-drained land. The technique will work for five years and then needs reploughing or more permanent measures, as shown in Figures 16.05b–e involving agricultural engineering.

Plastic-filtered cores can improve mole drain techniques for sports fields. The system relies upon a slot cut in the ground 50 mm wide and 300 mm deep. Taped lengths of polythene cores are pressed into the trench in pre-formed lengths and sealed by tape to main drains at the edge of the area. The system is ideal for individual games areas of, say, 60 × 100 m and plastic core units are placed at 3 m intervals

16.05 Land drains

a Plough for mole drains

a

b Mole drains

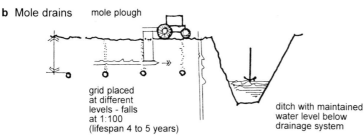

mole plough

grid placed at different levels - falls at 1:100 (lifespan 4 to 5 years)

ditch with maintained water level below drainage system

centres and depths as below

	depth mm	centres mm
heavy soils	460/510	1.800 to 2.700
light soils	460/510	3.600 to 4.500

c Lateral trenches and their spacing

Key section

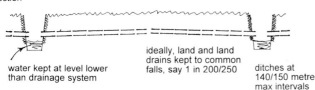

water kept at level lower than drainage system

ideally, land and land drains kept to common falls, say 1 in 200/250

ditches at 140/150 metre max intervals

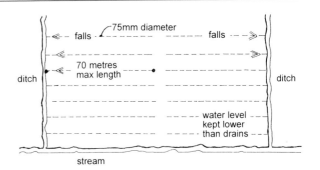

75mm diameter

falls — falls

70 metres max length

ditch ⟵ ditch

water level kept lower than drains

stream

d Spacing of branch drains

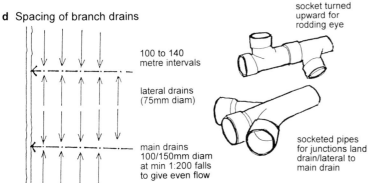

100 to 140 metre intervals

lateral drains (75mm diam)

main drains 100/150mm diam at min 1:200 falls to give even flow

socket turned upward for rodding eye

socketed pipes for junctions land drain/lateral to main drain

e Pipes for lateral and branch drains.

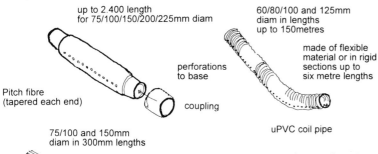

up to 2.400 length for 75/100/150/200/225mm diam

Pitch fibre (tapered each end)

perforations to base

coupling

60/80/100 and 125mm diam in lengths up to 150metres

made of flexible material or in rigid sections up to six metre lengths

uPVC coil pipe

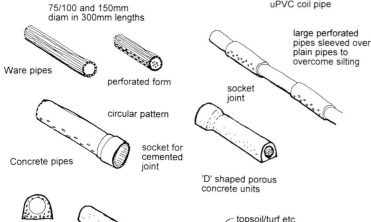

75/100 and 150mm diam in 300mm lengths

Ware pipes

perforated form

Concrete pipes

circular pattern

socket for cemented joint

Porous concrete unit

coupling sleeve

socket joint

large perforated pipes sleeved over plain pipes to overcome silting

'D' shaped porous concrete units

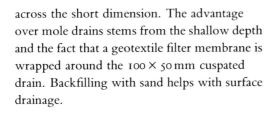

topsoil/turf etc.

25mm of 3-5mm chippings

10mm chippings

100mm tamped base layer

Bedding for uPVC pipes

across the short dimension. The advantage over mole drains stems from the shallow depth and the fact that a geotextile filter membrane is wrapped around the 100×50 mm cuspated drain. Backfilling with sand helps with surface drainage.

Lateral drains

The depth and spacing of lateral land drains needs to be reduced as the cohesive strength of sub-soil increases. The guidance given in Figure 16.05c covers pitch fibre pipes, but the concept could be applied to other materials. Conventional drain trenches require a sequence of operations, and the profile shown in the key section (see Figure 10.05a) would be formed as follows: firstly, trenching to give a working space for the drain layer, then bedding and surrounding the pipes with shingle or broken stone, and finally, screening with brushwood or plastic mesh and backfilling. The choice of pipe material depends upon the quantities required. Coils of plastic tube can only be purchased in long lengths, while pitch fibre or ware pipes are delivered in palletloads.

Branch drains

Branch drains (Figures 16.05d—e) are the essential link in the system and need to be carefully assembled to maintain the working life of the drainage network. Care has to be taken that seepage or settlement does not displace the pipes, so sleeved or socketed pipes are used. Tree roots can be a considerable nuisance as these invade broken or loose pipes, causing blockages. Concrete beds, mortar

16.2 Spacing of branch drains

Type of soil	Centres of branch drains	
	Depth of main drain to invert level	
	600−900	900−1,200
Sand	30,500−45,700	45,700−91,400
Sandy loam	25,900−30,500	30,500−45,700
Clay loam	13,700−16,800	16,800−19,800
Loam	22,900−25,900	25,900−30,500
Sandy clay	10,700−12,200	12,200−13,700
Clay	7,600−9,100	9,100−10,700

e Layout of lateral and branch drains

falls usually 1 in 250

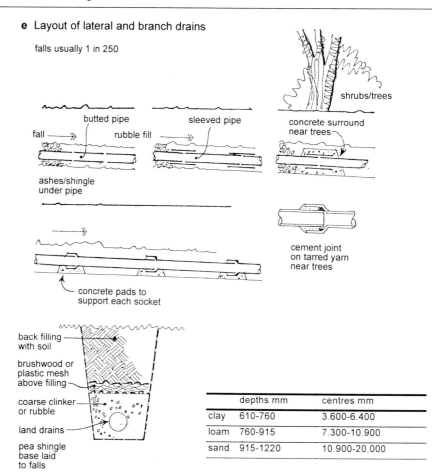

	depths mm	centres mm
clay	610-760	3.600-6.400
loam	760-915	7.300-10.900
sand	915-1220	10.900-20.000

jointing and concrete encasement at joints are advisable precautions where tree roots are found (see Figure 11.08b).

Pipes for lateral and branch drains

The various types of pipe components are discussed below (Figure 16.05f).

Unglazed ware pipes The traditional ribbed pattern is made in 75, 100 & 150 mm diameters, either plain or perforated, and is stocked by builders' merchants and supplied in small quantities. They are usually hand-laid, though agricultural machinery exists which ploughs a trench, lays pipe and backfills in one operation. The pipes are easily disturbed and can fall out of line, leading to ponding and silting. A laying method whereby 75 and 100 mm pipes are laid interlocking will give a more stable pipe run.

Concrete pipes These are superior to clayware as they are made with socketed connections and are available with flat bedding planes with perforations. Honeycomb concrete versions can be used to overcome problems of silt penetration. Branch and silt gully fittings

are made so that a complete system can be installed using one material.

Pitch fibre pipes Inexpensive and simple to install, the pipe joints are either made with cone-shaped couplings or else reliance is placed on interleafing two sizes of pipe. They are liable to be crushed under heavy loading or destroyed by rodents.

uPVC pipes Available in coil form or in 6 m lengths, perforated patterns are made for land drainage. Couplings exist for pipe ends and for multiple junctions between herringbone systems and carrier drains. The fittings include silt traps and access chambers. The pipes can be laid straight or curved, while machines exist which can lay coiled pipe in runs up to 150 m. Plastic components for couplings and fittings can be interchanged with clayware where traditional and modern systems of land drainage are combined. There is considerable advantage in using coupling fittings between land drains and the carrier system so that rodding can take place along the main drainage runs. Access can be provided via chambers, or the main drain can be turned upwards to ground level in a gentle curve to assist rodding and cleaning.

16.6 Drainage Principles

The sample layout in Figure 16.06a depicts a range of land drainage methods and the principles involved.

Field drains

Three forms are shown in Figure 16.06a: firstly the single-grid pattern run oblique to the contours, with the main drain (also called a carrier) discharging into a stream; secondly, the system can be extended as a herringbone design, as shown at the lower left-hand side; the third variation for wetter situations is a combination of mole drains and the herringbone pattern. Erosion at the stream side needs to be countered by providing abutments or splash plates, as in Figures 16.07a–b. Water authorities in the UK specify silt traps to protect streams from blockage. The same measures are used for 'French' drains, which are utilized for surface water disposal below embankments or steep inclines, and are commonly installed in road verges/shoulders. The stone filling will have to be cored out from time to time as the trench becomes mud-caked. Silt run-off from such drains is a nuisance, and silt traps are installed at connections with land drains or streams.

Surface water drainage from highways will be polluted by oil and petrol/gasoline. A typical installation comprises a triple-chamber silt trap with full access for cleaning. Individual roadside gullies are fitted with silt traps, either a deeper water chamber to hold debris and grit, which can be cleared using mobile mechanized pumps, or a bucket gully, which must be emptied manually.

16.7 Components and Details

Refer to Figure 16.05f for details of pipes and fittings, and to Figure 16.06a for the key plan.

Abutments and splash plates

Land drains need a collar of firm material at abutments to streams to prevent bank erosion. A splash plate of concrete or stone below the outlet also assists, and could form the foundation slab for a solid abutment of concrete, concrete blocks or stone rubble, as in

a Typical drainage layout

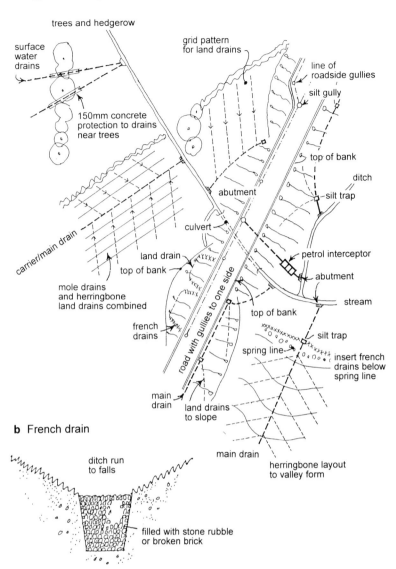

b French drain

16.06 Drainage principles

a Abutments and splash plates.

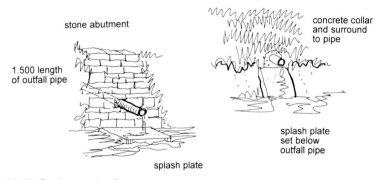

16.07 Drainage details

Figure 16.07a. Similar precautions are needed wherever open ditches or streams become culverts at roadways and other obstructions. The details in Figure 16.07b show a 'green' construction using turves, or more solid work using concrete blocks and rubble.

16.07b Culvert details

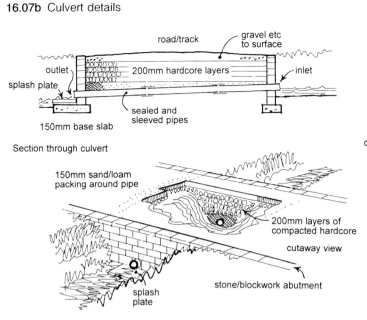

Section through culvert

d Silt trap for culvert or drain overflow

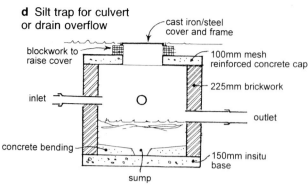

c Silt trap placed on the outlet side of a culvert or surface water drain.

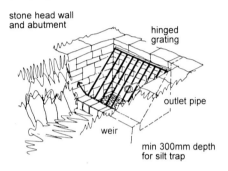

e Petrol interceptor.

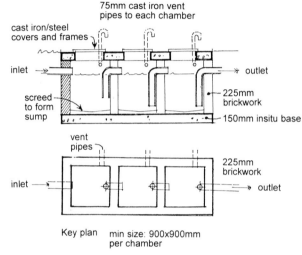

Key plan   min size: 900x900mm per chamber

A common defect with culverts is the precipitation of silt on the downstream side. A weir and trap will be effective at this location. The construction needs a concrete base slab to secure the enclosing walls. The front weir should entrap at least 300 mm of water, and the outlet pipe should be set at weir level. Greater depths of 900 mm or so are created to give a larger reservoir, but need gratings to prevent accidents. The traditional details in Figure 16.07c are shown in stonework, but could be replicated in brickwork or cast in concrete. The arrangement of a silt trap and drain outlet is similar where surface water or land drain carriers discharge into streams. Silt traps are also constructed where there is an extensive system of surface water drains discharging into a municipal sewer. The principle is similar to that shown in Figure 16.07c, but totally enclosed as with an access chamber, and often built in concrete with brickwork enclosing walls (Figure 16.07d). Standard precast concrete or plastic components can also be obtained for the purpose.

Petrol/gasoline interceptors

Petrol/gasoline interceptors (Figure 16.07e) are necessary to prevent oil or petrol/gasoline polluting surface water sewers and watercourses, and are specified in the UK by river/water authorities for public and private roads as well as car parks. Construction using concrete and brickwork is shown in Figure 16.07c. GRP formers are also manufactured for triple tanks, and are encased within cast in-situ concrete. The triple-tank system enables weirs to trap differing grades of pollutant. The size of catch pit needs to be engineer-designed, for large expanses of roadway, such as motorway/highway service areas, will be open ponds protected by mesh or steel grids.

Soakaways

Soakaways (Figure 16.07f) are made by excavating a shaft down to a permeable layer of subsoil and infilling with loose rubble or stone to form a filter for land drains or surface water

f Soakaway

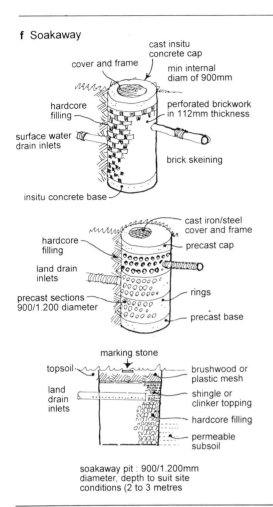

soakaway pit : 900/1.200mm
diameter, depth to suit site
conditions (2 to 3 metres

disposal. Once again the construction of soakaways is subject to river or water authority approval in the UK. It is useless to install soakaways in permeable subsoils if the water table is close to the surface, or in heavy clays where the water-filled shafts will make matters worse for adjacent land. However, there are many sites where soakaways sited downhill can alleviate ground conditions. Silt will eventually clog the rubble filling, and soakaways will need to be re-dug or re-filled. The latter process is best arranged by providing a honeycomb skin of brickwork or precast concrete surmounted by a slab and access cover. Typical sizes are 0.9–1.2 m internal diameter, with depths ranging from 1.5 to 2.1 m. Soakaways are not to be confused with cesspools, which are enclosed vessels for collecting sewage, designed either for collection by mobile pumps or for treatment on site. Connecting surface water drains to cesspools will be a disaster, either washing out the sewage treatment culture in times of storm, or else flooding the locality with untreated sewage.

16.8 Conclusion

Sound principles for water engineering and drainage are core activities in improving the environment. The land and reclamation seen around the former Zuider Zee in the Netherlands is one of the foremost examples in Europe. It is not without problems, however, as the pollutants from modern agriculture and industry have permeated the freshwater lake

16.08 The new polders in the Netherlands a enclosing dam

16.08b field drainage
c main canal drainage
d bank of sluices to sea
e map showing reclaimed land

created to replace the tidal basin. The lessons learnt have been applied to the Delta project at the mouth of the Rhine where the cleansing of the tidal waters continue with flood control ensured by moveable barriers and tide gates.

Figures 16.08a–e demonstrate the skills at work creating farmers' fields from a fisherman's realm. It is also a hopeful vision

where the fusion of arbiculture, engineering, landscaping and planning skills have created one of the outstanding achievements of twentieth–century civilization. The cost of the latest Delta project equalled the expenditure on the first 'moon shot' and reveals that earth bound priorities can provide better value for humankind and our future.

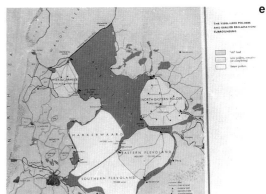

NOTES

Chapter 1

1 Bearing capacities for pavers in flexible pavements: clay pavers to BS 6677: Part 1, Table 3.

Type of paver	Minimum mean transverse breaking load	Minimum individual transverse breaking load
PA	3.0 kN	2.0 kN
PB	7.0 kN	4.0 kN

2 The following are key references for specifications of flexible brick and block paving work in the UK:

- Department of the Environment, Road note 29, 3rd edn, HMSO, London, 1970.
- BDA, Design note 5, *Flexible and calcium silicate paving for lightly trafficked roads and paved areas*, 1981.
- BDA, *A specification for clay pavers for flexible pavements*, 2nd edn, May 1988.
- *Concrete block paving for heavily trafficked roads and paved areas*, C & CA, 1978.
- *Concrete block paving for lightly trafficked roads and paved areas*, C & CA, 1980.
- Department of Transport, *Specification for road and bridge works*, HMSO, London, 1976.
- British Ports Associations, *The structural design of heavy duty pavements for ports and other industries*, 1985.
- Walsh, I. D., 'Skid resistance testing of clay pavers', *Chemistry and Industry*, November 1985.
- British Standards Institution, DD 155, *Method for determination of polished paver value of pavers*, 1986.

BDA-Brick Development Association
Publications from:
Woodside House
Winkfield
Windsor
Berkshire
SL4 2DX

C & CA CA-Cement and Concrete Association
(now called The Concrete Society)
Publications from:
Devon House
12–15 Dartmouth Street
London
SW1H 9BL

US standards are approximately the same, but have differing technical references.

3 Brick and block classification by method of manufacture

- **Claybricks and pavers** – made from clay or similar argillaceous material, which may be mixed with fuel or other additives and pressed, or extruded and cut, or moulded to the required shape, dried and fired.
- **Silicate bricks and pavers** – made from sand and lime, which is mixed with colour additives, pressed into moulds, dried and steam autoclaved, then air-cured.
- **Concrete blocks** – made from fine and course aggregate and cement (grey, white or coloured) mixed with water pressed into moulds and cured.

4 British Ceramic Tile Council
Federation House
Station Road
Stoke on Trent
Staffordshire
ST4 2RV

5 Swimming Pool Construction Swimming Pool and Allied Trades Association Ltd.
Spata House
Junction Road
Andover
Hampshire
SP10 3QT

6 British Standards for precast pavers
Refer to BS 7263: Part 1 (1990) for traditional sizes 450, 600 square and 600 × 750 and 900 either 50 or 63 mm thick. Small element flags are 300, 400 and 450 square. Other slabs comply with BS 368 and cover various finishes and manufacture.

7 Ibid.

8 Foreign standards for paving levels: USA and Germany
Details need to be studied for tolerances in laying and acceptable performance of levels between adjoining pavers.

Eurocodes may one day restore higher standards to the UK.

9 Thomas Church's influence resulted from his DIY manuals prepared for Sunset Books which dominated garden ideas in the USA. It could be said that if he had lived long enough the USA would have been decked over from coast to coast. A fine epitaph to Church is provided in his book, *Gardens are for People*, McGraw-Hill, New York, 2nd edn, 1983.

10 Sports and Playing Field Associations in the UK

- General points
  National Playing Fields Association
  Specification for outdoor sports and recreational facilities 1980
  25 Ovington Square
  London
  SW3 ILQ
  Landscape Techniques, A. E. Weddle (ed.), Heinnemann London, 1979
- Specialist firms
  Landscape Specification, 3rd edition, Landscape Promotions, 1991
- Advice
  Sports Council Technical Unit for Sport
  16 Upper Woburn Place
  London
  WC1H 0QP

Chapter 2

1 Key diagrams for tread-to-riser proportions according to Building Uses. (Under National Building Regulations in the UK). Refer to tables 2.2−4.

2 Technical terms
Standard definitions under the National Building Regulations (1989) in the UK.
Stairway Flights and landings included in this term.
Going The distance measured in plan across the tread less any overlap with the next tread above or below.
Rise The vertical distance between the top surfaces of two consecutive treads.
Pitch line May be defined as a notional line connecting the nosings of all treads in a flight. The line is taken so as to form the greatest possible angle with the horizontal, subject to the special requirements for tapered steps.
Pitch May be defined as the angle between the pitch line and the horizontal.
Final exit Termination of escape to a safe zone − street, open walkway or open space.

3 In the UK places for public entertainment or assembly (such as hotels, public houses, theatres, and stadiums) require licences which cover items such as emergency escapes. Buildings have specific requirements for escape in case of fire, and these can include external stairways and ramps, particularly where large numbers of people are involved (for example, theatres and stadiums). The licences granted are specific to the use of the facilities and the occupancy rate, and will govern the width and layout of stairs and ramps and the detailed design for guardrailing and handrails. Other points covered are emergency lighting and prevention of damage due to ice and snowfall. The licensing authority in the UK could be the local council or magistrate's court under the Home Office regulations.

4 Space prevents a comprehensive analysis of the spatial concept and the role played by oblique vistas instead of axial ones which follow one behind the other. One of the finest descriptions is by Le Corbusier in his chapters dedicated to the plan of the Acropolis and its architecture in *Towards A New Architecture*, Butterworth Architecture, London, 1970.

Chapter 3

1 Rainwater shed by gutters and pipes
Refer to UK National Building Regulations Sections N8 and 9.

Chapter 4

1 The principle of balancing lakes resembles that of land drains (see Section 16.5), where ditches are kept at prescribed water levels to maintain water tables in the surrounding land. Lakes can be used for a similar purpose as collecting points for land drainage. The lake levels are maintained by pumps and weirs, with flood plains such those as at York University. Winter and summer needs vary, hence the vertical embankments to the lake at 'pinch points' near buildings to prevent flooding.

2 Battery-powered fountain units are available which float below the pond surface. They will provide sufficient aeration for small ponds. They are not to be confused with the creation used in the Jacques Tati film *Mon Oncle*, where the fountain came into play when the bank manager made a visit.

3 Refer to the fountains at the Gardens of Shalamar Bagh, Kashmir, from the mid-seventeenth century, described in Geoffrey and Susan Jellicoe, *The Landscape of Man*, Thames & Hudson, London, 1975, Chapter 5.

Chapter 5

1 Illustrations are given in Dan Cruickshank and Neil Burton, *Life in the Georgian City*, Viking, London, 1990, and refer to posts erected along busy pavements for protection of the public, with engravings of High Holborn, London, and adjacent streets.

2 Refer to BS 1217 (1986): *Specification for Cast Stone*.

3 Refer to issues of the *Architectural Review* for 1950 and 1951. The 'gift' of setts, etc. occurred on the date of editor's birthday in 1951, the donors being the staff of the Design Research Unit. Refer to the collected works of Gordon Cullen in *The Concise Townscape*, Architectural Press, London, 1971.

Chapter 6

1 Refer to Raymond Unwin, *Town Planning in Practice*, concerning Hampstead Garden Suburb, London, Ernest Benn, 2nd edition, 1911. Chapter 9 contains advice on plots and the spacing and placing of buildings and fences, the most useful quotation being as follows:

When some form of fence is desired, probably the best is a simple trellis, preferably of intertwined laths, unobstructive in colour, and up which all sorts of climbing plants may readily twine; by the use of such fence it is possible to secure what would practically have the appearance of a well-grown hedge much more quickly than the hedge by itself could grow; but if people were willing to spend as much on the planting of the hedges as they usually spend on a dividing fence or wall, a much better grown hedge than one often sees to new houses could be secured at once.

2 Gravel board is a generic term for a base board in wood fencing, traditionally used for close-boarded forms to keep the open grain of the board facing 150–200 mm above the ground level. Gravel boards are also used in post and rail fencing where the lower edge of the mesh or windscreening needs anchoring. The board can be a 200 × 20 mm plank or a strip of external-grade plywood of the same size. It is often staked once or twice over its length to improve stability.

Chapter 7

1 Refer to Alistair Cooke, *America*, BBC, 1973, an expanded version of a BBC television series which takes the story of the USA from the time of Columbus to the 1970s. Chapter 7 contains references to farming and the enclosure of the wilderness.

2 The following BS codes cover agricultural and other fencing. It is important to check the precise wording of the BS documents – often choices are given which may not be suitable, being either too cheap or too elaborate.

BS 1722: *Specification for fences*:

- Part 1 (1986) Chain link fences.
- Part 2 (1973) Woven wire fences.
- Part 3 (1986) Strained wire fences.
- Part 4 (1986) Cleft chestnut pale fences.
- Part 5 (1986) Close-boarded fences.
- Part 6 (1986) Wooden palisade fences.
- Part 7 (1986) Wooden post and rail.
- Part 8 (1978) Mild steel (low-carbon steel) continuous bar fences.
- Part 9 (1979) Mild steel (low carbon steel) fences with round or square with round or square verticals and flat posts and horizontals.
- Part 10 (1972) Anti-intruder chain link fences.
- Part 11 (1986) Woven wood fences and lap boarded panel fences.
- Part 12 (1979) Steel palisade fences.
- Part 13 (1978) Chain link fences for tennis court surrounds.

BS 4102 (1986) *Steel wire and wire products for fences*.

There are also codes for gates and stiles which are useful in differing categories of work:

- BS 3470 (1975) *Field gates and posts*.
- BS 4092 *Domestic front entrance gates*.
  Part 1 (1966) Metal gates.
  Part 2 (1966) Wooden gates.
- BS 5709 (1979) *Specification for stiles, bridle and kissing gates*.

Chapter 8

1 British Standards Institution codes and standards:

- BS 729 (1971 & 1986) *Hot dip galvanised coatings on iron and steel articles*.
- BS 1052 (1980) *Welded mesh*.
- BS 1722 *Specification for fences*:
  Part 1 (1986) Chain link fences.
  Part 2 (1973) Woven wire fences.
  Part 3 (1986) Strained wire fences.
  Part 10 (1972) Anti-intruder chain link fences.
  Part 13 (1978) Chain link fences for tennis court surrounds.
- BS 4102 (1986) Link mesh.

2 There was a mature student at Kew Gardens who confessed that she had no difficulty in climbing three metre chain link fencing. Her previous job as an expatriate had been head mistress to a girls school in Uganda. She kept to a bare foot keep fit routine and claimed this enabled her leathery toes to climb in and out of school whenever the main gates were shut.

3 Orsogril are structural steel grilles formed of rectangular cross-section bars in one direction and circular cross-section rods in the other, at 90° to the bars. Bar cross-sections range from 20 × 2 mm to 30 × 4 mm and rod diameters are 4, 5, and 6 mm, the two being in the best productions electrofused together at spacings varying from 42 × 44 mm to 124 × 132 mm. The grilles are in large-scale production in mats of 6 × 1–2 m or ready-to-use panels, and because of their elegance, especially when colour powder-coated, are used for street furniture and pergolas cladding, as well as fencing.

Chapter 9

1 Microporous paints have been structured to give greater permeability than traditional oil-based coatings. All materials, including paint films, are able to absorb gaseous phases, and to some extent liquid phases. Different pore sizes can be engineered, but care should be taken to ensure that the resultant finish has microporous qualities relevant to the situation. Softwoods will need preservative treatment to prevent rot developing under exposed and weathered surfaces of microporous paints.

2 Plastic and powder coatings

Two broad groups of resins or polymers are used for powders to produce what are commonly called plastic coatings. These are thermoplastic polymers which can be heated without chemical change, and thermosetting polymers which, when heated, produce a permanent chemical change. Common polymers in the two groups are:

- Thermoplastic – PVC (polyvinyl chloride), nylon and polythene.
- Thermosetting — phenolics, epoxides and polyesters.

Although fairly large sections of steel can be coated with powder coatings, the most common use for the material is for components and smaller units. They are comparatively expensive to apply and problems arise where welding as required. The welded area, after cleaning, is often coated with an air drying paint, which tends to perform less well than the main plastic coating. Nevertheless, if properly applied, they can provide durable coatings for steel and may well be considered for special features such as balustrades.

3 British Standards relating to barriers for pedestrian and public spaces

- BS 6180 (1982) *Protective barriers to highways.*
- BS 3039 (1976) *Pedestrian guardrails.*
  This standard categorizes the differing classes of strength required in guardrail construction:

  Normal Strength (Class A): Rails 700 N/m Infilling 500 N/m.
  For public areas subject to vandalism (Class B): Rails 700 N/m; Infilling 1000 N/m.
  For crowd pressure (Class C): Rails 1400 N/m; Infilling 1000 N/m.

4 Grateful acknowledgement is given to help from the Timber Research and Development Association (TRADA), and for their permission to utilize their former publications, including *Finishes for Outdoor Timbers*. TRADA are a valuable source of information in the use of timber, and on constructional details for bridges, fences and preservative treatments. TRADA's address is:
Hughenden Valley
High Wycombe
Buckinghamshire
HP14 4ND

Chapter 10

1 The term ha-ha is said to have been coined by the French writer d'Argenville and relates to the surprise of finding a sunken wall – 'A-ha!'

declares the visitor. Whether this follows upon nearly falling down the ditch is not clear. Some consider that the French used the term *ha-ha* in this context, but in France the precise description is *saut-de-loup*, meaning a wolf's leap.

2 Refer to Raymond Unwin, *Town Planning in Practice*, 2nd Edition, 1911, Ernest Benn Ltd, London, Chapter 5.
The following is a key quotation:

where the ground is sloping, and the district adjoins a park or belt of open space, the retaining wall be a charming boundary, its monotony broken by garden houses and gates instead of old turrets and bastions. The ha-ha or sunk fence, too gives a good defining line.

The above paragraph was illustrated by the Great Wall on the southern boundary of Hampstead Garden Suburb (see Figure 10.04a).

3 Ernst May was an assistant to Raymond Unwin, working in Hampstead Garden Suburb 1910–12. He was City Architect for Frankfurt am Main 1925–30.

Chapter 11

1 The Brick Development Association represents brick makers and offers a wide range of technical detail and specifications upon the application of brickwork in landscape construction. One of the most useful references is their publication *Achieving Successful Brickwork*, June 1990. Their help is gratefully acknowledged in preparing information on brick paving for Chapter 1 and for brickwork walling in Chapter 11.

2 The term 'damp-proof course', refers to materials installed in walls to exclude the penetration of rising damp at the base of a wall and through saturation below a coping at the top of walls. The term can also apply to a continuous sheet of material installed vertically to backs of retaining walls. The horizontal form is usually of flexible material to cope with a slight settlement or movements. Typical sheet materials are lead-cored bitumen felts or else code 4 strip lead (4 lb) or bitumen polymer. Components such as roofing slates or engineering bricks (both laid in a double course) are often used where engineering requirements call for a non-compressible layer within the wall.

3 The BRE *Good Building Guide*, No. 14, May 1992, provides rule-of-thumb guidance for constructing free-standing brick walls. Regrettably it does not deal with panelled walls (walls with piers and infilling panels of thinner brickwork) nor with walls higher than 2.4 m, so the designer is best advised to call in a consultant engineer to design, a free-standing wall to prevent the risk of being sued for incompetence.

Documents produced by BRE from earlier times are, however, excellent sources, and the codes of practice they lay out are still relevant.

4 Cohesive soils suffer from expansion as freezing occurs, known as 'frost heave'. The depth of frost penetration varies from a high of 900 mm in the UK to 2–3 m in central Europe, Scandinavia and parts of North America. Builders in areas with severe frost problems avoid shallow masonry construction for landscape work by using timberwork or with foundation engineering which relies on piles and interconnecting beams.

5 This matter is complex, but in essence the planting of trees which cause root trespass onto a neighbour's land could be curtailed by the adjoining owner. In other words, the roots cut off and contained by a berm (sheet or concrete filling to a trench). A neighbour might also put an adjoining owner on a 'notice of care' regarding risks arising from trees by the adjoining owner. Existing roots are a different problem since cutting off may well cause ground heave when clay soils, formerly dry and infested with roots become moist and swell. The wise landscape designer tries to cause the least disturbance to ground conditions below neighbour's buildings.

Chapter 12

1 See reference 1 for Chapter 6.

2 The timber for small-profile members needs to be straight-grained and knot-free. Larch is an excellent material for this purpose as it is durable, and its life span can be extended to 70 or more years by preservative treatment. The timber features which adorn the pergola garden at Bodnant, North Wales, have survived since the early 1910s where a copper-based preservative was used. Figure 12.04c, d & e reveal the possibilities with contemporary preservatives, and the tonal contrasts which can be achieved for interwoven and patterned effects.

Chapter 13

1 Expanding bolts are inset masonry bolts to secure fixings in masonry or cast in-situ concrete walls. The basic form allows for a hole to be drilled into the masonry and the sheathed bolt inserted. The threaded sheaths are turned and expand to tighten the bolt within the mortise. Security is ensured by the tapered anchor on the bolt shank. Other bolt fixings rely upon glue capsules which break and then set and bond the metal to the mortise hole. Cast in-situ concrete work permits bolts to be incorporated as the concrete is poured, but this requires accuracy in setting out. All bolts that are exposed externally or set within external masonry should be of galvanized steel, or stainless steel in hostile environments.

Chapter 15

1 This principle was established at Radburn, New Jersey, by Henry Wright and Clarence Stein in 1929. An extensive garden city was laid out which embraced Raymond Unwin's concepts but adapted these to the motor age. In essence a periphery network of roads served the housing with cul-de-sac access. The pedestrian approach was via the rear gardens with a network of paths and 'commons'. The 'Span' housing of the 1950s, 60s and 70s used modified Radburn layouts to separate pedestrian from vehicle traffic and the fusion of private and public landscape was outstanding.

2 Refer to reference 3 in Chapter 2.

Chapter 16

1 One memorable disaster was the first heavy rains which beset Battersea Pleasure Gardens, London, remodelled for the Festival of Britain. The newly macadamized grounds became a paddling pool of considerable dimensions, and pumps were brought in to handle drainage until the drains were replaced.

2 Combined surface water drainage and foul sewers are no longer installed in the UK, though public sewers which work in combination still exist in Inner London and other cities. Rat infestation is a severe problem and water traps will be needed at all gullies and boundary access chambers.

3 The full titles are:

- BS 65 (1988): *Specification for vitrified clay pipes, fittings, joints and ducts.*
- BS 2494 (1988): *Specification for elastometric joint rings for pipework and pipe lines.*
- BS 8301 (1985): *Code of practice for building drainage.*

4 The full titles are:

- BS 437 (1978): *Specification for cast iron spigot and socket drain pipes and fittings.* (This is the basic guide and relates largely to cast iron pipes laid below buildings).
- BS 4772 (1988): *Specification for ductile iron pipes and fittings.* (Up-to-date reference for pipes designed for flexible connections).
- BS 6087 (1981): *Specification for flexible joints for cast iron drain pipes and fittings.* (This needs to be read in conjunction with BS 4772 (1988).)

BIBLIOGRAPHY

Ashurst, J. and N., *Practical Building Conservation*, Volumes 1–3, Gower, Aldershot, 1988

Aurand, G. Douglas, *Fountains and Pools: Construction Guidelines and Specifications*, Van Nostrand Reinhold, 1987

Brown, J., *The Art and Architecture of English Gardens*, Weidenfeld and Nicholson, London, 1989

Clouston, Brian, *Landscape Design with Plants*, Heinemann, 1989

Cullen, Gordon, *The Concise Townscape*, Architectural Press, London, 1971

Cutler, D.F. and Richardson, I.D.K., *Tree Roots and Buildings*, 2nd edition, Construction Press, 1989

Friends of The Earth, *Good Wood Guide*, 1990

Harris, C.W. and Davis, N.T., *Timesaver Standards for Landscape Architecture*, McGraw Hill, 1988

Ingels, J., *Landscaping; Principles and Practice*, Van Nostrand Reinhold, 1992

Jellicoe, Geoffrey and Susan, *The Landscape of Man*, Thames and Hudson, London, 1975

Klatt, F. and Landphair, H. *Landscape Architecture Construction*, Elsevier, New York, 1979

Landscape Specifications, published by Landscape Promotions, third edition, 1991

Laurie, Michael, *An Introduction to Landscape Architecture*, Elsevier, New York, 1986

Le Corbusier, *Towards a New Architecture*, Butterworth Architecture, London, 1970

Littlewood, Michael, *Landscape Detailing*, Architectural Press, London, 1987

Littlewood, Michael, *Tree Detailing*, Butterworth, London, 1988

Mosser, M. and Teysott, G., *The History of Garden Design*, Thames and Hudson, London, 1991

National Playing Fields Association, *Specification for Outdoor Sports and Recreational Facilities*, 1980

Pindar, A., *Beazley's Design and Detail of the Space between Buildings*, Spon, London, 1990

Sitwell, Sir George, *On the Making of Gardens*

Spon's Landscape Handbook, ed Derek Lovejoy Partnership, 3rd edition, Spon, London, 1986

Unwin, Raymond, *Town Planning in Practice*, 2nd edition, Ernest Ben, 1911

Weddle, A.E., *Landscape Techniques*, Heinemann, London, 1979

USEFUL ORGANIZATIONS

Brick Development Association
Publications from:
Woodside House
Winkfield
Windsor
Berkshire
SL4 3DX

The Concrete Society
(formerly the Cement and Concrete
Association)
Publications from:
Devon House
12—15 Dartmouth Street
London
SW1H 9BL

Sports Council Technical Unit for Sport
16 Upper Woburn Place
London
WC1 HQP

Sports and Playing Field Association
25 Ovington Square
London SW3 1LR

**Swimming Pool and Allied Trades
Association**
Spata House
Junction Road
Andover
Hampshire
SP10 3QT

British Ceramic Tile Council
Federation House
Station Road
Stoke on Trent
Staffordshire
ST4 2RV

**Timber Research Development
(TRADA)**
Hughendon Valley
High Wycombe
Buckinghamshire
HP14 4ND

INDEX